INCREASING ROLE OF TECHNOLOGY IN EDUCATION

INCREASING ROLE OF TECHNOLOGY IN EDUCATION

Editor

Sarita Kumari

ISHA BOOKS

DELHI-110 033

Increasing Role of Technology in Education

Rs. 790

ISBN: 81-8205-141-X

Published in 2004 in India by
Isha Books, D-43, Prithviraj Road,
Adarsh Nagar, Delhi-110 033

Laser Typesetting at : Shree Vaishnavi Creations, Delhi.
Printed at : Chawla Offset Press, Delhi.

Contents

Preface

The role of technology in education came to be emphasised greatly in the second half of the twentieth century all over the world. Today technology and education are inseparable. Intrusion of technology and the need of it in the field of education is ever increasing. In the beginning small tools of technology were used to aid the teaching and learning process. Today, we make use of advanced technology in the field of education. Mass media, both print and electronic, is utilised in a big way to make learning easy and enjoyable. Books, magazines, journals, radio, TV, satellites etc. are involved in the field of education.

Literature on education is vast and varied. The same is true of the literature on education technology. A large number of books have been and are being written every now and then. As technology is advancing, so does the educational technology. Hence the need for updating of literature. This calls for introduction of new books on the subject. This work is created keeping this in mind. The latest in the field of educational technology, the programmes and policies of government and the like, has been included to make the work useful to the students and teachers in the fields of education. The book is shaped as a semi-reference book and is useful both as a textbook and a reference book. The 'Review Questions' included at the end of each chapter make enquiries on the subject matter of the chapter and prompt the students to search out the matter and attempt to answer the questions. This makes the learning by the students more effective.

The language used in the book has been lucid enough to maintain the interest of the reader and avoid making the book dull and drab. The emphasis has been in line with the spirit of the national Policy of Education, 1986 and the revised NPE, 1992. The National Policy of Education aims at the maximum use of technology in the field of education.

This effort has drawn great support from the publishers and the same has resulted in giving birth to a quite useful product for the users. Enquiries and suggestions from the readers are welcome.

-Author

Introduction

The importance of educational technology for improvement of education, both quantitively and qualitatively, was recognised by the Ministry of Education, Government of India way back in 1974 and it was included in 5th Five Year Plan. The project had the following sub-schemes:

(i) Setting up an Educational Technology Unit in the Ministry of Education & Social Welfare.

(ii) Establishing a Centre for Educational Technology in the NCERT.

(iii) Assisting States in setting up Educational Technology Cells and their programmes on 100% basis.

(iv) Strengthening a few educational institutions for undertaking Educational Technology programmes.

In accordance with these, a Unit was started in the Ministry since 1971 and the CET in the NCERT was set up during 1973. Educational Technology Cells came into being in different States from 1972-73 onwards. With a view to strengthening selected educational institutions for undertaking Educational Technology programmes, some assistance was given to 50 Continuation Education Centres by the NCERT.

The Unit in the Ministry made all the planning, policy-making and providing funds for implementation of the Educational Project and the CET in the NCERT started functioning in the following areas:

(i) System designing and innovations.

(ii) Training in different areas of Educational Technology.

(iii) Prototype production of suitable hardware and software.

(iv) Research and Evaluation.

(v) Collection and dissemination of information data and consultancy services.

The establishment of ET Cells, however, coincided with introduction of ETV Programmes, mainly on account of Satellite Instructional

Television Experiment in the six States-Andhra Pradesh, Bihar, Karnataka, Madhya Pradesh, Orissa and Rajasthan from the 1st August 1975 onwards. The hectic preparation for implementing the time-bound SITE Project took most of the time and energy available with the ET Cells. However, the ET Cells functioned in the following areas according to the local demands and available resources.

(i) Planning programmes for making efficient use of mass media and modern educational technologies for education including schools and college education, open schools and open universities, further and continuation of education.

(ii) Co-ordination with local AIR and Doordarshan Stations for production of suitable educational programmes for radio and television.

(iii) Preparation of plans for production of educational films for all stages of formal education and for out-of-school informal adult and teacher education.

(iv) Organisation of training courses for scriptwriters, presenters and classroom teachers required for implementing ET programmes.

(v) Production of background literature and guidance materials required for effective use of educational radio and TV programmes.

(vi) Showing educational films in the classroom in relation to curriculum.

(vii) Exploring the possibilities of non-formal education, radio and television.

(viii) Production and utilisation of various audio-visual media and materials.

(ix) Liaisoning between the Government of India in the Ministry of Education, Centre for Educational Technology on one hand and the State Department of Educational Institutions and other concerned agencies on the other.

The ET Project was conceived as a broad-based and collaborative effort among the Ministry of Education, the Ministry of Information & Broadcasting, the Indian Space Research Organisation and other concerned organisations. It underlined the importance of inter-agency co-ordination, systematic planning, scientific evaluation and effective utilization. Operationally, the scheme sought to extend the benefits of technology to large groups, particularly those in rural areas. It aimed at improving the quality of education at all levels, to reduce wastage and stagnation and introduce new methods of teaching and innovations. The programmes of ET Cells were shaped mainly in two ways according to the pressing requirements and facilities available in: (i) SITE States, and (ii)

Non-SITE States.

SITE State Programmes

Although the project was initiated in 1971, it took off only with the launching of the SITE in 1975-76. The instructional television programmes were transmitted directly from the Satellite TV reception sets in 2,300 villages in the six States mentioned earlier. These programmes were transmitted in the morning to primary school students and in the evening to adult viewers.

The ETV Programmes were produced by the *Upagraha Doordarshan Kendras* and Indian Space Research Organisation. The TV Sets were installed mostly in primary schools, community halls and Panchayat Ghars. The ET Cell provided all management and supporting services and facilities for proper use of ETV programmes which include electrification of buildings, appointment of custodians, payment of their remuneration and energy charges, supply of programme schedules, support materials like teacher's notes, etc.

The ET Cells organised training courses for user teachers in the handling of TV sets and utilisation of ETV programmes. They also assisted in the planning of programmes and organisation of training courses for scriptwriters. The ET Cells actively participated in the massive training programmes for science teachers of elementary schools through a multi-media package developed by the CIET, NCERT. About 47,000 teachers were given orientation in science through such training programmes.

The ET Cells conducted research studies and evaluated various aspects of SITE individually and jointly in collaboration with other agencies. Some ET Cells undertook in-depth studies of the impact of educational television programmes. These studies have been useful for bringing about a better understanding of the implication of educational television. Consequently, the ET Cells acquired greater understanding, clarity and insight into the TV process.

They also planned and implemented various programmes for promotion of the use of radio, films and slides in education. Some employed radio and television in training primary school teachers in order to avoid dislocation, to cut down costs and maintain continuous contacts in service. Thus, they gained experience and expertise in organisational and management systems and logistics necessary for large-scale use of various media and materials in education.

Non-SITE State Programmes

The ET Cells in Maharashtra and Tamil Nadu have developed an infrastructure for production and utilisation of TV programmes. Telecasting of the programmes produced by them was, however, done by TV stations at Mumbai and Chennai respectively. Besides, ET Cells in Tamil Nadu launched a special drive for providing radio sets through voluntary assistance of the people and its achievement was remarkable. It also took several measures for integration of educational radio programmes with the school system. The ET Cell in Punjab planned a thematic approach to radio programmes.

The ET Cell in Gujarat launched a training programme involving 10,000 primary school teachers for improving their competence in teaching English. This programme consisted of a systematically planned series of radio programmes and printed materials. It was implemented in collaboration with AIR, State Institute of Education and H.M. Patel Institute of English. In Kerala, a radio-cum-correspondence teacher-training programme was organised since 1975 in collaboration with AIR, SITE and other State agencies. The encouraging experience of such programmes facilitated the development of ET Cells in the State.

Besides the six States (Andhra Pradesh, Bihar, Karnataka, Madhya Pradesh, Orissa and Rajasthan), Maharashtra, Punjab, Tamil Nadu, Uttar Pradesh and Jammu and Kashmir had their ET Cells by 1977-78. In the following two or three years, ET Cells were established in most of the remaining States like Himachal Pradesh, Nagaland, Manipur, Meghalaya, Sikkim, Assam, West Bengal and Mizoram.

Further Steps

As discussed earlier, the ET Cells in six States were mostly devoted to implementation of the SITE programmes during the period from August 1975 to July 1975. The Centre for Educational Technology, NCERT played a leadership role in planning and organising various educational technology programmes. The CET and ET Cells worked as catalytic agents in this field and heralded changes in the educational system. They tried out new approaches for the achievement of educational objectives such as universlization of primary education and removal of illiteracy. Thus a number of innovations were introduced and implemented both for quality and quantity of education.

The CET organised training programmes in order to develop expertise at the national and State levels mainly in the following areas:

(i) Orientation courses in Educational Technology.

(ii) Training courses for scriptwriting in ETV and Educational Radio.

(iii) Training courses for resource persons for media utilization.

(iv) Training courses for writing self-instructional materials.

(v) Training courses for system designing, animation graphics,etc.

The CET conducted a number of surveys and studies in the field of radio, television and other aspects of educational technology for effective planning, utilization and production of Educational Programmes. It also produced prototype materials and offered consultancy services in different aspects of Educational Technology.

The Ministry of Education launched some research studies on the qualitative appraisal of ETV programmes and their impact on enrolment and attendance in collaboration with States ET Cells and Doordarshan Kendras. In Orissa, for example, through intensive field work, data was collected from 1349 children and 238 teachers and inspection officers. The report of the study has already been published by the Ministry of Education. The findings of this pioneering study are felt useful and enlightening for production and utilization of Educational Television Programmes.

The ET Cells paid their attention to systematic planning for better production and utilization of radio and television programmes, slides and films. Training programmes were organised for radio and TV user teachers and scriptwriters. Workshops were held for developing self-instructional materials and graphics. Seminars and conferences were organised for generating awareness about and developing skills in educational technology. A good number of research studies and surveys were conducted by the ET Cells in the use and qualitative appraisal of Radio and TV programmes. The ET Cells also produced various kinds of support and publicity materials and brought out research reports in educational technology.

Experience gained during SITE period was quite encouraging for expansion of TV service in the country. This led the Government of India to decide on starting the SITE Continuity Community Viewing Programme. That is 40% of the villages within 40 Kms of radius were provided community viewing facility in six States SITE cluster areas by setting up terrestrial transmitters. It was also possible due to availability of the infrastructure and studio facilities developed during SITE period.

Thus, the terrestrial transmission was made available from 1977 to 1982 and Educational Television programmes were telecast in the morning hours along with other programmes in the evening.

During this period, consolidation took place in several States. Since only a skeleton staff consisting of an officer-in-charge, two programmers-cum-scriptwriters, two office assistants, one typist-cum-stenographer, a peon and a driver were sanctioned for all ET Cells, it was difficult to cope with the expanding works. All the States have Audio-Visual units/ departments started in 1950s. In such States these units were merged with ET Cells and in some States the officers-in-charge of AV Units were given the charge of ET Cells. In the remaining States both the ET Cells and AV units worked separately. With a view to avoiding duplication of work and waste of physical and human resources, the Ministry of Education decided to amalgamate both the units officially. Although this decision materilised in some States, it faced strong opposition in others on several grounds. Hence, diversity and variety were evident in the infrastructure and resultant activities of the ET Cells which functioned under the Secretariat or Directorate of SCERT(SIE).

Advent of INSAT

The Goverment of India launched an ambitious project, "Indian National Satellite System" in 1982 and decided to substantially improve the educational condition in the country by utilising new communication and information facilities provided by this system, INSAT. The Educational Technology Division in the Ministry of Education and Culture designed a project INSAT for EDUCATION covering the establishment of a Central Institute of Educational Technology (CIET) at New Delhi and State Institute of Educational Technology (SIETs) in all States. The CIET would provide the organisation framework, production capacity and training facilities to assist the SIETs develop and produce Educational TV Programmes relevant to the need and conditions of the target audience in their regions. In the beginning, programmes produced by SIETs were telecast via INSAT and appropriate support materials and utilization components were provided by the SIETs in collaboration with the CIET.

It was decided initially to establish SIETs in the six states-Andhra Pradesh, Orissa, Maharashtra, Gujarat, Uttar Pradesh and Bihar covered under INSAT for Education Project. Although the Government of India has provided substantial financial input to establish the SIETs, external assistance was available for: (i) Consultancy on production of ETV Programmes for alternate approaches in education, (ii) Study tours to give staff from the SITEs an opportunity to study similar activities in other countries, (iii) Fellowships to provide training in outstanding institutions abroad, and (iv) Equipment components that cannot be provided from indigenous sources.

The Indian Educational System has been geared to achieve the following major objectives:

(i) Growth, (ii) Modernization, (iii) Self-reliance, and (iv) Social Justice.

The Sixth Five Year Plan has identified improvement in the quality of life of the people in general and of the disadvantaged sections in particular during this Plan period. The Following educational priorities have been determined for realization:

(i) Universalisation of elementary education through both formal and non-formal means;
(ii) Non-formal education for adults linking education to economic and social needs;
(iii) Development of vocational and professional skills;
(iv) Popularising science with a view to developing a scientific outlook;
(v) Training for citizenship;
(vi) Promoting national integration; and
(vii) Providing information about themes of national importance such as population education, energy conservation, preservation of wild life, environmental sanitation, nutrition and health.

The INSAT system has been designed to provide a multidimensional basis for communication and information in education. The Division of Educational Technology in the Ministry has been performing the following functions:

(i) Preparing plans for the growth of educational and communication systems including various media;
(ii) Preparing plan for increasing utilization of radio and television for education;
(iii) Attending to budgetary work and arranging international funding;
(iv) Promoting policy research and organising expert meetings;
(v) Liaisoning among Ministries Departments and organisation at the national level;
(vi) Advising State governments on matters relating to implementation of the educational technology programme in general and INSAT for Education Project in particular; and
(vii) Promoting necessary co-ordination at the State level for implementing the CIET Project.

The Centre of Educational Technology and Department of Teaching Aids formed the Central Institute of Educational Technology for discharging the following primary responsibilities:

(i) Provision of the overall organisational framework for all INSAT education activities;
(ii) Establishment and maintenance of a Central ETV and radio production facility;
(iii) Production and evaluation of programmes of national importance and prototypes for regional applications;
(iv) Training of production, technical and evaluation staff of the SIETs

and other agencies;

(v) Overall monitoring and impact studies;

(vi) Initiating, coordinating and conducting of research studies; and

(vii) Information and documentation services.

As per the decision of the Government of India, the ET Cells in most of the States have been upgraded and in others were upgraded to State Institutes of Educational Technology under the overall umbrella of the SCERT/SIE. They are required to perform almost the same activities at the State level as the CIET does at the national level. In the beginning, permanent production centres for ETV and radio programmes have been started in the six States and gradually such facilities were provided to all the States in the country. Staff were recruited in the following three categories and steps were taken for training them:

(a) Academic and Production Staff;

(b) Engineering Staff; and

(c) Administrative and Supporting Personnel.

Current Scenario

Since the Ministry of Education and Culture (Now Ministry of Human Resources Development) have been providing 100 per cent financial assistance for manning and equipping the SIETs, progress has been evident in developing the infrastructure particularly in recruiting personnel in the six States of Orissa, Bihar, Maharashtra, U.P., Gujarat and Andhra Pradesh.

Although all emphasis has been laid over these years particularly on production of ETV programmes for the children in the age-groups of 5-8 years and 9-11 years and teachers of primary schools, the status of production or the quantum of ETV programmes, on the whole, is far from satisfactory. In comparison to huge expenditure incurred on payment of staff salary, installation of costly equipment and other recurring as well as non-recurring expenditure, the outcome is very negligible. Besides, the SIETs are required to train the teachers, scriptwriters and others concerned with production, utilization and evaluation of ETV programmes, to conduct studies and produce support materials to ensure better utilization of such programmes. But unforunately the progress in these aspects has not been encouraging at all.

These SIETs and ET Cells/ Departments working in various States are expected to work for production and utilization of other media and materials like radio and audio programmes. Various appropriate technologies are now used and developed for improvement of school and teacher education. But such activities are not satisfactory in most of the States. Hence, the programmes and problems of these agencies or organisations should be reviewed without further delay and immediate steps be taken for the total reorientation and revamping of the functionaries. Otherwise the very purpose of setting up these institutions will be defeated and valuable human as well as materials resources be wasted without realising the laudable objectives kept in view.

Educational Technology flourished in this country as a centrally sponsored scheme and various kinds of facilities like colour TV sets, Radio-cum-Cassette Players (RCCP), VCR, VCP etc., were provided to different schools. The six autonomous SIETs in Utter Pradesh, Bihar, Orissa, Maharashtra, Gujarat and Andhra Pradesh were funded by the Central Government., and more financial support was extended to the CIET, NCERT for producing programmes for the schools for telecasting/broadcasting through Doordarsan/Akash Vani. CIETs and SIETS were funded under the scheme for producing ETV and radio programmes for education. The Educational Technology programmes tried to bring about qualitative improvement and widening the access to education. By 1999-2000 approximately 3,92,438 RCCP and 75,001 colour TV sets were provided to the States and Union Territories for primary and upper-primary schools. CIET & SIETs produced as many as 683 video and audio programmes. The importance of educational technology and its expansion is increasing with every passing day.

1

Understanding Education Technology

In the view of Eric Ashby (1967), mankind is now in the midst of the Fourth Revolution in Education - the Age of Electronic Media which comprises radio, television, audio/video recorder, computer and so on. The NPE '86 has therefore added (p.22) "In the villages without electricity batteries or solar packs will be utilised to run the programme." It has also suggested that in order to avoid structural dualism, modern educational technology must reach out to the most distant areas and the most deprived sections of beneficiaries simultaneously with the areas of comparative affluence and availability. The Programme of Action (POA), 1986 (P.180)[1] has rightly pointed out that several efforts have been made in the past to use technological aids for improving the quality of education. Audio visual units and film libraries were set up at the Centre and in States for promoting the use of educational films and projection aids. Educational Technology Centres and Cells were established at the national and state levels respectively for facilitating the use of various media, particularly radio and television. Although School Broadcast programme has been in vogue for more than four decades, it has not yet been accepted whole-heartedly and in massive scale throughout the country. Educational Television Programme, in spite of its glamour and potentiality, has not yet been popular in the educational institutions.

In many states and union territories, State Institutes of Educational Technology (SIETs) and at the national level the Central Institute of Educational Technology have been producing, utilising, monitoring and following up the television and radio programmes for improving the quantity and quality of education. Under the project "INSAT for EDUCATION" launched in 1982, the SIETs have been generating educational software for children. The Audio Visual Research Centres (AVRCs) and Educational Media Research Centres (EMRCs) have been producing Educational TV Programmes for college/university students. Some Technical Teacher Training Institutions (TTTIs) have also been developing facilities for production of TV as well as other media programmes. Video Technology has made a headway in the field of education. The Electronic Trade and Technology Development Corporation (ET & TDC) has formulated a TELETEACH Project to prepare software on video-tape. A good number of secondary schools have been selected by the Ministry of Education for equipping them with VCRs and viewing equipment to work as viewing centres.

Computer Education has been popular in the country at various stages of education. The Computer Literacy and Studies in Schools (CLASS) Project has been implemented in hundreds of Schools and with availability of microcomputers there, the students have been familiarised with the application and potentiality of computer as learning medium. Computer eduction courses are now available in many universities besides Ph.D., M.Tech., and B.Tech Programmes conducted by the IITs and other technological institutions. Diploma level courses are being offered by a few dozens of polytechnics. Although educational broadcasting has the inherent advantages of greater reach, management, convenience and cost effectiveness, the non-broadcast/non-project media and materials are more oriented to individual learning and more appropriate to the indigenous clientele and developing economy. These media would also help in enriching the learning process. Large scale use of audio and video programmes in broadcast and non-broadcast modes would generate enormous demand for qualified manpower to work in educational media set-ups. It would be necessary to develop maintenance structure and train "technician entrepreneurs" for taking up such responsibilities. As enunciated in the POA (1986) "Education requires media support which is related to the curriculum as well as enrichment. Curriculum-based education also requires materials which the teacher can draw upon in the course of this teaching. This could be provided in the form of charts, slides, transparencies etc. Video technology offers considerable potential for improving the quality of education especially at higher levels."

Similarly computer technology is likely to influence education enormously and can play an important role in enhancing the efficiency of the teaching-learning process, making children more creative and providing them with an individualised learning environment. Computer literacy would be crucial in preparing children to cope with microcomputer explosion which has the same potential for social change as the Industrial Revolution. It is essential to integrate the same progressively with the school curriculum.

Meaning

The modern world is confronting two general problems which are not only affecting the pattern of human life, but also inflicting their full impact on education. These two problems are called "information explosion" and the "population explosion." They are like two horns of dilemma in education-more things to learn and more people to be taught.

The term "information explosion" really means an explosion of knowledge. We all know, new frontiers of knowledge are opening day by day and the horizon of human knowledge and understanding is expanding very fast. In most of the subjects, moreover, knowledge is cumulative, so that every now and then, there is more to be learnt. Especially in arts subjects, new facts and figures take their place along with the old. In sciences although new knowledge or information often supersedes the old, the students and scientists have to learn both. Besides, closer relations among countries of the world resulting from wide international communications make information explosion more acute and complicated.

The second problem is "Population Explosion" which is immensely affecting traditional pattern of education. The problem of population explosion is more serious in the developing countries than the developed ones. For example, in India population has been increasing in geometrical progression. India now has more than 1000 million people.

Michael J. Apter (1968 p.10)[2] has rightly observed, "The increase in population has of course tended to occur fastest in the developing countries. For this reason the problem it poses for education is the greatest in these countries. Conversely, the information explosion has the greatest immediate effect on the technologically advanced countries. Fortunately, no country has experienced the full effects of both at the same time. Nevertheless, there is a fair degree of overlap between the effects of the two." The developing countries like India, however, are facing serious difficulties both from population as well as information explosion. Because they have to provide education for a larger population year by year and cover more and more technical and scientific ground for making up the deficiency. Since most of the countries are confronted more or less with the problem of more persons to be taught and more information to be learnt, this general problem is called "Education Explosion."

Narrow and Wider Meanings

Educational technology, in its global sense, includes the entire process of the setting of goals, the continuous reforms of curriculum, the tryout of new methods and materials, the evaluation of the system as an integrated whole and resetting of goals on the basis of the findings of evaluation and innovations. But it is often identified as pointed out by Spaulding, with various devices and processes which make possible the recording, storage, manipulation, retrieval, transmission and display of data, information and printed and photographed materials with an efficiency and speed unheard of, even 20 years ago. If these capabilities are considered as part of a broad curriculum for research and development design, they have tremendous potential in education.

Technological materials and methods useful in the teaching-learning process range from chalkboards to television sets. Technology of education involves books and blackboards, paper and pencils, models and maps, charts and globes, tapes and slides, radios and televisions, projectors and computers. It comprises both "hardware" and "software" and both audio and visual materials. It also includes decisions about the educational objectives to be achieved and decisions about the size of the learning group, the learning sequence, teaching methods and selection of media.

In its wider perspective, therefore, educational technology deals with the systematic application of the resources of scientific knowledge to the process that each individual has to pass through in order to acquire and use knowledge. "Educational Technology" writes Geoffrey Hubbard (1974), Director of the National Council for Educational Technology, England "is the complement of curriculum reform concerned with the Method where curriculum reform is concerned with the content... Given an acceptance of the concept of educational technology as the process of improving learning method, we are faced with the problems of encouraging innovation in an educational system whose greatest strength is in decentralisation and autonomy. Certainly nothing will be achieved by elaborating authoritarian solutions. Wnat is needed is more discussion of the contribution the different elements of the system can make to the problems facing education. Widespread dissemination of experience (both successful and unsuccessful) of innovations and supporting services, including training, consultancy and information activities are necessary to assist the teacher in the selection and introduction of the new methods appropriate to his own particular situation."

According to GOM Leith "Educational Technology is the application of scientific knowledge about learning and the conditions of learning to improve the effectiveness and efficiency of Teaching and Training. In the absence of scientifically established principles, educational technology implements techniques of empirical testing to improve learning situations." Hence educational technology seeks to apply scientific knowledge about learning and the conditions of learning for improving its effectiveness.

Nature and Characteristics

We find that a large number of new methods and media constitute educational technology. But there is no proper co-ordination and articulation in their use. That is why, no satisfactory results are achieved by such a wide range of materials due to lack of a systematic planning and organisation. Henri Dieuzeide (1970), Director of UNESCO's Division of Methods, Materials and Techniques has aptly remarked. "The new techniques do in fact offer a vast range of possibilities, but their field of application often seems to be a wasteland scattered with spare parts which no one knows how to put together to form an efficient system. Here it is useful to discuss the difference between technology in education and technology of education. We have to move from one to the other, i.e. from the former to the latter. Technology in education is concerned with equipment, preparation of adhoc messages and integration with traditional teacher-centered activities. But as discussed earlier, technology of education deals with the active use of mass media and computer science for the individual pupils learning process under the teacher's supervision. Hence the latter one i.e. educational technology is more scientific, more psychological and more pedagogical than the former one i.e. technology in education."[3]

With the advance of science and technology there are new learning aids which have revolutionized the learning process in particular and education as a whole. In modern society with its emphasis on mass education and successful citizenship training, the requirement is for efficient learning. Education has now become an assembly-line like mass production factories. A nation can prosper if its education can be made effective. Education can be made efficient, if it uses modern technology. Technology in education will be useful, if it is properly planned and organised on psychological and pedagogical principles. Henri Dieuzeide has rightly observed, "The transition from technology in education to the technology of education involves a through appraisal of the existing educational system, of its objectives and of the means used to attain them, before any decision is reached to employ these new techniques for specific teaching purposes. The teacher-turned technologist can then gradually assume the functions of an 'educational engineer' whose job is to increase the output of the entire scholastic machine."

Although educational technology can be interpreted in a rather narrow sense as the use of sophisticated hardware in teaching or in a broad sense as the use of any new educational technique, in fact the concept means more than the sum total of all the media and methods, materials and techniques used for better teaching and learning. It involves or should involve greater psychological and pedagogical preparedness, a scientific attitude and a coordinated approach to the educational process as a whole. It should reflect one's professional interest and zeal for making experiments and innovations for development and success of education.

Educational Technology implies the use of all educational resources-men and materials, methods and techniques, means and media in an integrated and systematic manner for optimizing learning. According to the modern educationists, learning not teaching is the crucial task of the entire educational process and emphasis of teachers is regarded as a system which facilitates learning and makes learning effective as well as efficient. Efficient in the sense that the learning with the use of Educational Technology becomes easy and interesting, durable and comprehensive. Efficient in the sense that it is economical and financially viable. In fact, effective communication of educational messages in an economic way is the main objective of educational technology.

Hardware v. Software

Educational Technology is not a new-comer, although the concept as such is comparatively new in the field of education. The educational process was teacher-centred, the method of rote-learning was important, a few textbooks were the main resource and chalkboard was the only aid. Subsequently, a number of audio-visual materials were introduced and used in the teaching-learning process. It was usually thought that teaching machines, film-projectors, slide-projectors, language laboratories, tape-recorders, cassettes, radio, television, video-tape recorders, computers and so on, are educational technology. In brief, all the audio-visual equipments are regarded as the Educational Technology. But this is only one aspect of educational technology and is called hardware component. Another aspect is new-methods of teaching, tested principles and practices, innovation e.g., programmed learning, micro-teaching, team-teaching etc., are called software component of educational technology. Both software and hardware constitute the concept of educational technology and both of them go hand in hand to maximise the effects of teaching-learning process. Thus increased efficiency of the process is the keynote of the Educational Technology.

Scope of Education Technology

Following are the factors leading to growth of educational technology:

i) appearance of a number of audio-visual aids which needed to be put together in order to avoid confusion and wastage of resources i.e. multimedia approach to education.

ii) increasing influence of science and scientific knowledge and skills of education.

iii) development of programmed learning approach.

iv) explosion of numbers and knowledge, facts and figures.

v) teaching revolution and recent development in pedagogy.

vi) expansion of educational broadcasting and computers.

vii) emergence of a systems theory.

Various Dimensions

Although in a narrow way educational technology means little more than the use of sophisticated hardware in teaching, including overhead projectors, tape-recorders, televised films, cassettes video-discs, gramophones etc., in a broad way it may be interpreted to mean the use of any new technique or methods of teaching. Technology of education would include the entire process of setting the goal, the continuous renewal of curriculum, the trying out and use of new methods and materials, the evaluation of the system as a whole, and the resetting of goals in view of the changing circumstances. It is also often identified with various devices and means or recording, storage, manipulation, retrieval, transmission and display of data and information with high efficiency and speed. They are considered as an integral part of a broad curriculum for research and development design amounting to tremendous potentialities in education.

Technological media and materials useful in the instructional process range from simple varieties of helping teachers to develop and present his lessons more effectively in traditional classrooms to sophisticated machines and mechanisms completely changing the classroom teaching structure and situations. A number of technological media and materials can be useful in both teaching and in the management of administrative data that is necessary in modern mass education. The computer, for example, can be used in the instructional process by efficient manipulation of instructional materials (computer-assisted instruction) and at the same time can be used to make new kinds of administrative strategies possible (making the complicated individual tests of students, the flexible scheduling of classes feasible and so on).

Areas of Influence

ET exercises direct influence in following areas:

i) Curriculum and development.
ii) Revolutionary change in teaching and learning methodology and practices.
iii) Shift in emphasis from teaching to learning.
iv) Media application in education and the development of media taxonomy.
v) Quantitative and qualitative expansion of education.
vi) Emphasis on non-formal education and special education systems.
vii) New assessment criteria and procedures.
viii) Emphasis and research, continued evaluation and recycling process in education.
ix) New role and position of teachers and an increasing emphasis on in-service training of teachers.
x) Appearance of resource libraries and teacher's centers.
xi) Changes in structural patterns of educational organisations to facilitate interaction between programme producers, course designers and users.
xii) Application of economic considerations and cost-effective criterion in education.
xiii) Use of ET in the field of lifelong and continuing education.

Comprehensiveness

The use E.T. encompasses all types of education-formal, non-formal and informal education, primary, secondary and higher education, adult and continuing education. ET has been applied largely in the field of distance/open learning system. Thus, educational technology is very comprehensive and all pervasive, covering all stages of education. Its scope is very broad, flexible, open and ever-widening. It is an emerging field that includes all modern methods, media and materials that are being invented every now and then, and being utilised for improving the quality and quantity of education.

Technology's Role in Improvement of Quantity and Quality of Education

"The house of education which we want to build is of course going to be different than the cottage in which we are living till this time. We know the present cottage does not fulfill our needs at present and certainly not going to cater for the needs in the coming decade" said I.J. Patel, President, Indian Association for Programmed Learning in his keynote address at the Fourth Annual Conference on Programmed Learning and

Educational Technology, Bombay, with reference to changing circumstances. What are these reforms then?

Educationists now-a-days realize that in education 'learning' is more important than 'teaching.' Learning is concerned with pupils whereas teaching is concerned with pupils and teachers. In the olden days, a teacher was the only source of knowledge. The students learnt what the teacher taught. With the advent of textbooks and other learning aids, the teacher's personal knowledge though important, ceased to be the only or even the paramount source of learning. Hence, the textbook, author, the radio programmer, the film-producer and many others now assist in the learning process.

The traditional classroom with one teacher teaching 30 or 40 students which was mainly one-way communication of information, is no longer effective for modern times. The two general factors- "information explosion" and "population explosion" are bringing about changes in the developed and developing countries. Both of them have posed critical problems for education. More things to be learnt and more individuals to learn. It is not possible to solve them by conventional means. For solving these problems successfully, educational technology consisting of various media of mass communication, suitable child-learning process and modern testing and evaluation techniques are required. Especially in developing countries like India, it has to be mastered and utilized by educationists, if they are to keep pace with each other and catch up with developed nations. As such, both quantitative expansion as well as qualitative improvement of education can be facilitated and accelerated with the help of educational technology. As Apter has succinctly pointed out, "Today a technology of education is being developed with the aim not only of making education more widely available, but also of improving the quality of education which is already available."

Curriculum Development

Any kind of educational improvement should be preceded by suitable curriculum reforms. Curriculum is the sum total of learning experiences provided by school. It is called the "stuff of education." It is what we teach, what the students learn, what we examine for and what we give degrees or diplomas for when students pass through. But we should make it relevant to and continuous with the changing needs of the present and challenges of the future. It must be defined in terms of what and how we want the students to know, do, think, feel and appreciate when they are in or outside the school. While determining objectives and defining their respective learning experiences, we must keep in mind what kinds of knowledge, skills, thoughts and feelings the children bring with them when they come to the school. We should also consider what kinds of things are happening to them outside the school or inside the society where they are likely to go and what they will probably do after their schooling.

Seth Spaulding (1970 p.11)[4] has very rightly observed that one of the reasons for current student unrest throughout the world is the fact that curriculum reform has not been continuous and the curriculum has not been entirely relevant, neither to what the student brings to it, nor to that the student expects from it. The student in today's secondary school and university is a very different kind of person from the student of a generation or two ago. The information explosion has enormously affected the younger generation. The secondary school student has probably learned more out of school than he has in school and the university student often feels much closer to the problems of his nation than does the professor who lectures to him. Yes the curriculum has changed little to reflect the changing nature of the students and the society in which education exists.

Which subjects constitute the curriculum for secondary schools? Many of the subject-matters may be outdated or irrelevant. But it must be agreed that we should teach our students to know, do, think and feel about democracy, population problems, pollution problems, and so on for future development of the country.

On the basis of broad objectives, curriculum planning should be done and suitable subject content, behavioural outcomes and other learning experiences be put in for making curriculum comprehensive. It should be based on the findings of curriculum research and be enriched by interdisciplinary collaboration among experts different subjects. All this would contribute to the design of a total school curriculum that is complementary as well as comprehensive. Spaulding has added, "This kind of curriculum building process would represent a scientific approach to the applied art of teaching. It would make possible a 'system approach' to curriculum planning (or at least a systematic approach) where-by various goals as seen by different sectors of society are considered and a matrix of goals agreed upon. These broad goals are then spelt out into behavioural goals in concrete terms. Suitable methods, strategies and materials would be suggested and tried out and then improved upon. Accordingly, teacher training programmes would be formulated and implemented for training teachers to enable them to manage with competence the new content, new media and new materials.

Future Perceptions

It goes without saying that the use of various new methods and devices is desirable for helping the teacher to do his work better whatever he has traditionally been doing for long time. With this aim in view the audio-visual movement has been launched for the past two generations. But due to lack of co-ordination and sincere efforts, the audio-visual materials have not been used adequately. Many of such aids have been found lying idle and dusty and some have been out of order for most of the time. Of course, there are some teachers who take keen interest in it and make optimum use of the audio-visual materials available with them. Spaulding (1970 p. 18) has rightly remarked, "These first generation educational technologies have suffered (and continue to suffer) from ineffective utilisation because they are usually not conceived of as part of an entirely new strategy of instruction which requires new kinds of administrative support, new kinds of curriculum materials (software) and suitable for presentation via the devices (hardware) and new ways of managing the materials so that they are easily available to the teacher."[5]

In the beginning, the audio-visual materials were only put to marginal and individualized uses. Subsequently they were applied as a stop-gap treatment for deficiencies in the system. There was neither any coherent thinking nor a scientific organization of these materials in the educational process. The new techniques used were very slow in finding their way into schools. Their increased use has been mainly due to interest and initiative of certain teachers. Gramophone and radio have been used for singing and games; projectors have been used to illustrate history, geography, tape-recorders for oral expression, pronunciation and narrating stories either individually or in groups and television for teaching any subject-item.

Thus educational technology materials have proved to help in clarifying concepts, stimulating group and individual activities, developing a collective critical awareness, changing attitudes, imposing a new structure or organization on certain subjects and encouraging originality and creativeness. Henri Dieuzeide (1970 p. 5) has also added, "The use of these techniques has even sometimes made it possible to progress beyond a mere change in the educational climate and, for example, to encourage problem-solving abilities either collective or individual or develop self-evaluation processes."[6]

There has been no systematic use of technology in education. Pupils are exposed to "sporadic bursts of audio-visual information." Only the half-hearted attempts are made to apply the techniques to conventional school activities. Use of these aids, as already said, depends entirely on the teacher himself and becomes meaningful and relevant only when carefully fitted into an educational pattern decided by him. Therefore, teachers have to be properly motivated and made interested in the use of such materials. And also mere interest will not help much. They have to be trained and oriented in the adequate use and maintenance of the materials.

Educational Technology has to be taken up as a comprehensive and continuous programme. It has, of course, to be used as a remedy for inherent deficiencies in the system, in on place to offset the teachers' lack of qualifications by regular broadcast demonstrations or by programmed documents for the pupils; in another to speed up the introduction of new subjects or new methods of teaching, to take over activities on which schools have fallen down and so on. Teacher-training programmes can thus be improved by radio and television broadcasts.

In many modern countries like the U.S.A., U.K., and France, attempts were made through special programmes of radio and television to eliminate the maladjustments between the school and the community by making up the cultural handicaps of certain classes of children. These broadcasts are intended to prepare them for school environment and to make up the "cultural lag" of certain classes of people in the society.

It is often found that these devices or media have been hurriedly introduced and used without sufficient planning and forethought. With the plea of urgency they have often been put to use for which they were not designed. For instance, television has some times been used simply as a means of verbal communication without any visual content thus repeating the old-fashioned teaching practices like lecture method or verbal teaching learning by heart, encouraging passive attitudes, autocratic teaching, etc. Therefore, the media are criticised as "retrograde innovations" which have tended to displace or disguise problems rather than solve them.

Moreover, the half-hearted combination of technology with a traditional system, by stressing to the point of caricature the worst features of the system, has forcibly emphasized the need to re-examine its aims and its methods.

With the development of research in cognitive and child psychology, educational technology has come to be immensely influenced as well as developed. Modern psychology in general and Piaget's work in particular on the behaviour and aptitudes of children, learner's readiness and needs, has everywhere been felt. At the same time, Skinner's work on learning and the development of programmed learning have had an equally wide influence on education. The users of the new technologies have been led to state education problems in more precise terms as regards aims, organisation of the subject to be taught, nature of learners' activities and evaluation methods in relation to educational aims and objectives. This Copernican revolution in teaching has transferred the center of gravity of educational thinking and activities from the teachers' functions to the pupils' activities and as such has enlarged the prospects opened up by "Educational Technology."

Educational Technology can promote a certain amount of flexibility into the functioning of the school system which has been in a rut for decades. For imparting in-service training to teachers and improving their professional growth, educational technology provides ample opportunities. It also works as a means of rapid dissemination of education on a massive scale and of increasing the effectiveness of education by making learning a more individual process. Moreover, educational technology implies assembly-line methods for the production of teaching materials and a division of talent in their uses.

The development of educational technology would open up the prospect of creating and recreating new types of educational institutions in future radically different in structure and function from those of the traditional ones. It would help in reducing wastage to a minimum, which is a great drainage of resources both physical and human. Since the society of tomorrow is to be founded on lifelong education, the self-teaching or self-study centers would grow-up, which can possess various educational technologies. Even the formal teaching would no longer mean a matter of forcing information upon inert pupils in an authoritarian method, but one of exposing self-motivated youth to the practices of self-teaching or self-learning.

The misgiving that the role of teachers will be reduced, is not at all entertained by the exponents of educational technology. Rather it is affirmed that teachers will be made more receptive and will be placed in a more central position where pupils can more easily approach him with their individual problems. Henri Dieuzeide (1970 p.13) an expert of international distinction on the matter has rightly asserted, "In this connection, we cannot stress too strongly the fact that the use of educational technology far from implying any qualitative decline in the role of the teacher frees him from certain purely mechanical tasks of exposition and repetition, thus enabling him to devote himself to the noble and irreplaceable functions of stimulation of interest, diagnosis, motivation and advice."[7]

Implementation of NPE, 1986 and Revised NPE,1992

According to POA (p. 183) "Educational Technology offers the means to reach numbers in remote and inaccessible areas, remove disparity in educational facilities available to the disadvantaged and provide individualized instruction no learners conveniently suited to their needs and pace of learning". All these technologies require adequate infrastructure, supporting staff, trained personnel, suitable building (even in urban areas), willing teachers etc. Since in the rural areas assured electricity supply is not available NPE, 1986 (p.22) has suggested, "In villages without electricity, batteries or solar packs will be used to run the programme. Thus alternative arrangements need be made for avoiding frustrations and dislocation in the teaching-learning process."[8]

The Ministry of Human Resource Development (MHRD) and the Ministry of Information & Broadcasting should jointly plan for long-term and effective use of media usage. The CIET and UGC should also make coordinated efforts in providing leadership and guidance in production of software, conducting research and evaluations as well as training the personnel for production and utilisation. The State governments and their agencies should take up production of locally relevant programmes and materials providing equipment and receiving systems, monitoring and evaluating the utilization of such technologies at various levels. Voluntary agencies of such technologies should be involved as far as possible in the production and utilization systems. Both hardware and software facilities should be provided by these agencies and mutual cooperation should be ensured for their effective maintenance and application.

During the 9th Plan the National Policy on Education, 1986 and POA, 1986 were reviewed and recast. Most of the SIETs were made autonomous. Particularly, the Central Institute of Educational Technology (CIET) and 6 SIETs in Uttar Pradesh, Bihar, Orissa, Gujarat, Maharashtra and Andhara Pradesh were strengthened and continued to produce ETV Programmes since 1988. During 8th Plan it was found that the working of SIETs and their output was not up to the mark. Hence, an attempt was made to improve the quality of producation and increase their output. The ETV Programmes were mainly of an enrichment type. The number of Non-Government Organisations (NGOs) was not substantial so far in this field and an important initiative was taken in distribution of radio-cum-cassette players and colour TV sets in primary schools. Programme were also produced for Adult Education and Teacher Training, particularly, for orientation and enrichment. The lecturers in ET and Teacher Educators of

DIETs were trained by CIETs and other Institutions. The teacher training institutions like DIETs, CTE and IASEs were provided with VCRs and colour TV sets and efforts were made to produce and make suitable software available for their optimal utilisation.

At higher education level, IGNOU continued to provide a half-hour slot on the national TV network every day. Country-wide Class Room Programme of the UGC continued its transmission daily. The UGC created 15 Educational Media Research Centres (EMRCs) and Audio-Visual Research Centres (AVRCs) which produced programmes for higher education. The UGC also developed and set-up an Inter-University Consortium for Educational Communication (IUCEC) for providing co-ordination and leadership among the above institutions. Some NGOs also came forward to produce software material with the UGC assistance. In technical education, 4 Technical Teacher Training Institutes (TTTIs) and some IITs were provided reasonable production infrastructure and they produced programmes suitable for technical education. The Ministry of Human Resource Development made expert assessment of the needs of programme production and personnel training and made initial attempts for improving the existing conditions. With the availability of INSAT, more transmission capability was acquired and the GRAMSAT Project was implemented by the Department of Space.

Computer Education was promoted in schools under the CLASS Project. Computer Literacy Programme was encouraged in most of the schools by the professional agencies. The CBSE pioneered Computer Science Education at higher secondary stage and some State Boards followed suit. The UGC also started the programme by providing PCs, introducing diploma and degree courses in computer science and providing research and higher studies in this field. The CLASS Project expanded its area of operation. Besides MHRD, Ministry of Information and Broadcasting, Department of Space, Department of Electronics and Finance Ministry augmented transmission facilities for educational programmes and set up educational channels. The CIET and UGC co-ordinated and monitored training and production facilities and State Governments were involved in the funding and management of educational technology programmes.

References

1. Government of India. *The Programme of Action*, (MHRD), Education, 1986, p. 180
2. Apter, M.J. *The New Technology of Education*, MacMillan, London, 1968, p. 10.

3. Dieuzeide, Henry, *Educational Technology and Development of Education*, UNESCO, IEY No. 8, 1970.
4. Seth, Spaulding. *Advanced Educational Technologies*, Vol. 1, No. 3, 1970, p. 11.
5. *Ibid*, p. 18.
6. Dieuzeide, Henry, *op.cit.*, p. 5
7. *Ibid*, p. 13
8. Government of India. (MHRD) Education, *The National Policy of Education*, 1986, p. 22.

2

Role of Technology in Different Stages of Education

Pre-school Education

Communicating anything to young children calls for special skills and experience. Communication means sharing of ideas and feelings. It involves interaction that encourages give and take. Since it is a two-way process, mutual sharing and interaction are essential. Various media facilitate such communication and ensure its effectiveness. Gone are the days when the teacher was a dictator and children were only silent listeners. In the past, children were seated as rows of butterflies transfixed with pins and were stuffed with inert ideas. Teachers were used to verbalism and students were forced to rote learning. Therefore the teaching-learning process was dry, dreary and drab which resulted in mostly ineffective exercise.

The modern education is paedocentric and emphasis has shifted from subject of instruction to the nature and needs of children, Learning is given more importance than teaching. That is why, science of teaching or pedagogy has given way to science of learning or mathematics. At present, educational programmes are to be devised and media used according to the mathematic principles or theory of behaviour of children undergoing the process of learining.

Needs of the Pre-school Child

The world-famous psychologists like Comenius, Rousseau, Pestalozzi and Piaget have arrived at the conclusion that every child has the built-in physiological and neurological mechanism for learning. This mechanism has to be exploited fully and learning experiences be provided adequately. Benjamin Bloom has also observed that environment during early years of life is very significant for cognitive development. Therefore all kinds of facilities should be provided to the child to explore, to enquire, to play and to interact with his peers, parents and teachers for optimum education.

The pre-school years of a child is the period of its maximum learning and intellectual development and hence of great potential educational significance. Especially in view of the poor family conditions and deprived communities as well as environment, pre-school education has assumed more importance. In the context of universalisation of elementary education it has additional significance. Dr. S.K. Mitra, a psychologist of national repute, has pointed out that if children were made to take interest in learning right from the tender age, then it would appreciably bring down the present high percentage of wastage and stagnation during early years of primary schooling. The Education Communication, 1964-66 have also mentioned[1] that the pre-primary schools are required to provide suitable environment to the boys and girls hailing from urban facilities whose small tenements or flats are hardly appropriate for the children's proper growth. These schools also seek to compensate for the unsatisfactory home environment of children from slum areas of poor families. With the use of suitable media the teaching-learning process can be made more interesting and school situation more attractive.

Classification of Media

All the media are aids to teaching or learning. They are roughly classified into (i) audio, (ii) visual and (iii) audio-visual. Tape/cassette, records, gramophone records, radio programme etc., of the first category; pictures, charts, slides, film-strips etc., are of second category and video recording, TV programme, activities etc., belong to the third category. These aids are mainly divided into - (i) projected and (ii) non-projected media. Films, filmstrips, slides, overhead transparencies etc., are example of the projected media, whereas pictures, charts, sound/audio recordings, models etc., are the instances of non-projected media.

Wilbur Schramm has classified all kinds of media into two. One is big media like films, television, video cassettes/records and little media like radio programme, audio tapes, gramophone records, slides, graphics. Media are again divided into six categories as follows:-

(1) *Graphic media* : Pictures, photographs, flash cards, charts, posters, graphs, maps, diagrams etc.

(2) *Display boards*	:	Chalkboards, flannel boards, bulletin boards; peg boards etc.
(3) Three-dimensional media	:	Models, objects, specimens, puppets etc.
(4) *Projected media*	:	Slides, film-strips, transparencies, TV, video tapes, films, etc.
(5) *Audio media*	:	Radio, audio cassettes, gramophone records, etc.
(6) *Activity media*	:	Field trips, dramatization, demonstration, role-playing etc.

Assessing Media

It is not possible to discuss the advantages and limitations of each medium in this chapter. But just to have a cursory views on this problem, we may discuss the broad categories of media: (i) visuals, (ii) audio and (ii) A.V. aids including activities. Media is by far a primary source of information. There is a saying " I hear and I forget, I see and I remember." It is also said that a picture should be lively, clear and meaningful. The pictures should be clear, precise and bold. Models and specimens are useful for making ideas and structures comprehensible, but the scale down sizes should be properly explained to the audience e.g., model of tsetse fly in Africa. Similarly, magnetic board or flannel board is useful for displaying visuals, but it should be used with proper understanding of the viewers. Otherwise simple and unsophisticated children and people will be merely amazed by the magnetic power without understanding the actual message. A slide is called "a headful in a handful" since it can explain many things, but it has to be prepared with proper sequence and relevance.

Activities like field trips, excursions and dramatization should be properly planned and well-organised. Otherwise, time and resources are wasted and educational gains or learning outcomes are not satisfactory. Even films or TV programmes with all the glamour and music if, fail to get if the audience fail to get the real message. Radio or audio tape/cassette recording is very powerful, inexpensive and very easy to handle. But it demands ample indulgence from the audience as it is mainly aural and one-sided. These materials have to be made interesting and supported with discussion. There should be adequate interaction with the audience and the programmes should be relevant and meaningful.

It must be realized that media are aids to communication and particularly useful to young children for making the teaching-learning process interesting and meaningful. But all care and precautions must be taken in planning, preparing and utilizing these media as effectively as possible. Like too much verbalization, too much pictorialisation is bad. Every medium should be used in right time, in right place and in right manner. Active participation as well as interaction should be promoted in the classrooms. Reasonable feedback should be provided for improving the media as well as ensuring success of communication process. Children are inquisitive, curious and active by nature. They are sensitive as well as possessive. Therefore, adequate scope and facility should be provided to them for free participation, discussion and activities. More actively they are involved in the process, more will be the success of the teaching-learning process. Media materials may even be prepared by children themselves under the guidance of teachers as far as possible. Because this will promote their ego involvement, belongingness and awareness about the various aspects of subject matter. Media, however, should be made slaves, not masters of the situations.

Primary Education

Childhood years are significant for intellectual growth and personality development. It is the period of maximum learning and as such is crucial for education of the child. Every child is endowed with the built-in physiological as well as neurological mechanism for learning. This mechanism is, however, to be exploited fully by providing learning experiences adequately. The foundation of all values, attitudes and even achievement is laid in the early years of an individual. Further, development of all kinds, intellectual, emotional, social and physical, is very rapid during this period and any deprivation or stimulation is most active either causing obstruction or acceleration in the growth process.

Although both nature of heredity and nature or environment play their parts in the development of personality in all its facets- intellect, emotion, values, attitudes, physiques and so on, ceiling for ultimate development is determined not only by the inherited potentials, but also by environmental stimulations, particularly received during childhood. Thus, the child's development ceiling becomes lower or higher according to the extent and quantum of nurturing facilities. Primary education provides necessary amenities for such development.

Improving Primary Education

This holds good for children from any country or culture. But in India, it is more important as a high percentage of population are deprived and disadvantaged both socially and economically. The environment of most of the Indian children is poor and unstimulating. The child is in many cases the first generation learner and does not get adequate stimulation and support from his parents, peers and siblings. He is left to himself for development and education. The research findings in this field reveal that our children when they enter primary schools have serious handicaps in learning. Their vocabulary is very limited, their concept formation is very poor and their psychomotor co-ordination is quite inadequate. When these children are required to respond to certain standard of learning in the schools, they start disliking and develop a kind of aversion towards rigid system of early education. This leads to heavy dropouts and stagnation particularly at the primary stage. All the attempts made for universalisation of primary education are, therefore, found mostly unfruitful and inadequate.

It is, therefore, felt imperative to make primary school an attractive place for children and to make its programmes interesting to them. Learning in the primary school should be made joyful and entertaining instead of making it dry and drab. Gone are the days when the teacher was an autocrat and pupils were mute subjects; he was only to talk and they were to hear silently. Children need not be stuffed with facts and figures only and be treated as empty vessels to be filled up with knowledge by teachers. It has been rightly said that an ordinary teacher tells, a good teacher explains, a superior teacher demonstrates and an exceptional teacher inspires. Especially, the teacher in a primary school should love his children and inspire them in their learning activity. Once children are inspired and motivated, they must take interest in learning from the tender age and that would bring down the present high percentage of wastage and stagnation at the primary stage.

The Education Commission, 1964-66 have also suggested[2] that children should be provided with suitable enviroment, so that they will be interested in learning and dropout rates will come down. Pre-primary schools should be set up along with primary schools and they should compensate for the unsatisfactory home environment of children from slum areas and poor families. With a view to making learning interesting as well as effective, various media and materials should be used in the primary schools. They should be inexpensive and easily available. Education and entertainment can be well integrated through their use and children's learning can be a joyful activity.

Play-way Method and Materials

It has been confirmed by all concerned that play-way method

enables the teacher to teach effectively and pupils to learn efficiently. In this context, various play materials like toys and games can be utilized, with profit for educational purpose. In our country, even in remote rural and tribal areas, there are a good number of materials and games which are of great educational implication and potentiality. But unfortunately, our schools have not tapped them in the teaching-learning process and have remained isolated from toys, games and activities of the community.

Games and Toys

The National Council of Educational Research and Training, New Delhi through its Children's Media Laboratory Project has made laudable attempts to identify and replicate the indigenous toys and games which are educationally very useful. Teachers are being trained and manuals are being developed for effective use of these materials for education.

Graphic Materials

Some research studies conducted in our country have shown that Indian children experience a great deal of difficulties in learning to read. Besides, in various development tasks like concept-formation, auditory discrimination, discrimination of forms, colours etc., our rural and tribal children are found deficient to a great extent. Language development is proved to be of crucial importance for other congnitive development. Adequate provision of picture books, story books, rhyme books, children's magazines and illustrations help language development and making up the deficiencies mentioned earlier. With UNICEF assistance the NCERT at the national level and the SCERT at the State level are bringing out a large number of well-illustrated story and poetry books for children.

Audio Programmes

Children love to listen to stories and poems which are also educationally useful. There are a good number of folk tales and songs, nursery rhymes and puzzles in different parts of the country. They are being collected and printed in books and journals for children. Stories, poems and features developed by talented writers according to the interests and needs of children are being recorded and played back by radio and tape/cassette recorders. These are very appealing to children. Training courses and workshops are being organized by various national and State organizations for effective production and utilization of these audio materials.

TV and Video

Attempts are being made for production of suitable programmes and materials for children. Special care has to be taken to blend enlightenment with entertainment, inspiration with interests and needs with joy, so that these TV and video programmes, slides and films can be made really useful to children. It is hoped that all these methods, media and materials which constitute educational technology would make primary schools attractive and their programmes interesting. These would enable children to play, to enjoy, to read, to write, to talk and to sing. Thus, primary education can be made really entertaining as well as enlightening and can be universalized in true sense of the term.

The National Policy on Education, 1986 and the revised NPE, 1992 provided a golden opportunity to provide essential aids and materials under the Operation Blackboard Scheme, as the Central Government came forward for financing the project in a big way.[3] Unfortunately, of course, due to the nasty politics in many States, this scheme did not have a smooth sailing and has faced a lot of hindrances in its implementation. The present education system, in spite of emphasis on paedo-centricism, has remained teacher-centred. Our teaching-learning process has to be made child/ learner-centred in order to be effective. Children have to be involved not only in utilization of the audio-visual aids, but also in their preparation for making their learning more meaningful and interesting.

Secondary Education

Educational Technology includes all kinds of modern media, methods and materials that are used for optimization of learning experiences. It aims at making the teaching-learning process effective, efficient and interesting. After Independence various steps were taken to modernize the educational system and improve the quality of education in our country. Particularly, through the Extension Services and Audio-visual Units, educational films, and slides were projected in high schools for updating and orientating the knowledge and skills of teachers. School Broadcast Programmes were meant for improving the quality of secondary education. But unfortunately, these programmes produced by AIR were not utilized by the high schools to the reasonable extent. During 1971, the Government of India in the Ministry of Education and Social Welfare realized the importance of Educational Technology (ET) for qualitative improvement of education and included the ET Project in the Fifth Five Year Plan. The project had the following objectives: (i) Setting up of an Educational Technology Unit in the Ministry of Education and Social Welfare, (ii) Establishing a Centre for Educational Technology in the NCERT, (iii) Assisting States in setting up Educational Technology Cell 100% basis, and, (iv) Strengthening a few educational institutions for undertaking ET programmes. Accordingly steps were taken to implement various schemes at the States and National levels.

In 1975, ET Cells were set up in 6 States of Andhra Pradesh, Bihar, Karnataka, M.P., Orissa and Rajasthan, and started functioning *inter alia* for coordination with local AIR and Doordarshan stations for production of suitable programmes on radio and TV, production of educational films for all stages of education and organization of training courses for better script writing and effective utilization of these programmes.

Audio Media

The All-India Radio introduced programmes for children from Bombay Station in 1929 and from Madras Station in 1930. The pioneering SB programme was started in 1932 by Madras AIR Station and followed by other stations. The SB programmes are mostly syllabus-based and almost all subjects are covered under this project. The AIR in collaboration with Central Institute of English and Foreign Languages and other State Institutes produced and broadcast a series of radio programmes in English. AIR also made many attempts for producing specific enrichment programmes for secondary school teachers during orientation programmes.

Video Media

The first move towards Educational TV was made by AIR in January-March, 1960 and an experimental programmes was telecast for school children of New Delhi every Tuesday from 3 to 4 PM. A Ford Foundation Project actually laid the foundation stone for ETV Programmes for secondary schools in Delhi subsequently. This Project was evaluated and found quite satisfactory and ETV programmes for high schools are still telecast in Delhi. But unfortunately ETV programme for high schools has not so far taken roots, although primary education and the higher/university education have their countrywide classroom and IGNOU ETV programmes very well structured and well founded.

Computer Education

During eighties, computers were introduced in the secondary schools under CLASS Project. Although the initial coverage was modest with 2,598 schools, it has generated increasing awareness of computer literacy among the students, teachers and parents. Now, as reported in the POA (1992 p. 101) "a close scrutiny of the implementation strategy and achievement of the project schools that the project has not met with desired degree of success, mainly on account of shortcomings in the implementation strategy." It is mainly due to (i) multiplicity of agencies involved, (ii) over emphasis on hardware, (iii) inadequate training, (iv) want of curriculum and teaching material and (v) indifferent maintenance.

Educational Technology is being "employed in the spread of useful information, the training and retraining of teachers, to improve quality, sharpen awareness of art and culture, inculcate abiding values, etc., both in the formal and non-formal sectors. Maximum use will be made of the available infrastructure" (NPE, 1980 & Revised 1992). In India, like other developing countries, people are more enamoured with glamorous electronic media like TV and computer, neglecting "little media" like radio, slides etc. which should be utilized with more profit and relevance. That is why, "appropriate technology" is proved more suitable and effective for our education system. It has been rightly observed by the NPE (1986/1992), "Educational Technologies have the potential to bypass several stages and sequences in the process of development encountered in earlier decades." But for achieving these potentialities coordinated and collaborative efforts need to be made by all agencies and organizations like Department of Secondary Education, Board of Secondary Education, AIR and Doordarshan/SIET. Especially, state governments should prepare plans for effective and efficient use of Educational Technology in improving the quality of education in general and of secondary education in particular, involving all the above agencies and also educationists and media men with experience and expertise.

Higher Education

Educational Technology is an emerging field meant for improving the quality of education as well as expanding the same in every nook and corner of the country. It has therefore been emphasized as an essential input in the modern educational planning and management. The National Policy on Education 1986 (p. 22) has rightly observed. "Educational Technology should be employed in the spread of useful information, training and retraining of teachers, to improve the quality, sharpen awareness, inculcate abiding values etc., both in the formal and non-formal education." The Programme of Action, 1986 (p. 183)[5] has therefore expounded the methods to reach the vast number of people in the remote and inaccessible areas and remove disparities by extending educational facilities to the disadvantaged and providing individualised instruction to the learners conveniently suited to their needs and conditions of learning. The modern methods, media and materials should be deployed for achieving universalisation of education, eradication of illiteracy and for improving the standard of education at all levels of education, particularly higher education.

Educational Technology is aimed at maximizing learning experiences. The teaching-learning process should be made effective and efficient for meeting the two dilemmas : (i) Explosion of Knowledge and (II) Explosion of Population. Not only the quantum of knowledge in almost all subjects has increased but also many of the concepts and theories have become outdated and obsolete. Similarly, the number of learners has increased not only in school education but also in higher education. With a view to counteracting these problems of quantity and quality, it has been felt necessary to bypass various stages in the existing system of education with the help of Educational Technology, not only for providing formal education but also for organising programmes, both pre-service and in-service most effectively.

The Programme of Action 1986, has therefore, enunciated, "Education requires media support which is related to the curriculum as well as enrichment. Curriculum based education also requires materials which the teaching can draw upon both through various materials and media. Learning experiences can be provided through maps, models, transparencies etc. Audio and Video Technology offers considerable potential for improving the quality of education especially at higher levels. Thus educational technology can play an important role in increasing efficiency of the teaching learning process and for making education more creative and innovative."

At the stage of higher education, educational technology is expected to play a more important role not only to provide meaningful learning experiences to the students but also to reorient teachers with the latest developments in the respective fields. Gone are the days when teachers were to use only 'Chalk and Talk' in the classrooms. They are to utilize at present various media and materials for making the teaching learning process more effective and interesting. Modern teachers are not the only source of knowledge. Therefore are multifarious media and agencies for providing learning experiences both knowledge and wisdom.

Big and Little Media

Wilbur Schramm in his important work 'Big Media and Little Media" has laid more emphasis on small format technology particularly in the developing countries for improving the standard of education.[6] Educationists have felt that unless educational technology is applied to education in a big way, we cannot make up the deficiencies in the field of education. It would enable educational system to bypass several stages and sequences and overcome constraints of time and distance. The projects like Country-wide Classroom, Computer Literacy and Studies in Schools (CLASS) INSAT for Education. TELETEACH, etc., are being implemented in the field of education, in order to achieve objectives of education most efficiently and effectively.

Distance Education in Higher Education in expected to cater to the needs for the deprived people of the society who are not able to go to the campus of the university/colleges. Indira Gandhi National Open University (IGNOU) has been set up for providing this education in the country on a mass scale. Television Programmes and Telefilms of educational nature produced by BBC and other organisations like Educational Media Research Centres (EMRCs), Audio-Visual Research Centres (AVRCs) and so on are being telecast by the UGC. But due to lack of adequate planning and management, these programmes are not utilized upto satisfaction.

Role of Teachers

Teachers are to play a crucial role in this situation. The attitude of teachers should change and management should make provisions for the proper use of media that are available for improving quality of higher education. Besides management, proper monitoring and evaluation are necessary for ascertaining the extent of utilization and quality of such programmes so that on the basis of their findings necessary improvement can be brought about in the process of production and utilization. Both hardware and software should not only be made available but also necessary provisions should be made for their effective utilization in the field of education.

Teachers are not always born. They are also made better teachers with training and orientation in the methods and techniques of teaching, and use of various media and materials so that they can not only improve their quality of teaching but also ensure optimization of learning experiences. They should develop: interest in learning skills; in adopting various methods of teaching like discussion, demonstration interaction, problem solving, seminar reading and so on besides traditional lecture methods of teaching. Teachers should promote learning among the students than merely teaching themselves. That is why, Pedagogy, the Science of Teachers Behaviour has given place to Mathetics, the Science of Learners Behaviour. They have to play, in fact, the role of "friend, philosopher and guide of students and inspire them with higher values of life and promote in them the ethos of a new culture through self-learning, lifelong education and deep human commitment so that they can effectively counteract the challenges of the 21st Century.

Application of Educational Technology

Educational Technology is no longer a dream vision or mirage in the field of higher education. It has successfully been used for improving the quality as well as expanding the frontiers of higher education in the country. It has broken the monopoly of oral communication and invaded the classrooms of the colleges and universities. It has proved a richer support or an essential input in the curriculum of higher education.

Prior to seventies of the 20th Century, various audio-visual aids and media were used in the arena of teacher education, science and technology. But their application was very limited and was not so much well-planned and well-integrated with the classroom teaching. A few educational films produced in the foreign countries were shown in the educational institutions on some special occasions or cultural functions. Computers were used in a very few educational organizations for publication of results and for data processing in research studies. Hence various audio-visual aids and media were received in the field of higher education as guests, not friends or as members of the family.

Since August 15, 1984 the University Grants Commission launched the project "Countrywide Classroom" and has been investing huge amounts on establishing Production Centres providing TV sets, producing and purchasing suitable ETV programmes and supporting the institutions engaged in training, production and utilization of audio-video programmes. The ETV Programmes are produced at the different Media Centres namely Educational Media Resources Centres (EMRCs) located at Ahmedabad, Hyderabad, Pune, MCRC located at Jamia Millia Islamia, New Delhi. Audio Visual Research Centres (AVRCs) located in Calcutta, Hyderabad, Jodhpur, Madurai, Madras, Roorkee, Srinagar, Patiala, Imphal, Indore and so on. A Mass Communication Bureau has also been functioning at the UGC New Delhi and ETV Production facilities have also been developed in the Technical Teachers Training Institute (TTTIs) located at different cities of India.

Video Technology has also appeared on the educational horizon in a big way. Various firms have started producing video programmes for schools and colleges. For example, the Electronics Trade and Technology Development Corporation (ET & TDC) has formulated the

"TELETEACH" project to produce educational software on audio and video tapes. VCRs and viewing equipment would be provided to larger number of schools, colleges and universities. The Ministry of Human Resources Development has also identified certain sub-areas in which educational software would be developed by these production agencies.

As reported in the Programme of Action (1986, P.181)[7] Computer-education courses at the Master's level (MCA) are being offered in several universities in addition to the Ph.D., M.Tech and B.Tech programmes conducted by the IITs and other technological institutions. Diploma level programmes are being run in many polytechnics. With the introduction of the Computer Literacy and Studies in Schools (CLASS) Project, computers, for long the preserve of select research & technological institutions, have transcended these barriers and entered the classrooms. Various educational institutions ranging from secondary schools to university Postgraduate Departments have been provided with different ranges of computers including micro and super-computers to familiarise students and teachers with the computer applications and their potential as a learning medium.

Indira Gandhi National Open University (IGNOU) has been setup as an effective alternative model of higher education on September 20, 1985 by an Act of Parliament. The Instructional System of IGNOU is different from that of conventional universities as it adopts a multimedia approach to education. Besides self-instructional print material, counselling, assignments, assessments etc., it utilizes video-audio programmes as well as broadcasting facilities. All the audio and video study materials are produced by the Communication Division of the university. All the necessary infrastructural facilities have been developed in the Communication Division for the purpose. These facilities are TV Studio, Radio Studio, Video Editing suites, Duplication facilities, associated technical areas and so on.

The Communication Division has produced hundreds of good quality audio and video programmes copies which are available at the Study Centres for students use. These programmes in cassette form are available for sale at ET & TDC. Now ETV & radio programmes are being telecast through the national network of Doordarshan and All India Radio, so that students have the added advantage of receiving the same in their homes. Under the Technical Cooperation Programme with the Government of Japan, the IGNOU has set up a Post-Production Centre consisting of state-of-the art facilities like computer graphics, digital video effects, telecine and standards converts.

The wider application of Educational Technology in the field of higher education would bring about socialization and democratization which must promote both quantitative expansion as well as qualitative improvement. The National Policy on Education, NPE 1986 rightly emphasized that "In order to avoid structural dualism, modern educational technology should reach out to the most distant areas and most deprived sections of beneficiaries simultaneously with the areas of comparative affluence and ready availability." This approach as viewed by the Programme of Action (1986 Pp.182-3)[8] would intrinsically favour the use of broadcast methods, with their inherent advantages of greater reach, convenience of management and cost-effectiveness over the non-broadcast methods largely oriented to individual learning. The radio & TV programmes can be used for distance learning and enrichment of the learning process in the formal system. This is, of course, inter alia, dependent on transmission capability of the national broadcasting network and the rational utilization of these programmes at the institutional level. Large-scale use of audio and video Programmes would be desirable and for that there would be enormous demand for qualified manpower to work in educational media setups.

It has been aptly said in the POA (1986) "Education requires media support which is related to the curriculum as well as enrichment. Curriculum based education also required materials which the teacher can draw upon in the course of his teaching. This could be provided in the form of charts, slides, transparencies etc. Video technology offers considerable potential for improving the quality of education especially at higher levels."

Education and training in computers would be necessary for human resource development programmes, for improving efficiency of the teaching-learning process, for making students more creative and providing them with an individualized learning environment. However, all technology requires supporting infrastructure and committed teachers for its success. Unless adequate facilities, both physical and human are developed and willing teachers as well as supporting staff are trained property to utilise the various media and materials in right places, in right time and in right manner, it may not be possible to take full advantage of the modern technologies.

References

1. Kothari, D.S., Quoted in Report of the Education Commission, 1964-66
2. *Ibid.*
3. Government of India, (MHRD) Education, *The National Policy of Education, 1986* and *Revised NPE, 1992*

4. *Ibid.*
5. Government of India, (MHRD) Education, *The Programme of Action*, 1986, p.183
6. Schramm, W. *Big Media, Little Media*, Agency of International Development, New York, 1974
7. The POA, *op.cit.*, p.181
8. *Ibid*, pp.182-83

3

Role of Technology in other Areas of Education

Teacher Education

The Ministry of Education document "Challenges of Education: A Policy Perspective" has mentioned, "Teacher performance is the most crucial input in the field of education. Whatever policies may be laid down by Governments at the national and State levels, in the ultimate analysis, these have to be interpreted and implemented by teachers as much through their personal example as through teaching-learning processes" (1985, P.54)[1]. Further, we have reached the threshold of the development of new technologies which are likely to revolutionalise the classroom teaching. Unless capable and committed teachers are in service, the education system cannot utilise them for bringing about desired national development. Teachers should be well equipped professionally in order to make education a potential instrument of social change. The National Policy on (1986) Education has aptly observed, "The status of the teacher reflects the socio-cultural ethos of a society; it is said that no people can rise above the level of its teachers. The Government and the community should endeavour to create conditions which will help motivate and inspire teachers on constructive and creative lines. Teachers should have the freedom to innovate, to devise appropriate methods of communication and activities relevant to the needs and capabilities of and the concerns of the community" (p.25).[2]

The NPE, 1986, has, therefore, suggested that the entire system of teacher education should be overhauled and the new programmes of teacher education would emphasize continuing education and the need for teachers to meet the thrusts envisaged in the policy. It has also added that educational technology should be employed, *inter alia*, in "the training and retraining of teachers, to improve quality, sharpen awareness of art and culture, inculcating abiding values etc., both in the formal and non-formal sectors." Thus, teachers should be provided with pre-service and in-service education by means of various media, methods and materials constituting educational technology.

Although teachers were held in high esteem in the past, during the British period their position was degraded. The reasons for such diminished status of teachers are attributed to deterioration in their service conditions, lowering standard of teacher education, poor impression of the public about sincerity and competence of teachers, unprecedented expansion of education at all levels resulting in its low standards, changes in the value-system in the society etc. The Programme of Action (1986) has rightly pointed out, "The status of teachers has had a direct bearing on the quality of education, and many of the ills of the latter can be ascribed to the indifferent manner in which society has looked upon the teacher and the manner in which many teachers have performed their functions".[3] Government of India and many State governments have taken some tangible steps for according adequate recognition and respect to teachers by improving their service conditions, giving national and state awards and providing various facilities. But the quality of teacher education has to be improved and teacher' professional growth should be ensured by different programmes. The NPE also emphasizes the teacher's accountability-to the pupils, their parents, the community and to their own professions.

There are at present several institutions for training of elementary school teachers and for preparing secondary school teachers. But a large number of these institutions suffer from inadequate facilities-human, physical and academic to provide good professional education. Curricula of teacher education are also felt outdated and teaching practices unsuitable as well as undemocratic. Besides improving these facilities, it is necessary to provide modern media, materials and methods for accelerating the teaching-learning prccess and energizing the training practices at various levels.

Eric Ashby's Opinion

According to Eric Ashby (1967) we are now in the midst of the Fourth Revolution in Education-the age of electronics. The first revolution took place when the human society began to differentiate adult roles and the task of educating the young was shifted partly from parents to teachers and from home to school. The second revolution occurred when the written word was adopted as a tool of education and the oral instruction continued to coexist with written materials in the classroom. The third revolution set in with the invention of printing technology and the subsequent mass production of books and journals. The Fourth Revolution has commenced with the development in electronics like radio, television, audio/video recorder and computer. The social scientists are also of the opinion that these electronic media should be utilized effectively for optimizing learning experiences. The International Commission on the Development of Education (1972) has mentioned, "In communications man was limited for thousands of years to the distance his voice or a drum-beat could carry or the time it took to deliver a written message. In the 1960s, hundreds of millions of people heard astronauts speaking from space and saw them the moment they stepped on the moon. There is every reason to believe that this progress in human knowledge and power, which has assumed such dizzying speed over the past twenty years, is only in its early stages. It is likely to gather still greater momentum as teaching in all countries becomes more democratic and particularly as educational progress in developing countries produces many more researchers in fields related to man's knowledge and his control over the environment" (p.90).[4]

The Commission has also aptly added, "Further qualitative leaps forward may be predicted not only in inventive activity but in productivity, reliability and quality. Progress in electronics, coupled with the coming of computer is the basis of a revolution comparable to the invention of writing" (p.90). Hence in the existing position, as well as in future situations education cannot afford to ignore the utilization of electronic equipment both for its quality and quantity.

At present many All India Radio Stations are producing and transmitting educational programmes for teachers in order to improve their competence and awareness in the modern trends and problems, psychological and philosophical issues, methods and techniques of teaching and so on. Similarly, Doordarshan Kendra in general and Central Institute of Educational Technology, New Delhi in particular are producing and telecasting educational TV programmes for catering to the professional needs of teachers under the "INSAT for Education" Project which was launched in 1982.

State Institutes of Educational Technology (SIET) have been set up initially in the States of Andhra Pradesh. Bihar, Gujarat, Maharashtra, Orissa and Uttar Pradesh, Besides, a Central Institute of Educational Technology (CIET) has been established in the NCERT with 100% central assistance, to generate educational software in general and for teachers in particular for updating teachers' knowledge and skills and improving their professional growth. A good number of agencies and organizations have been set up for producing and conducting research into the ETV Programmes. Important among them are Technical Teacher Training Video Laboratory, Electronic Trade and Technology Development Corporation. Particularly, the latter has been trying to produce suitable video programmes under the TELETEACH Project. The National Seminar on Educational Television as an Alternate System of Education (CIET, New Delhi, February 24-27, 1986) has rightly suggested, "A teacher should realize the importance of ETV programmes. These programmes enrich him. A textbook is mere skeleton; these programmes provide flesh to the skeleton" (p.22).[5] The following types of programmes will help to enrich it:

1. Programmes that expose them to innovate practices in real situations. Duplicating these methods by teachers may fetch good dividends.
2. Programmes on difficult concepts and topics along with methodology.
3. Programmes that expose them to places where actual field trips are difficult to arrange.
4. 'Programmes that develop parents' concern in child's development, importance of activities like games, exploratory and experimental activities etc.
5. Programmes that will illustrate that time spent in such activities is really useful in life and is not a waste.

Besides media and materials, the teacher of today is to acquaint himself with and acquire adequate skills in various modern methods like micro-teaching, programmed learning, computer-assisted education and so on. Education should be "child-centred" or "pupil-centred" in true sense of the term in place of "teacher- centred" as it is today. Emphasis should be more on "how" than on "what" of the teaching-learning process. Learning is to be given more importance than teaching. The science of teacher's behaviour is called "pedagogy" and that of pupils' behaviour is known as "mathetics." Now more stress is to be laid on mathetic principles in contrast to pedagogic principles.

The teacher is thus required to restructure his environment for promoting effective learning and utilizing educational technology in an integrated manner. Educational Technology seeks to integrate the relevant principles of psychology, sociology, linguistics, communication and other allied fields. It also attempts to incorporate the management principles of resource development, systems analysis and cost-effectiveness. Thus, the teacher should master educational technology in order to use it as a means of bringing about improvement in all aspects of his transaction- teaching, class management, school organization and so on. It has to be realized that teachers are not always born, they are often made. For "making" teachers, various media, methods and materials should be utilized appropriately "in right place, in right time and in right manner." Educational Technology should be rightly regarded as the handmaid of the teaching profession.

The National Policy on Education emphasizes "In order to avoid structural dualism, modern educational technology should reach out to the most distant areas and most deprived sections of beneficiaries simultaneously with the areas of comparative affluence and ready availability" (1986, p. 22)[6]. Programmes that expose them to innovate practices in real situations. Duplicating these methods by teachers may fetch good dividends. This approach would intrinsically favour the use of broadcasting both radio and TV with their inherent advantages of greater reach, cost- effectiveness, convenience of management and attractiveness. These media can effectively be used both for enriching as well as supplementing the teaching-learning process. The POA (1986, pp.182-3)[7] has rightly mentioned, "Education requires media support which is related to the curriculum as well as enrichment. Curriculum-based education also requires materials which the teacher can draw upon in the course of his teaching. This could be provided in the form of charts, slides, transparencies etc. Video technology offers considerable potential for improving the quality of education especially at higher levels."

It has also added that educational technology offers the means to reach large numbers in remote and inaccessible areas, remove disparity in educational facilities available to the disadvantaged and provide individualized instruction to learners conveniently suited to their needs and pace of learning. However, all technologies require supporting infrastructure like adequate physical facilities, trained manpower, competent and committed teachers. Unless all these are ensured, success would be a too-far cry. It is hoped that the establishment of District Institutions of Education and Training (DIETs) and upgradation of colleges of teacher education to comprehensive institutions of excellence would be immensely helpful for improving teachers competence at the primary level and secondary level respectively. They can ensure appropriate infrastructure and desired human resources for effective and efficient utilization on educational technology for improving quality of education at all levels.

Community Education

"Education, normally one of the largest employers in any country, is one of the industries which has not undergone a technological revolution. We must help to move it out of the handicraft stage. With the terrible and growing shortage of qualified teachers all over the developing world, we must find ways to make good teachers more productive. This will involve investment in textbooks, in audio-visual materials and above all the use of modern communication techniques (radio, television and film) for teaching purposes." This is remarked by Robert F. McNamara, former President of the World Bank addressing the Board of Governors in 1968. What is the nature and scope of this "technological revolution" to be brought about in the industry of education as visualised by the world famous economist? Why has he emphasized the use of modern communication techniques for teaching purposes? In what way will this contribute to community education or solve the problems of the community? These are the questions we have tried to answer in this chapter.

It is beyond doubt that technologcial revolution in education will occur only through educational technology which in a broader sense includes the entire process of curriculum development, the setting of objectives, the planning of curricular programmes and practices, the try out of new methods and materials, the evaluation and feedback of the system as an integrated whole and resetting of objectives on the basis of findings and experiences out of evaluation and innovations. Any kind of educational improvement should be preceded by suitable curriculum reforms. Curriculum is the sum total of learning experiences provided by the school. It is what we teach, what the pupils learn, what we examine for and what we award degrees or diplomas when students pass through. But we should make it relevant to and continuous in consonance with the current needs of the present and probably challenges of the future. It must be defined in terms of what and how we want the students to know, do, think, feel and appreciate when they are in or outside the school. While determining the objectives and defining their respective learning experiences we should also keep in mind what kinds of knowledge, skills, thoughts and feelings the children bring with them when they come to the school. At the same time we cannot close our eyes to what is happening to them outside the school or inside the community where they are likely to go and work after their schooling.

Seth Spaulding (1970, p.11)[8] Director UNESCO Department of School and Higher Education has rightly observed that one of the reasons for curriculum reform has not been continuous and the curriculum has not been entirely relevant either to what the student brings to it or to what the students expect from it. The student in today's secondary school and university is a very different kind of person from the student of a generation or two ago. The "information explosion" has enormously affected the younger generation; the secondary school student probably learns more out of school than he does in the school and the university student often feels much closer to the problems of his nation than does the professor who lectures to him.

With a veiw to making the curriculum relevant and meaningful, not only necessary reforms have to be brought about, but also suitable media and methods are to be adopted without delay. This necessitates greater psychological and pedagogical preparedness, more social concern and community involvement, a new scientific attitude and a coordinated or integrated approach to the educational process as a whole. Here comes in the scope of Educational Technology which seeks to have a happy conglomeration of all the media, methods and materials used for better teaching and learning. Thus Educational Technology comprises of methods from textbooks teaching to micro-teaching and deals with media and materials ranging from chalkboards to television or computer. As a matter of fact, technology of education involves books and blackboards, models and maps, tapes and slides, radio and televisions, projectors and computers. It includes both 'hardware' and 'software' and audio as well as visual materials.

It has rightly been pointed out by Geoffrey Hubbard (1974, p. 14) Director, National Council of Educational Technology, England "Educational Technology is the complement of curriculum reform concerned with the Method where curriculum reform is concerned with the content... Given an acceptance of the concept of educational technology as the process of improving learning process, we are faced with the problem of encouraging innvoation in an educational system whose strength is in decentralisation and autonomy." This leads us to think that the methods of learning i.e., learning how to learn the habits of self-study, independent thinking etc., have to be emphasized. The learner has to develop a continuing concern for his freedom and his self-responsibility and his quest for self-fulfilment should come from within and without.

The International Commission on the Development of Education 1971 (UNESCO p. 75)[9] has rightly observed, "Education is all the more democratic when it takes the form of a free search, a conquest, a creative art; instead of being as it so often is, something given or inculcated a present or a constraint." The method of independent learning or self-study is thus a direct corollary of the use of educational technology. Hence the technology of education is not only more scientific, but also more psychological and more pedagogical. With the advance of science and technology there are now several learning aids which have revolutionised the learning process in particular and education as a whole.

Importance of Use of Modern Technologies

Modern world is faced with two crucial problems: (1) Knowledge Explosion and (2) Population Explosion. New frontiers of knowledge are being opened every now and then and more knowledge is being added to the already accumulated mass of information through ages. Similarly population of the world particularly in the developing countries is increasing by leaps and bounds. These two problems have raised a large number of difficulties in the field of education.

It is estimated in the world as many as one third of the children of school going age have not yet been in the school. If at all they enter the schools, only less than one third of them will be able to complete primary education. It is also said that as many as fifty percent of the student population are only repeaters. Thus wastage and stagnation also lead to the increased number of illiterates and semi-literates. Many developing countries including India, inspite of their maximum investment in education, are finding it difficult to reach the quantitative targets like physical facilities, provision of teachers and enrolment of students. Our country is a Sovereign Democratic Republic. Education is intended to prepare the youth of this country, for effective citizenship. Suitable elementary education i.e. education of children between 6 and 14 years of age is expected to make them intelligent and responsible citizens. That is why the fathers of our Constitution desired to make this education universal. But more than five decades are now over and we have not yet been able to achieve the target even for the age group 6-11 years. We are all aware of the reasons for this. The poor economic conditions, social superstitions and natural barriers like forests, hills, rivers, deserts etc., stand on the way to realise this Constitutional Directive.

Educational Technology like films, television and radio programmes will not only serve the students living in far flung areas but also make their education effective and interesting. This will help in imparting primary education besides increasing enrolment and reducing wastage and stagnation.

The standard of education is apparently going down day by day. Educationists, in a large number, are deeply concerned about the irrelevance and inadequacy of education in the modern society. Many portions in the curriculum are becoming outdated very rapidly; many contemporary issues are also not properly dealt with in the programmes and practices of schools. Unless the students are made throughly familiar with the burning problems of the society and sufficiently capable of tackling them successfully, they will fail to be true citizens of the world in future and their education will be deemed to be a failure.

In this context, educational technology will be of immense importance. Because successful teachers will be able to influence and motivate a larger number of pupils with the help of mass media, expertise of a limited number of persons can be made available to innumerable students; an inadequacy of physical facilities like laboratory expensive materials and many other things can be made up through the use of modern technologies. Consequently the quality of education will improve. But we have not yet done this upto the mark. Seth Spaulding (1970, p.10)[10] has therefore said "Although education has shared in the creation of technological age, education itself has not learned how to use quality of its own institution. In attempts to 'catch up" quanitatively, education has usually attempted to multiply what has gone on in a pre technology system of schooling."

Thus the teaching-learning process will be improved to a great extent with the help of new media and materials through clarification of concepts, stimulation of groups and individual activities, development of critical awareness, changes of attitudes and encouragement of originality and creativeness. The role of educational technology, both for quantitiative and qualitative improvement of education, has been very clearly stated by Henri Dieuzeide (1970, p.15)[11] Director of the Division of Educational Methods, Materials and Techniques, UNESCO, "Educationalists in the developing countries will be more inclined to see educational technology as a means of rapid dissemination of urgently needed education on a massive scale to large groups, whereas the developed countries will see it as a means of increasing the effectiveness of education by making learning a more individual process."

Advantages of Educating through Educational Technology

As discussed in the precdeeing pages. Educational Technology will not only revolutionise the entire educational process of the young learners but will also immensely influence life systems of the community, It goes without saying that young students of the present are the adult citizens of the future. Hence education of the young pupils is in a sense an integral part of the community education. It has been found that poor enrolment, irregular attendance, wastage and stagnation are largely due to mass illiteracy. If parents or guardians are literate and aware of the value of education, they will not allow their children to be illiterate or without education. It is rightly said that "A literate mother will never allow her child to become a school dropout. Therefore, in the early period of American Independence the popular slogan of the senators was "Let us educate our masters." This was accepted not merely as a slogan, but as a clarion call for the nation, not only in America but in other countries of the world as well.

This problem can be solved with more systematic and well integrated schemes of non-formal education based on psychological principles, functional needs and interesting methods. In this context, educational technology with modern means, media and materials will be of enormous significance. The mass communication media like radio, TV and films have already been used in the rural community. The SITE and INSAT Projects have *inter alia* the fundamental objective of mass education and the TV has proved its potentiality as an agency of community education through various evening programmes besides morning programmes for children and UGC programmes for higher education. In India the number of out-of-school youth in the age group 15-25 is very large. This is a group of vital importance for every country from cultural, demographic, economic, political and social points of view. It is therefore felt very necessary to develop a programme of non-formal education for this age group. The content of the programme will be psychologically sound and adequately need-based. The various films radio and TV programmes suitably designed and produced for the purpose will make the non-formal education attractive as well as effective.

In order to make various developmental programmes like family planning, agriculture, health etc., quite successful, community education has to be given more emphasis. A study was made by the Community and Family Study Centre of the University of Chicago to find out the reasons for unsatisfactory results of family planning programmes. The overall conclusion of the study is the lack of effective communication of the message of these programmes. The study therefore suggests ways and means to improve the use of radio, television, direct mail and posters. Yash Pal, the erstwhile Director of the Space Application Centre, ISRO similarly said about agriculture, "Millions of people learn better by seeing. The farmer is very conservative because he has done certain things for hundreds of years. He is not going to do things differently until he sees that these things are beneficial."

Educational Technology has been a part of the wider mass communication media and materials. If we accept Marshal Me Luhan's theories of technological determinism - namely that changes in the technology of communication lie at the bases of all social changes, then modern technologies of education will undoubtedly effect the community life and learning. Since our future society is going to be a "Learning Society" and education has been deemed to be a "lifelong process" we cannot understimate the role and importance of educational technology, which has to be taken up as a comprehensive and continuous programme for the well-being of the community."

Workers Education

Education has been acknowledged as one of the potential instruments of social change and an important means of bringing about national development. But the expenditure in education is yet to be treated as an investment by the planners and administrators at the helm of affairs. It is still to be realized that human resources are more valuable than the material resources. A host of economists like T.W. Schultz, John Vaizey, John Sheehan, H.G. Johnson have accepted the concept of human capital emphasizing thereby the expenditure on education as an investment. According to them the procedure as followed for estimating physical capital formation can be followed for the formation of human capital, that is, by the expenditure to produce them. As the expenditures help in increasing knowledge and skill, they also increase the value productivity of human efforts and yield a positive rate of return. The important means of improving human efficiency are, *inter alia*, health facilities and services, on the job training, formal education and adult education programmes for workers.

A number of studies has also established a close correlation between the workers' education and their efficiency in terms of production. All the developed countries and even many developing once have laid stress on workers education. For example, in Russia with a view to helping young specialists study systamatically all the time. An extensive State-operated system of advanced training has been set up and a large number of refresher institutes, departments and courses are being organised throughout the year and in various places to keep them abreast of the advances in their respective fields. V. Yelutin, Minister for Higher Education and Specialised Secondary Education of the USSR has said that combining work and study, though not easy, is increasingly popular. The government gives evening and correspondence students an annual 20-day to 40-day leave of absence from work with full pay, to do study assignment and take examinations, on a paid four-month leave of absence from work on the diploma thesis or project. Students also get leave of absence to take their final State examinations and the State pays part of their travel fare. According to the International Commission set up by UNESCO in 1972, lifelong education means that business, industrial and agricultural firms will have extensive educational functions. The Commission have aptly observed, "Economic circles in industralised countries have realized the need for improved training and generally agree that expenditure on it is a worthwhile investment. Many developing countries, however, still tend to under-estimate the importance of training-within-industry" (p.198)[12]. They have further added that young workers with a professional or technical education still need complementary training, and also have to learn to adopt to the conditions and rhythm of work in industry. They can do so on the job. It would be logical for different firms to take responsibility for various types of subsequent training, such as specialization, improvement of qualification, courses preparatory to promotion, retraining and training of executive and other personnel in other higher skilled jobs. In so far as education is to be carefully shaped to meet the needs of the economy, it is imperative for educational institutions and industries to work hand in hand. In many countries both private and public undertakings allocate a portion of their profits to educating and training their employees. The Commission have recommended that this practice should be more widely adopted.

Improving Efficiency through Education

Continuing education has been emphasized by the educationists for improving efficiency of workers. This means that individuals who are put on jobs after their general education may take up higher examinations as private candidates. Suitable arrangements of part-time evening and correspondance courses should be made for them. This will promote "educationalization of vocations" which implies that persons put on jobs first, subsequently are provided with facilities for higher studies. On the contrary, the present practice is "vocationalization of education" which connotes persons are given education in vocations and then are appointed on the jobs. Thus in near future "vocationalization of education" will be replaced by "educationalization of vocations."

Technical and vocational education should be provided largely through apprentiship training and in-service training courses to be organised under the auspices of the industries and factories. Both government and private enterprises should impart such training on the job or in workshops. A number of industries or a complex of factories may in collaboration organize common training programmes providing for both theoretical instructions and practical skills. They may also set up their own training institutions.

Workers' Adult Education

In India there is a high percentage of illiterate workers. Unless they are provided with adequate facilities for getting themselves not only literate, but also educated, their capabilities cannot be improved and democracy cannot be a success. In order to enable them to effectively participate in the development programmes, it is imperative that they should be given suitable education on the job during their off-time. They need not go to educational centres, rather education should come to them. For many of them adult education is a substitute for the primary education, and a complement to elementary or professional education. For a few it may be prolongation of education for furthering their efficiency and capacity not only as workers but also as citizens.

As mentioned by the International Commission on Education (1972) the present facilities are lagging far behind the adult population's educational and cultural needs. Step by step progress is therefore not enough. What is required is a giant leap forward. This can only be achieved if both private and public bodies join in contributing their resources and efforts to the maximum. The National Adult Education Programme inaugurated on October 02, 1978 was therefore a promising step and utilization of both government and voluntary resources, intra and inter-departmental endeavours are aimed at achieving the target.

Use of Educational Technology

Adult Education for workers requires specific strategy and methodology and spcial institutes and courses are desirable to bring about desired results. As an illustration, Yugoslavia's workers universities may be taken for the purpose where attempts are made to find answers to many questions arising in the field of workers' education today. These institutes provided both formal and non-formal education and open to all workers whatever their earlier training and education. Courses are offered at all levels ranging from elementary education to specialized training for highly qualified workers. There must be flexibility in courses which means that a worker may combine components of individual methods or group methods. The programmes may be adopted to the environment and diversified according to individual and socio-economic needs. Thus functional education for professional and civic growth is as important as the workers' general and cultural development.

As the workers spend major part of the day's time in the factory or office, they cannot be expected to be fairly receptive and interested in education. To change over from the world of work to the world of study is strenuous for them. But they possess immense wealth of experiences and are good conversationalists. Therefore they are to be motivated to discuss their experiences, problems and suggestions with the teacher freely and frankly. This will be the suitable method of teaching for these adults. The traditional ways of lecturing and teaching from textbooks will not be effective for them.

Besides, media and materials should be selectively used in the right place and time. All the means, methods and materials that may be used for learning effectively and efficiently are in general called educational technology. To make learning interesting as well as successful it is necessary to utilize suitable media and materials for adults in general and workers in particular. The International Commission for Education have aptly opined, "However, systematic use of educational technology has in some cases made it possible to step up work on earlier plans for educational development and so gain time. It has also helped to redistribute and make better use of qualified teaching personnel, and to improve the system's internal efficiency and yield by reducing the number of dropouts and repeaters" (1972, p.211)[13].

Education and work are intimately connected and one influences the other to a great extent. Schooling is the main institutional experience shared by the young, while work is the principal institutional experience of adults. Most jobs and occupations have educational requirements for entry and advancement. In the industralized societies work education has to be made effective for improving productivity. Exposure to work situations and experience in the actual conditions add to relevance and effectiveness of the work education particularly for the personnel in service.

Radio, TV and other media bring to their listeners and viwers programmes on current issues and problems and news on developmental activities. For women, for example, there are programmes on housecraft, childcare, nutrition etc. For farmers there may be programmes on good agricultural practices, use of fertilizers, availability of new seeds, equipment etc. Not only in developed countries but also in developing countries like China, radio and TV are being used in the field of workers education very effectively. For example, Television Colleges came into operation in some provinces and municipalities in China in the sixties.

As reported in the International Encyclopaedia of Education[14] (Torsten Husen, 1989, p.44) "In 1979, the Central Radio and Television University was set up, jointly sponsored by the Ministry of Education and the Central Broadcasting Administration. With 28 other Television Universities at provincial or municipal level, a national network of television higher education has been formed. These Television Colleges mainly enroll in service workers, cadres, scientific and technical personnel, school teachers, army and also a certain number of senior high school graduates who have neither been admitted to formal universities nor employed."

In our country, regular broadcasts and telecasts are specially designed for the general orientation and countinuing education of farmers and industrial workers. A project called "Radio School for Farmers" has been operating from a good number of response from the clientele. With a view to providing school as well as tertiary or higher education to the workers of the firms and factories, housewives and otherwise employed persons, the concept of open, spare-time and own-time education came into prominence. The British Open University-model was adopted by the Govt. of India and the experiment began with the establishment of an Open University in Hyderabad, Andhra Pradesh in 1982 with courses leading to B.A., B.Com., and B.Sc., degree correspondence courses/lessons were supported by audio cassettes. Indira Gandhi National Open University (IGNOU) was set up with open courses in various degrees and diplomas.

The Open School was established in New Delhi for providing secondary education and also primary education in some places for the deprived sections of the society. A scheme of non-formal primary education is being implemented in the rural areas for working children in the age group 9-14 years. The National Policy on Education, 1986 has also visualised the provision of Open and Continuing Education of all types. A variety of skill-based in-service education programmes are being implemented for the primary and secondary stage dropouts. In India the Central Board of Workers' Education with regional branches has been oragnising education and training programmes and utilising various modern methods, media and materials for making their programmes more effective and interesting. Both "big as well as little media" in the words of Schramm, both projected and non-projected audio-visual aids and dynamic as well as activities based methods should be used as far as possible.

Modern media like radio and television would immensely influence the quality and quantity of workers education. The programme of Action, 1986 (p.182)[15] observed, "Large scale use of audio and video programmes in broadcast and non broadcast modes would also generate enormous demand for qualified manpower to work in educational media set-ups. In the long run, it would be desirable and probably essential that maintenance structures be decentralised, both organisationally and geographically, and local technician entrepreneurs, could be trained for such responsibilities." Thus the extensive use of media would not only improve the quality of workers' education, but also create employment opportunities at different levels. Educational technology rightly acts as two-edged sword and exerts profound influence on education in general and on workers' education in particular.

All the audio-visual materials ranging from books to television, from chalkboards to computers have their own limitations. If they are not used in time and with due care, instead of serving as aids they turn to be obstructions and create psychological hazards. As literacy is necessary for understanding printed words, visual literacy is also essential for comprehending graphics, films and television. The workers should be oriented to enjoy and understand. Otherwise these adult learners will not be able to make any sense and the message that is intended to be communicated falls flat on most of the clientele. Radio and television programmes may be specifically produced and used for the worker community. The printed materials, tape recording, slides and film strips are to be used for clarifying certain concepts and explaining the points through discussion and demonstration. Last but not the least in importance is the inter-personnel communication or face-to-face conversation for teaching workers. All these are not exclusive but complementary to each other and are to be used suitably as in an orchestra to have desirable impact on the adult learners. Adequate feedback and extension activities should also go hand in hand for the effective use of eductional technology in order to make learning efficient and adult education for workers a success.

References

1. Government of India, Ministry of Education, "Challenges of Education: A Policy Perspective", 1985, p.54
2. Government of India, *National Policy of Education, (MHRD)*, Education, 1986, p.25
3. Government of India, *The Programme of Action, (MHRD)*, Education, 1986, p.185
4. UNESCO. The international Commission on Development of Education, 1972, p.90
5. Government of India, 'The National Seminar on Educational Television as an Alternate system of Education (CIET), New Delhi, 1986, p.22
6. Government of India, *National Policy of Education*, *op. cit.*, p.22
7. Government of India, *The POA*, o*p. cit*, pp.182-83.
8. Seth, Spaulding, *Advanced Educational Technology: Prospects in Education,* 1970, p.11
9. UNESCO, *op. cit,* p.75
10. Seth, Spaulding, *op. cit,* p.10
11. Dieuzeide, Henri, *Educational Technology and Development of Education* IEY, 1970, p.15
12. UNESCO, *op. cit,* p.198
13. *ibid,*. p.211
14. Husen Torsten, (Ed), *International Encyclopaedia,* Pergamon Press, Oxford, 1989, p.44
15. Government of India, *The POA*, *op. cit.*, p. 182

4

Methods and Techniques in Teaching

Higher education has to provide the right kind of leadership in all walks of life and identify gifted youth and help them develop their potential to the full by cultivating physical fitness, developing the powers of the mind, right interests, attitudes and values. The objectives of higher education are to develop those capabilities in an individual which would help him to conceptualise a phenomenon or situation and enable him to contribute to societal development through his knowledge, skills and knowhow, as well as by generating new knowledge. Accordingly the objectives of education at the undergraduate and postgraduate levels are:

i. developing critical and analytical abilities;
ii. imparting in-depth knowledge of the subjects concerned;
iii. developing the ability to relate and use this knowledge in real life situations;
iv: developing vocational and professional skills,
v. developing social, cultural and aesthetic values.

According to the "Challenge of Education" (1985) the teaching practices in our universities continue to be the same as in forties and methodologies in the teaching learning process should lay emphasis on learning and developing analytical, critical and conceptual abilities rather than on memorisation and reproduction. The National Policy on Education 1986, (NPE 1986, p.14) has aptly enunciated that higher education provides people with an opportunity to reflect on the critical, social, economic, cultural, moral and spiritual issues facing humanity. It contributes to national development through dissemination of specialised knowledge and skills. It is therefore a crucial factor for survival as well as development and being at the apex of the educational pyramid, has also to play a key role in producing teachers for the education system.[1]

Why Methods are Needed?

These objectives are reflected in the curriculum and syllabus which are again transacted through instructional materials and teaching-learning activities. Teachers are the key agents who translate the abstract into concrete and dreams into realities. Whatever may be the subject matter or content or message of communication, suitable tools and techniques, media and methods are of prime importance for realising the objectives most effectively and efficiently. The report of the Secondary Education Commission (1965, p.85) has clearly pointed out, "But every teacher and educationist of experience knows that even the best curriculum and the most perfect syllabus remain dead unless quickened into life by the right methods of teaching and the right kind of teachers."[2] In discussing the problems of right methods, the above commission has opined that a method is not merely a device adopted for communicating certain items of information to students and exclusively the concern of the teacher who is supposed to be at the "giving end". Any method, good or bad links the teacher and his pupils into an organic relationship with constant mutual interaction. It reacts not only on the mind of the students but also on their entire personality, their standards of work and judgement, their intellectual and emotional equipment, their attitudes and values. Good methods which are psychologically and socially sound may raise the whole quality of their life and bad methods may debase it. Good methods of teaching should aim at realising all the objectives, cognitive, conative and affective.

At the school stage, trained teachers are usually exposed to a number of methods of teaching, some of which are demonstrated by teachers, educators and trainees themselves during their term of practice lessons or student teaching. But college teachers are not exposed to different models and methods of teaching. Lowman[3] (1987-Preface) on the basis of his own teaching experience in USA has observed, "Few college teachers receive instruction in how to present intellectually exciting lectures, to lead engaging discussions or to relate to students in a way that promotes motivation and independent learning."

A model of effective teaching is based on two assumptions: (i) the college classroom is a dramatic arena first and a setting for intellectual discourse second and (ii) it is also a human arena, wherein the interpersonal dealings of students and teachers - many of them emotional, subtle and symbolic - strongly effect student morale, motivation and learning. College teachers need be made "skilled artists" and it is a long standing art, a time taking process. Lowman (1987) has cogently stated, "Excellent teaching captivates and stimulates students' imaginations with exciting ideas and rationale discourse. Students satisfaction and enjoyment are stressed here as important criteria for successful teaching." Thus successful teaching and student satisfaction as well as motivation are strongly correlated and teaching and learning are not thought of as cold and technological, but warm, exciting and personal. Rather college teaching should be persotime taking process. Lowman (1987) has cogently stated, "Excellent teaching captivates and stimulates students' imaginations with exciting ideas and ring captivates and stimuing captivates and stimulates students' imaginations with exciting ideas and rationale discourse. Students satisfaction and enjoyment are stressed here as important criteria for successful teaching." Thus successful teaching and student satisfaction as well as motivation are strongly correlated and teaching and learning are not thought of as cold and technological, but warm, exciting and personal. Rather college teaching should be persotime taking process. Lowman (1987) has cogently stated, "Excellent teachhing has been viewed as two dimensional (i) Intellectual Excitement and (ii) Interpersonal Rapport. The former has again two components: clarity of an instructor's communication and his positive emotional impact on students. Clarity of communication is related to what one presents, and positive emotional impact results from the way in which material is presented. Besides this intellectual arena, classroom is a highly emotional and interpersonal arena, which includes students motivation, morale, liking and disliking. These two dimensions are however intermingled and overlapping for bringing about effectiveness in teaching. An important parameter for improving the quality of education lies in the art of imparting education or, in other words, on teaching methods or teaching style. It is perhaps necessary to have a look at the various methods of teaching which are followed in different university/ college classes.

Teaching aims at facilitating learning. Every teaching is therefore required to plan and direct the promotion of learning among students and with that purpose in view a variety of activities are undertaken by him. But a college teacher is more obsessed with "what" - his subject matter, than "how" the methods and techniques of presenting the subject matter. Methods of instruction at the higher education level may fall into two broad categories, namely, the mass method and the individual method. Mass methods comprises lectures, demonstrations, practical experience, syndicate method, group discussions and the use of audio-visual aids. Individual method comprises mostly individual assignments, programmed learning and computer assisted instruction. Teaching techniques vary from the Expository to Discovery (or Enquiry) methods and somewhere in between there are techniques like discussion which are partly Expository and partly Inquiry. Expository techniques of teaching are teacher-centred and suitable for large groups. Examples of such methods are lecture, demonstration, symposium, radio/television talks. Inquiry methods of teaching are student-centred and meant for individual students. Each student works by himself and learning on his own using inquiry approaches. Instances of this method are self-study, field work, student assignment, individual experiment/project and so on. Group discussion techniques are interactive and participatory in which students and teachers are involved equally more or less. Conferences, tutorial group, role-playing, group project, simulation etc., come under this category.

At the higher education stage, expository approaches or techniques are more often adopted as a large quantum of knowledge or information can be communicated to large groups in a short time by these methods. However, inquiry or group approaches or techniques are used for teaching science and other practical subjects. These methods should be encouraged more and more for promoting effective student learning and many laudable objectives. A proper mix of expository and inquiry techniques can be more successfully adopted in higher education.

Basic information may be transmitted through the former, for example, lectures to large classes, but group discussion should be held and practical workshop activities can be organised in groups individually. Individual students should be encouraged to make progress according to their ability through assignments, problems and projects. It has now been realised that an important parameter for improving the quality of higher education lies in the art of imparting education or in teaching methods or styles or approaches. Teachers must be fully aware of and well conversant with the various methods or techniques of teaching as soldiers are required to be conversant with the use of various arms and ammunition for fighting effectively. Which methods or approaches they should use at a particular time or for teaching a particular topic or for realising a particular objective will be determined according to their individual judgements or decisions. There should not be any set formula to dictate how to teach and no methods or techniques should be rigidly followed at any stage or level of education. The right methods or approaches need be decided, rather adjusted to the dynamic needs of human nature and classroom situations.

Teachers of higher education generally give most importance to acquire and transmit knowledge. They never care to know how far students have assimilated or grasped their new ideas. They are not concerned about their abilities to communicate their strategies effectively and evaluate their own performance from time to time. More often they don't feel the need to evaluate their abilities. All efforts are made to cover the syllabus rather than uncover it for the students to explore, analyze and critically study in order to assimilate the knowledge and make it their own.

Many teachers do not treat teaching as a complex process calling for competencies in various knowledge and skills. They should master different teaching skills and understand the adolescent psychology, classroom management, pedagogy and methodology. Their postgraduate degrees showing their mastery in a particular subject and their research experience cannot ensure good teaching. Imitation and emulation are the only methods through which young teachers learn the teaching skills and other "tricks of the trade" for improving their professional competence, It is therefore felt essential to expose teachers to various teaching methods and models. They should be encouraged to try out the methods found useful and favourable. Proper guidance and supervision can be provided to them by experienced and skillful teachers.

Methods may vary from subject to subject, from topic to topic and from teacher to teacher. An adequate knowledge and practice of vital principles of teaching methods and learning theories can help the teachers to improve their performance in classrooms. Modern media and materials like radio, television, films, slides etc., have made the teaching methods more interesting and lively. The "broadcasting" in true sense of the term has made the teaching of good teachers available to many living in far-flung areas. Thus the methodologies are likely to be revolutionalised by increasing and imaginative use of various audio-visual aids, most of which are electronic and have now caught the attention of students as well as teachers.

Different Types of Teaching Methods

You will now have a different taste of Educational Technology which may be taken as the hardcore software and quite different from the theme of most of the units. That is, you will be introduced to various methods of teaching, of course only a sample of a few including traditional and modern methods of teaching such as Lecture Method, Project Method, Seminar Method, Discussion Method and Demonstration Method.

An attempt has been made here to discuss the need for using different methods, the characteristics and uses of these methods along with their limitations. Lastly, integration of different methods of teaching has been discussed.

Objectives

On completion of this part, you can

i. get the meaning of various methods

ii. know the necessity for using various methods in teaching

iii. acquaint yourself with the nature and characteristics of the selected methods of teaching

iv. identify the types and advantages and requisites for these methods of teaching

v. see whether integration is possible between the methods.

vi. state the limitations of these methods

According to the Challenge of Education (1985) the teaching practices in our universities and colleges of education continue to be the same as in forties, and methodologies in the teaching-learning process should lay emphasis on learning and developing analytical, critical and conceptual abilities rather than on memorisation and reproduction. The National Policy on Education (NPE, 1986, p. 14)[4] has aptly enunciated that higher education provides people with an opportunity to reflect on the critical, social, economic, cultural, moral and spiritual issues facing humanity.

Developing such reflective, critical and analytical power should be the chief general objective of higher education that contributes to national development through dissemination of specialised knowledge and spirit. This will actually ensure the effectiveness of higher education. Higher education is to realise its objectives through suitable methods and techniques. These are mostly reflected in the curriculation and syllabus which are transacted through various teaching-learning activities. The Report of Secondary Education Commission (1965, p.85) has aptly observed, "But every teacher and educationist of experience knows that even the best curriculum and the most perfect syllabus remain dead unless quickened into the life by the right methods of teaching and the right kind of teachers."[5]

A method is not merely a device adopted for communicating certain items of information to students. It links the teacher and his pupil into an organic relationship with the constant mutual interaction. It motivates and reacts not only in the mind of the students, but also on their entire personality, their work and judgement, their intellectual and emotional equipment, their attitude and values. Good methods which are psychologically and socially sound may raise the whole quality of their life and bad methods may debase it. Good methods of teaching should aim at realising all the objectives, cognitive, conative and affective, besides the various specific objectives.

Teachers need be "Skilled Artists." An American Teacher Lowman[6] (1987, Preface) has cogenty stated, "Excellent teaching captivates and stimulates students imagination with exciting ideas and rational discourses. Students satisfaction as well as motivation are stressed important criteria for successful teaching." Thus successful teaching and student satisfaction are strongly correlated ar»d teaching and learning are not thought of as cold and technological, but warm, exciting and personal. Rather college teaching should be personal and an incisive enterprise involving human beings and their personalities. It should not be compared to mechanical cause and effect relationship. Modern electronic media and materials like radio, television, films and computers have revolutionised the methods of teaching by making them innovative, interesting and successful. By imaginative use of audio-visual aids, the methodology becomes more effective and efficient. Moreover, multimedia package and multidisciplinary approaches can make the teaching-learning process more productive, cost effective and time-effective.

There should be adequate scope for students' participation, interaction and activities. Wise and experienced teachers know how to balance the individualised and group methods. Good methods must enable students to acquire the qualities of leadership, initiative, cooperation, discipline etc., and should develop problem-solving ability, capacity of personal achievement and independent work, besides team/group activities.

Necessity of Multiplicity

Methods of teaching vary according to the size of learners groups. For instance, lecture or seminar method is followed effectively in a big class of 40 to 50 or above and role-playing or brainstorming techniques can be adopted with profit in a small group of 15-20. There are some age old methods like lecture, discussion etc., which are followed invariably in most of the classrooms, particularly at the stage of higher education. In a class there is scope for interaction, collective perception, emotional cohesiveness, shared aims and so on which contribute to the effectiveness of group teaching in more than one way. But learning according to individual capacity is possible only in individual teaching like programmed learning, or assignment or tutorials. But group discussion, simulation exercises buzz group techniques etc., are efficiently adopted in small groups. Activity Method, Heuristic Method, Project Method etc., can promote practical skills and abilities. Hence, variety and multiplicity of methods should be encouraged in classroom practices.

Lecture Method

Lecture method is generally followed in the colleges and Departments of Universities. It is the most commonly and traditionally used method through ages at the higher education stage. It is mostly a teacher-centred and expository method involving one way communication and transmitting good quantum of knowledge or subject matter to a large number of individuals. Lecture is also found to be a feasible method of teaching in higher classes to the students who are motivated and required to achieve the desired learning objectives. The advantages and limitations of this method may be discussed here for providing necessary insight and guidance to teachers.

Features of Lecture Method

The lecture method has the following characteristics which have to be capitalised for better outcomes.

i) Imparting good amount of content knowledge: Since the lecture method is mostly one way communication process and meant for adult learners, a big quantum of content knowledge can be transmitted and many teaching points can be covered through this. Thus economy of time and energy is ensured in this method.

ii) Providing better opportunity for clarification of concepts: While teaching through the lecture method, a teacher knows the background and reception of the students from the attention and interests shown by them. He can assume and ascertain to what extent they have been able to appreciate and understand. Accordingly, he can clarify the difficult points or repeat the point not got by students properly. Thus he can carry the class with him getting proper feedback.

iii) Vitalising dry and dead ideas: Spoken words are more effective than printed ones. In a lecture a teacher not only speaks but also changes tone, gestures, postures and facial expressions. He can thus use various devices for bringing in life, blood, colour, vivacity and vividness to the dead, dry and dreary material.

iv) Making presentation more psychological than logical:

A lecture can present the subject matter according to psychological and educational principles and not merely logically as is done in writing textual material. It, therefore, becomes emotionally appealing and psychologically sound.

v) Ensuring flexibility and adaptability: The lecture method can ensure adequate flexibility according to the needs, ability, interests and previous knowledge of the pupils. A lecture is not just a straight jacket readymade method or material. It can be adjusted or adapted, suiting to the requirements and capability of students for whom it is intended.

Limitations of the Method

The lecture method has the following limitations which should be taken into account for improving the same.

i) Lack of feedback: Since the lecture method is a one-way communication. The lecture proceeds to deliver a speech without getting or without caring to get the reaction from the audience. This delimits the effectiveness of a lecture.

ii) Want of active participation of audience: Learning is an active process. But in the lecture method, students become passive audience without getting any scope for interaction and participation. This does not provide adequate environment for learning.

iii) Developing dry monotony: Since the lecture method does not wait for interaction or discussion with the students, it develops deadening monopoly in the class. But very invigorating speeches make the class interested and involved in the process.

iv) Substituting the teacher only: Lectures are generally presented as various chapters of a textbook. Heavy dose of content knowledge is imparted without giving scope for creating interest and curiosity among the students.

Utility of Lecture method

As discussed earlier, the lecture method is generally used in the higher classes where students are of higher age-group, adequately knowledgeable and properly motivated to listen to lectures attentively and benefit from the knowledge packed exposition of teachers who are mostly subject experts. However, in order to make lectures effective, some supporting and supplementary inputs are given by good teachers. These kinds of lectures are discussed as follows:

Although there are several limitations to a lecture, it has been accepted as a popular method of teaching particularly at the stage of higher education. It has proved its effectiveness for transmitting a good quantum of knowledge at a time and for covering a vast area of subject matter. With a view to overcoming the draw back, however, lectures occasionally are modified and enriched or supported with different features and materials which help in enhancing the learning experiences of students. These modified forms of lectures are, for example, lecture-cum-demonstration, illustrated lecture, lecture cum buzz sessions and lecture cum discussion. These are discussed below:

(i) Lecture-cum-Demonstration: A lecture is sometimes supported and enriched by demonstration which provides scope for students to observe and understand certain object or system in action and operation. Demonstration enables them to learn skills and get concepts clarified. The lecture explains the various parts of the material and different steps of an operation showing the actual objects of relevant audio-visual aids. Such lecture cum-demonstration method is found quite useful for teaching science, language and different skill subjects involving practical activities.

(ii) Illustrated Lecture: Various types of illustrations may be used by a lectuer in course of his presentation. These illustrations may be projected ones like slides, film strips, transparencies etc., and non-projected ones like models, charts, maps, pictures, diagrams and even blackboard writing. A lecturer carefully selects or prepares various AV aids to show and explain different concepts, ideas and objects in the classroom. The illustrations must be related to the topics and properly sequenced and planned so that these can be used in right time and at the right place. Otherwise instead of helping, these may hamper the acquisition of learning experiences.

(iii) Lecture-cum-Buzz Session: A topic is presented in a lecture at first and about ten to fifteen minutes before it is concluded, the entire class is divided into some groups of five to ten students for discussing and rinding solutions to certain problems involved to give practical suggestions for improving the existing condition. Such discussions in small groups are called buzz sessions which may last for a few minutes, generally for five minutes. Then the group leaders present their views

or findings in the class and the lecturer tries to moderate and conclude their observations.

(vi) Lecture-cum-Discussion: Since a lecture is a one-way communication, attempt is made to discuss some salient points with students in order to involve them and elicit their reactions. Such discussions may be held intermittently or at any stage of the lecture according to the need and convenience. In this process questions are asked by the teacher or the students and the method of interaction, the lecture, is able to clarify some important points through discussions and lecture is modified after getting feedback from the students. Thus, the rigid structure of one-way communication is broken and the subject matter is made meaningful through introduction of adequate freedom flexibility and feedback.

With a view to making the lecture method more effective, the teachers should consider the following guidelines meant for necessary activities at three distinctive phases i.e. (i) Preparation (ii) Presentation and (iii) Evaluation.

Preparation for the Lecture

(i). The first step in the process is to define the objectives in clear and specific terms. The lecturer should be aware of the purposes for which he is going to teach.

(ii) The lecturer should be clear about nature of the audience or the students, their background, needs, interests, and so on. This will help him to plan his lesson accordingly.

(iii) He should know the duration of the period during which his lecture will be delivered. This will enable him to decide the quantum of content to be covered during that period.

(iv) The lecturer should prepare sufficient subject matter or teaching points for dealing with the students. It is better to collect more material than is usually required for teaching a class in a particular period, so that he may not run short of content before the lapse of time.

(v) It is advisable to develop a synopsis of the lecture giving the important teaching points at various steps along with a list of reference materials. This will save the teacher from pointless digressions and save students from undue distractions. Thus, it can save time and energy of the teacher and the taught.

(vi) The lesson of the lecture should be planned in a sequential manner which will facilitate logical presentation of facts starting from known to unknown and from concrete to abstract.

(vii) Relevant audio-visual aids can be thought of while planning and adequate preparation for their use in right time and place be made earlier to presentation.

Presentation of the Lecture

(i) The lecture should create curiosity and motivation among students from the very beginning and should continue the same throughout the class. That is the introduction should be interesting as well as motivating, and similar atmosphere may be sustained in the class.

(ii) Various techniques of creating interest and motivation should be utilised according to the proficiency of the teacher. Some of these examples are narrating illustrative stories, anecdotes, contemporary incidents, newspaper items of relevance, visual presentations, highlight of the previous lecture etc.

(iii) There must be variation in the style of presentation like voice modulation, change in speed of delivery, pausing for emphasis or emotion and combining auditory with visual presentation. A well modulated voice and combination of various techniques are desirable.

(iv) Unnecessary movements, gestures or postures which are named as mannerism should be avoided as far as possible during the lecture. Some teachers, for example, move up and down in front of the class or unnecessarily make some gestures or use some words more frequently.

(v) Blackboard writing as an art needs special skills. Important points-names, year and drawings should find place on the blackboard during presentation. A lecturer should however should not show his back to the class longer than is necessary. The use of overhead projector at present has reduced this difficulty.

(vi) The lecturer should distribute his attention throughout the classroom That is, he should look at various places and individuals in the class, not at any place or anybody particularly. He should also convey thanks for encouragement and reinforce responses by a smile or similar non-verbal techniques.

(vii) Too many facts and figures should be avoided in the lecture which lead to boredom or drudgery. The lecturer should know that there is explosion of knowledge of course, but the sources of knowledge also are so many, starting from conversation among friends and peers to radio and television programmes.

Evaluation of Lectures

(i) The lecturer should always try to get feedback to his lecture, so that he can improve upon the methods and techniques followed in the same.

(ii) He can get readymade feedback from the interest evinced and attention paid to his presentation by the students or audience. The faces in front of him can reflect the same like living mirrors.

(iii) Besides such informal methods of evaluation, the teacher can develop a proforma or a small questionnaire for formal evaluation by collecting views or reaction of the students on the lecture delivered in the class.

(iv) The sole objective of this evaluation is not to test the students but to ascertain the effectiveness of the lecture and to improve the learning experiences of students. The proforma and questionnaire should contain specific items and rating scales indicating the degree of response.

(v) Such evaluation can be done in the beginning or in the middle to know students' entry behaviour or status of their knowledge on the topic. But it is usually done at the end of a lecture to assess its effectiveness and locate the level of understanding and difficult concepts or ideas of students.

(vi) A colleague can be requested to assess the effectiveness of a lecture with the help of a checklist or proforma. The teacher can also use a self-evaluation proforma or checklist to ascertain such effectiveness of his own lecture.

(vii) Like in micro-teaching, recording of a lecture can be done with the help of a tape recorder or video recorder so that it can be played back and the lecture can be evaluated on the desired aspects or points.

Project Method

The Project method is a dynamic and democratic approach to teaching, particularly suitable to the stage of higher education.

This method centres round a project which is a practical unit of activity having educational implications and aims at achieving not only knowledge, but also understanding, application and skills. It involves investigation, documentation and solution of problems. This is a student-centred method and planned by the student with the help of the teacher and conducted in a natural and real life situations.

Features of Project Method

An educational project is defined by Stevenson as "a problematic act carried to completion in its natural setting." According to Kilpartick "A project is a whole-hearted purposeful activity proceeding in a social environment." It has been defined by Good (1973) as "a significant practical unit of activity having educational value and aimed at one or more definite goals of understanding, involves investigation and solution of problems" and is carried to completion by pupils and teachers in a natural real life, manner.

The characteristics of the project method are as follows:

(i) The project method aims at teaching the students to get the best out of life and to prepare them for life. It is not meant merely for the future living, but also as a part of the present living.

(ii) This method is an attempt to utilise experiences as the truest and best lesson which cannot be forgotten.

(iii) It brings out the best of the potentiality in the student and provides opportunities for self-expression.

(iv) This method enables the learners to translate theories into practices. It not only solves problems, but also the activity is actually carried to completion.

(v) In this method the activity chosen becomes the core and all learning experiences become incidental. The curriculum is reset and all barriers of subject matter are broken in organisation of the project.

(vi) This method provides opportunities of working out purposeful projects of any character according to learners taste and interest viz., presenting a play or producing a class magazine. It may increase technical knowledge or motor skills.

(vii) Although a project is undertaken with all sincerity and seriousness, a relaxed atmosphere prevails through this method. Inspite of hard work, a project gives more satisfaction to the learners.

(viii) In the project method, the workshop techniques are followed through which learners acquire more learning experiences according to the principle of "learning through doing."

(ix) A project is usually organised in a life-like situation which provides actual and meaningful experiences to the student like "that of an apprentice learning his trade" as remarked by Dewey.

(x) The project method naturally implies group activity which means co-operation, fellow feeling, sense of responsibility, mutual sharing and respect for others.

Utility of the Method

These are uses of the Project Method:

(i) The method follows the psychological principles of learning. For example, the law of readiness, the law of exercise and the law of effect are very well taken care of in organising a project and providing learning experiences through it.

(ii) It gives ample freedom to the learners which is so valuable for self-direction, self-learning and self-satisfaction. In absence of external direction and imposition, the learners plan, implement, experiment, explore and learn according to their interest and ability.

(iii) It enables pupils to derive social values like cooperativeness, sharing responsibility, dignity of labour, respect for the individual etc., which are possible usually in a project work.

(iv) It provides training in citizenship which is very essential for success of democracy. Since the students select their project, plan the same, distribute responsibility among themselves and organise with understanding and cooperative spirit, they are practically trained in citizenship.

(v) It is generally a problem solving activity in which pupils are made active, responsive, involved, motivated and responsible. Students try to sort out a particular problem in a cooperative manner. They get practical experience as well as insight into the solution of a problem.

(vi) This method gives a sense of reality as a consequence of its practical and social implications. In this method school activity is related to social needs and situations which make students' learning experiences more realistic and relevant to their life.

(vii) It gives a feeling of satisfaction of completing the whole task by sharing a part of it. A project is divided into various tasks and series of activities are distributed among the students according to their interest and ability. But as the project is completed, the individual students feel the satisfaction of fulfilling their objective and completing the whole activity.

(viii) It is economical and efficient as learners are made interested and motivated in learning through participation and sharing in the project work. In an atmosphere of spontaneity and freedom, they learn more within the short time. Further, whatever is learnt by them is retained.

(ix) It gives dignity of labour in particular and dignity of the individual in general as the students are required to work personally in completing their assignments of various kinds small or big, manual or mental. That is why, this method is more democratic and dynamic than any other method.

(x) This method is particularly successful and effective in teaching of science, geography, language, art and craft in which students are required to do some practical work.

Limitations of the Method

(i) In the project method, systematic learning may not take place. Actual learning is apt to be incidental and accidental as teaching is not possible in an organised manner and many things are left to the interest and initiatives of students.

(ii) Progress of instruction may not be upto the mark or as per schedule, as the students are likely to waste more time in planning and organising activities. That is why, the course cannot be covered in time and students may experience difficulty in the formal examinations.

(iii) In this method, communication plays a minor role. Emphasis is laid on activities. In this age of knowledge and information explosion, unless adequate facts and figures are given in the shortest possible time, students will face problems in competition and evaluation.

(iv) This method is time consuming and cost-intensive as the project for proper organisation must call for more materials, more accommodation and more facilities. All students are not adequately motivated and involved and teachers cannot control their progress and activities.

(v) This method may not be suitable to the bright students who need speedy progress and efficient acquisition of knowledge and skills. That is why, they may lose interest and feel bored with the unsystematic and time consuming process.

(vi) This method is likely to leave gaps in the pupils' knowledge as learning does not follow a logical and systematic arrangement. The teachers are required to keep note of these gaps and fill up the same in time.

(vii) This method needs more correlation of topics and objectives in order to make learning effective. But such correlation is not always possible, particularly in academic subjects.

(viii) This method should be followed occasionally and as sparingly as possible since progress cannot be made adequately as per schedule.

(ix) In this method the teachers' role is quite significant and proper guidance as well as directions are to be provided by him. For this resourcefulness, training and experience of teachers are essential. Otherwise, the teaching-learning process is apt to the haphazard and superfluous.

Seminar Method

The English author Francis Bacon rightly said long ago, "Reading make the full man, writing the exact man and conference the ready man." That is the skills of reading, writing and speaking are essential for development of the personality. These skills are well combined and well developed through the Seminar Method. The term "Seminar" generally refers to a structured group discussion that may precede or follow a formal lecture. It may be either in the form of an essay or a paper presentation. It may be done by experts or academicians at a seminar or conference organised by an institution or an association or by individual students in a class or group of peers as a part of the source of work. In any case, the audience critically examine the paper and discuss the content or findings of the paper. They make queries -for clarification or elucidation on any point and the writer of the paper is required to clarify these queries with further facts and figures. The special nature and the professional setting distinguish the seminar from group discussion. The seminar method is very suitable for higher education or professional discussion when the level of attainment of the group is relatively high and the nature of discussion is expected to be analytical and technical.

Features of the Seminar Method

(i) The seminar method is stimulating and motivating.

(ii) It is an effective mode of testing the students' understanding and knowledge in the subject or the topic.

(iii) It evaluates their skills in arranging, formulating and presenting facts in a systematic manner.

(iv) It develops the sense of responsibility and cooperation as well as the powers of self-reliance and self-confidence.

(v) It is an advanced means of socialisation and instruction involving students' participation, preparation and interaction.

(vi) It breaks the monotony of traditional teaching and promotes academic excellence.

(vii) It stimulates and tests the students power of comprehension and understanding.

(viii) Seminar is mostly subject oriented and deals in depth a particular topic and issue at hand.

(ix) The presenter or the teacher is tested in his skill of arranging ideas in a sequence and sustained manner.

(x) Seminar promotes the power of delving deep into the matter and deriving principal from the context.

(xi) Questioning power is developed through participation in this process of intellectual model.

(xii) Seminar develops self-reliance, self-confidence, sense of cooperation and responsibility.

(xiii) It is an advanced technique of socialization and serves the very useful purpose of creating interest in intellectual pursuits.

Utility of the Seminar Method

The teacher concerned of the college or department should take initiative and acquaint the students with the objectives of the seminar. In case of a professional organisation or association the head or chairman gives an idea about the purpose of the seminar and a backdrop of relevant activities or progress made so far. The students and participants should be made aware of the potentialities of the seminar and motivate them to actively participate in the same..

The student or scholar who is required to present his paper has to prepare himself in all respects. He has to search and research the relevant material and develop the paper which needs proper sequencing of facts and figures and effective reporting. The teacher may give guidance in locating literature or references and preparing the paper in an objective as well as scientific manner. He may suggest the audio-visual aids to be used for presenting the paper effectively.

. A seminar can be held for two-three hours, and about 30-45 minutes may be devoted to presentation of the paper. Participants should also be encouraged to seek clarification or elucidation on various aspects of the paper. Thus discusssion may take one or two hours giving adequate time for interaction according to the degree of interest shown by the students or participants. Necessary facilities should be provided for the use of various projected and non-projected materials.

Like other intellectual and academic activities, seminars may be evaluated formally or informally. The presenters of papers should be able to get adequate feedback for improving their paper and removing the defects or deficiencies there in. An observation schedule can be developed for getting formal feedback and objective assessment of the paper and participation of the students or audience. The data collected may be analysed and interpreted for further discussion or guidance of the presenters and teachers concerned with the programme.

Discussion Method

It is said that "two heads are better than one." When a number of heads combine to solve a problem, results become wonderful. Discussion Method makes use of these tests particularly in teaching Social Sciences. An issue or a problem in which there is a difference of opinion, becomes a fit topic for discussion method of teaching. In this method ideas are initiated, expressed and exchanged, and the factual basis is traced out. The participants are engaged in interaction, interpretation and interpolation of facts. A kind of "Competitive Cooperation" takes place. Agreement is the declared purpose of such discussion. If it fails to achieve an agreement at all, there is value in discussion for clarifying the concepts and widening the horizons of knowledge and understanding the issue in question.

Feature of Discussion Method

Discussion as a method of teaching may have the following purpose.

(i) Laying plans for new work.

(ii) Presenting facts and figures from various angles.

(iii) Sharing and exchanging information and data.

(iv) Respecting various points of view.

(v) Clarifying ideas and concepts.

(vi) Inspiring interest.

(vii) Taking decisions in the matter,

(viii) Evaluating the progress from time to time.

According to some characteristics, discussion takes different forms viz., classroom discussion, debate, symposium, panel discussion and round table discussion. In the classroom discussion the teacher initiates presentation of a topic or issue giving the background and then elicits points of view and ideas from the students. In the debate usually a group of students argue in favour of, and another group against the issue or topic in question. In the symposium, different specialists or speakers make presentations dealing the topic from different perspectives. Such presentations may be written. A panel discussion raises issues, provides facts and stimulates interests in a selected topic. A panel of experts or speakers interact with each other on various aspects. In a round table conference, similarly, arguments are made from two opposing groups to seek solution to a current problem.

Some other characteristics are as follows:

(i) This method can be used both for junior and senior age-groups.

(ii) This method enables students to learn together, make suggestions, provide facts, share responsibility and comprehend the topic.

(iii) It clarifies the issue and sharpens curiosity to know further.

(iv) It crystallises the thoughts and concepts relating to the topic.

(v) It helps students in discovering what is not known already

(vi) It is an intellectual team-work for working out the details and seeking solution to the problem.

(vii) It helps the teacher to identify the potentiality and talent of students for promotion.

Utility of Discussion Method

Discussion method, in order to be effective, has to pass through the following stages.

(i) Planning: Considerable planning is necessary for holding successful discussion. Discussion for producing the desired results follows a well-directed procedure which can be divided into three stages, such as preparation, discussion and evaluation.

(ii) Preparation: The teacher should at first introduce the topic and may read out the method purposefully and critically. Points need to be arranged in a sequence logically. The points may be written on the blackboard for rereference of the students. The problem to be discussed should be a burning problem.

(iii) Discussion: The teacher should see that discussion is conducted in a disciplined manner. Face to face talk should be arranged. Adequate data and information has to be presented, and viewpoints exchanged by the students freely and frankly. It must be ensured that everybody takes part in the discussion. Queries may be made and comments made for clarifying the concepts and sorting out solutions to the problem faced. The teacher should see that discussion is made in a relaxed and cooperative manner. He has to discourage heated exchanges and wild comments. He ought to ensure that proper support is created for cooperative and unbiased discussion.

(iv) Evaluation: Discussion aims at achieving certain specific results. It is to be evaluated whether these results have been secured through discussion, whether knowledge has been increased, prejudices have been removed and interest increased in the burning issue.

Limitations of the Method

(i) Discussion Method is time-taking and often taxing.

(ii) It requires active participation of all which is not so easy.

(iii) The teacher should be more alert, careful and skillful for making discussion logical and systematic.

(iv) Students coming from various backgrounds and having various levels of interest cannot contribute to discussion adequately.

(v) This method can be followed sparingly as the entire Course of Study cannot be covered through this method only.

Demonstration Method

Demonstration Method lays emphasis on demonstrating experiments for teaching a particular topic, usually in science. The teacher performs all kinds of experiments in the classroom or science laboratory and explains the use of apparatus, chemicals and operations. This method, although mostly teacher-centred, encourages students' participation in conducting experiments. Many unfamiliar things become familiar and many abstract things become concrete, when students see with their own eyes and handle some of the apparatus and chemicals themselves. Since students are motivated to see new experiments, they observe attentively and learn everything critically.

Demonstration method proved to be one of the best methods in explaining new concepts and anecdotes. But the demonstrations are to be well-planned and rehearsed by the teacher. Otherwise, if all experiments fail in the classroom, it will have a very bad effect on the students. Once all experiments are well conducted, demonstration becomes successful and teaching becomes effective for achieving the objectives.

Features of Demonstration Method

There are several characteristics of the Demonstration Method which may be taken as criteria for ensuring success in teaching. These are as follows:

(i) Demonstration Method makes use of several experiments involving a series of operations.

(ii) These experiments need to be well-planned and rehearsed well in advance.

(iii) Success of experiments encourages and their failure discourages students in learning.

(iv) Students need encouragement to participate and involve themselves in conducting experiments.

(v) The teacher and students should be clear of the institutional objectives in lessons delivered.

(vi) The teacher must have adequate confidence and preparedness for demonstrations.

(vii) Students have to observe the operations with attention and know all apparatus with interest.

(viii) He should involve students as much as possible and seek their cooperation in perform ing experiments.

(ix) Questioning should form an important part of demonstration in order to get feedback from students about their understanding and assimilation.

(x) Difficult or new concepts need to be explained to them in simple and clear-cut language and style.

(xi) Important points and terms are to be mentioned on the chalkboard which is to the back of the teacher and in front of students.

(xii) The apparatus for demonstration should be arranged earlier in a sequence.

(xiii) The experiments need to be visible to the entire class and for the purpose, the demonstration table should be higher than students' desks/tables.

(xiv) Demonstration should fit in the timetable and according to the season/occasion.

(xv) Students' interest should be maintained throughout demonstration.

(xvi) The teacher should see that students write in their notebook what is written on the chalkboard and found in the experiments.

Utility of Demonstration Method

(i) Demonstration Method is found to be economical in time and money.

(ii) It is psychologically based as the pupils are shown all apparatus and operations conducted in their presence.

(iii) Students' participation is encouraged and their involvement ensures effectiveness.

(iv) Abstract things are made concrete by teachers and observed by students.

(v) The teaching-learning process becomes very efficient and meaningful through experiments.

Limitation of Demonstration Method

(i) Students often do not get chance to perform the experiments themselves in the classroom.

(ii) "Learning by Doing" maxim becomes ineffective in Demonstration Method.

(iii) Unless the teacher rehearses the experiments and plans them in sequence, there may be delay and failure in conducting demonstration bringing about adverse effects on students. With adequate planning and rehearsals, however, these limitations can be overcome.

Criteria for Selection of Methods

The Secondary Education Commission (1965, pp.84-90) has laid down some objectives of good methods of teaching which equally hold good for higher education also. According to the Commission good methods should aim at:

i. inculcating among the students desirable values and proper attitudes in habits of work;

ii. creating in their minds a genuine attachment to work and a desire to do it as efficiently, honestly and thoroughly as possible;

iii. shifting the emphasis from verbalism and memorisation to learning through purposeful, concrete and realistic situations;

iv. providing opportunities for the students to make practical application of the knowledge they have acquired in the classrooms;

v. training the students in the techniques of self-study and the methods of acquiring knowledge, personal effort and institution;

vi. developing the capacity for clear thinking and clear expression in speech and writing;

vii. expanding the range of the students' interests so that they might be able to explore different fields of creative activity and choose one, if necessary, for specialization at a later stage.

It is desirable on the part of teachers to create adequate interest and initiative among students through methods of teaching. Self-learning is the best learning method and students once motivated can acquire knowledge through self-activity. One important principle which may be borne in mind by the teacher in planning his method of teaching is that it is not the amount of knowledge that matters, but the efficiency with which it is acquired by the students. The Commission has rightly observed, "with the great increase in knowledge that has taken place in every single field, it is quite impossible for a student - not only in secondary school, but even in the university - to acquire even one hundredth of the most essential knowledge in any particular field of studies. Any attempt, therefore, at an encyclopedic approach, however, watered down, is foredoomed to failure. The teacher must concentrate on two things - quickening of interest and training in efficient techniques of learning and study. If, through proper presentation and the realization of the relationship between student life and what he is learning at school (even college) his curiosity and interest have been aroused, he will always be able to acquire necessary knowledge, on the spur of felt need, in his later life. On the other hand, the static readymade knowledge, which is forced on him, not only fails to irradiate his mind but is also quickly forgotten - as soon as it has been unburdened in the Examination Hall."

The emphasis should therefore, be shifted from the quantum of knowledge to the right methods of acquiring it. For this purpose it is essential that every student should be trained in the art of study. This basic skill of "learning to learn" should be acquired by students at the school stage and be developed at the higher education level. These skills cannot be acquired automatically, but have to be consciously practised. It is also felt essential to train the students in the habit of working and reading independently. If students are trained to do so, it will discourage cramming and make it unnecessary for the teacher to cover the entire course or to teach the whole book through formal oral lessons. The teacher could then concentrate on the essentials, show the inter-connections of topics and arouse intelligent interest leaving some part of the course to be studied by the students independently. Assignments, projects etc., can be given to them according to their individual interest and ability. Such training is necessary not only to develop their capacity for independent work but also to adopt instruction to individual differences.

These individual differences are the most significant part of the psychological data with which the teacher has to deal with and if he fails to adopt his methods of work and presentation to the psychological needs and mental range of students, he can neither win their interest nor their active co-operation. The present practice of mechanically applying the same methods to dull, average, as well as bright students is responsible for much of the ineffectiveness of the instruction given in schools and colleges. Various groups of pupils should be allowed to proceed at their own appropriate level/pace and the methods, approaches or techniques of teaching need to be properly adjusted to it. It will save the dull students from the discouragement and the bright ones from a sense of frustration. In this context the Secondary Education Commission has given the instances of the United Kingdom where curriculum is organised in three streams - A, B and C for bright, average and dull students respectively. The Commission has also added, "But we recommend that this idea of adjusting the curriculum to students of varying ability should be explored and what is equally important, methods of teaching should also be similarly adjusted. The brighter children will, for example, be able to respond better to methods involving greater freedom, initiative and individual responsibility than the dull or the average children who may require atleast in the early stages, a greater measure of planning and guidance by the teachers" (p.89).[7]

There should be balancing between individualised and group methods of teaching. A wise teacher knows how to balance the claims of individual work with co-operative and group work. In actual life to acquire the qualities of leadership, initiative, co-operation, discipline etc., is as important as to possess the capacity of personal achievement and independent work. The former qualities are better developed in the well organised group work like problem-solving activities, projects and community service programmes. Teachers at all stages of education, particularly at higher education level, should organise such group work through various methods which have been discussed in the relevant chapters. The Commission has therefore recommended that "the teachers should be so trained that they are able to visualise and organise atleast a part of the curriculum in the form of projects and activity units which groups of students may take up and carry to completion. Such activities would promote give and take of shared experiences and emotional satisfaction among students. The project would break the academic isolation of educational institutions and bring the students as well as teachers into vital rapport with the life and problems of the community. The chemistry of purification of water may lead to the study of the Municipal Water Supply System and the Civics of democratic organisations may take the teachers and students to the study of the functioning of local Panchayat Samities. Such interaction and interface of the educational institutions with the surrounding community would vitalise the educational system and create a sense of belongingness and social responsibility among the teachers and students. In this process community resources can be utilised for effective education and educational institutions can contribute to the development of the community. These practical and pragmatic methods of teaching or organising curricular programmes will be mutually enriching and rewarding for both educational institutions and society.

An important parameter for improving the quality of education thus lies in the part of imparting instruction in adopting right methods for organising various curricular programmes. Dynamic methods of teaching e.g., project and problem-solving activities need be adopted by the successful teachers besides following stereotyped techniques of giving lectures in the classroom. Interactive and innovative methods like seminars, symposia and brainstorming sessions should be tried out as far as possible. Learning by living and learning by doing should be the main objective as well as the process of education. There should be adequate scope for flexibility and freedom in the system for facilitating the growth of sterling qualities of initiative, co-operation, leadership, free thinking, dignity of labour and social responsibility among teachers as well as students. This can break the academic isolation of colleges and universities which have been defamed as 'Ivory Towers' keeping themselves aloof from the community problems and national issues. Teachers should be exposed to these various methods of organising programmes in and outside the classrooms through their staff/faculty development courses being implemented by Academic Staff College and other institutions concerned with the improvement of the quality and relevance in higher education.

Integration of Different Methods of Teaching

It is to be borne in mind that not a single method should be adopted in teaching. The method has to be selected according to the nature of the topic. But very often, one or two or more methods are to be followed for making teaching effective and efficient. For example, unless the lecture method is used for initiating teaching, for giving the background knowledge and explaining certain content, demonstration or experiments cannot be effective or understood properly by students. Hence lecture-cum-demonstration method is usually adopted in teaching science subjects. Similarly, discussion method is also followed along with lecture method.

Project method is to succeed the lecture method which is used by the teacher to introduce the problem, lay down guidelines, forming groups and giving some ideas about the project earlier. In the seminar method also, the teacher may be required to initiate and conclude the discussion and deliberation of the points relating to the project. Unless the scattered points are properly summed up and inferences are drawn, the entire exercise may fall flat on the students. Therefore, methods have to be properly integrated for making the teaching-learning process successful and meaningful.

Different objectives and criteria for good methods have been spelt out here for developing an insight and purposes of these methods. You have been told about the necessity for using various methods in different contexts. The characteristics, uses and limitations of Lecture Method, Project Method, Seminar Method, Discussion Method and Demonstration Method have been discussed and you have been made familiar with the merits and demerits of these methods. Now, you can select any method found, suitable for transmitting the knowledge, skills, attitudes and interests in teaching a particular topic. Sometimes you may find an integration of one method with another benefitting the students more than in any one method.

References

1. Government of India, Secondary Education Commission, 1965, p.85
2. Government of India. *National Policy of Education (MHRD)*, Education, 1986, p.14
3. Lowman, J. *Mastering the Techniques of Teaching*, Prentice Hall of India, New Delhi, 1987, Preface.
4. Government of India, *NPE*, *op.cit.*
5. Government of India, SEC, *op. cit.*
6. Lowman. J. *op. cit.*

5

Teaching-Learning Process

Teaching

We cannot measure the significance of teaching by mercenary standards, but in terms of emotional and psychological satisfaction. Teaching is not a mechanical process of transmitting knowledge and information from the teacher to the students. It is not a monologue but a dialogue. In the dialogue one may be vocal and another not so vocal, but can give vent to his feeling in the form of queries through facial expressions and some sounds of exclamation or irritation. Teaching is regarded as an art. Like a piece of music or painting, it touches the heart, brightens the mind and gives pleasure to everybody. It has to inspire and motivate the learner to go ahead on the road of exploration and discovery, to open new vistas and to reach new horizons. But traditionally teaching is equated with telling. The old concept of teaching as giving of information has been discarded by the modern psychologists. Now the educationists feel that teaching is to motivate the student to learn and acquire the desired knowledge, skills and also desirable ways of living in the society. The main objective of teaching is to enable the pupil to respond to his environment effectively.

Teaching, to be precise, is a process of communication for achieving certain objectives. These objectives, of course, should be desirable and specific to various groups of learners. Teaching is defined as "the process wherein conditions are deliberately created (environment organised) to enable a specified learner (or a group of learners) to behave in a specified manner to perform or to experience certain desired objectives." Teaching thus aims at helping learners to learn or change their behaviour in a relatively permanent manner and involves arrangement of situations for facilitating learning. The important general maxims of teaching are: it should proceed from the known to unknown, from analysis to synthesis, from simple to complex, from whole to part, from concrete to abstract, from particular to the general, from empirical to rational, from psychological to logical and so on.

Good teaching recognises individual differences among students; it should be interesting and need based. It should be challenging as well as sympathetic to the learner. It ought to promote productivity and self-study. Teachers should take the social and psychological background of pupils into account. Good teaching should be dynamic and well-planned. Teachers in order to make their teaching effective need to acquaint themselves with curriculum, school routine, standard of the class and if possible, brief bio-data of students. Successful teachers should project themselves as sympathetic and sincere, warm and friendly persons to their pupils.

Learning

As we grow, we learn, we are apt to learn more than any other living beings. We adjust with our environment better than any other being. We influence our environment and the environment also influences our living styles. The interaction between the living being and environment results in the change of behaviour and such change is learning. That is why, learning is called the modification of behaviour. It implies change in knowledge, understanding, skills, interests, habits, attitudes and so on. Learning thus consists of all changes in thinking, feeling and doing in course of life. The human child is the most helpless of all creatures and his helplessness is again longer than that of any other living being.

It is said that such helplessness of the human child gives a greater scope for learning. The world is full of problems. The human being faces problems in his everyday life. But he tries to solve them with his own knowledge, insight, reasoning, skills and techniques of adjustment. Human life is thus a continuous process of learning, a series of experiences gained through living. Skinner has therefore defined learning as "a process of progressive behaviours adaptations." Crow & Crow has considered learning as "the acquisition of habits, knowledge and attitude." According to Munn learning is "more or less permanent incremental modification of behaviour which results from activity, special training of observations." McConnel has precisely defined learning as "the modification of behaviour through experience."

Summing up all these elements, learning means "relatively permanent change in behaviour which occurs as a result of experience or practice.

On the whole learning can be defined as the process of effecting changes in behaviour that brings about improvement in our relations with environment. Learning is rightly called the pivotal issue in education.

The main aim of education is to effect desired changes in the behaviour of students. Learning is thus a natural outcome of the individual as attempts to meet his basic and normal needs." The learner cannot afford to be passive in the process. He has to interact with his environment. Learning is a complex process by which an organism faces new problems, acquires new knowledge, develops new mode of behaviour which tends to persist and create a general behaviour pattern of organism in more or less degree. All this brings about changes in behaviour - in doing, expressing one's thoughts, feelings and attitudes called learning.

As regards its main characteristics, learning is growth through experience; it is an adjustment to the environment; it is a synthesis of old and new expressions; it is purposeful and intelligent; it is both individual and social; it effects conduct of the learner. There is a difference in adult learning and child learning. For instance the adult learns through concentration of mind on essential and useful rejecting the useless. Children on the other hand, learn through all senses in a natural and active way. The vastness of adults experience may help or hinder their learning, whereas children's learning is immensely promoted due to their strong spirit of curiosity, inquisitiveness and free and frank mind towards the outside world. Therefore children should not be forced to learn in adult ways and methods with narrow utilitarian objectives.

Behaviour

The behaviour is roughly of three kinds: (i) thinking, (ii) feeling, and (iii) doing, which are technically known as cognitive, affective and psychomotor objectives. Cognitive objectives involve the leaner in thinking processes like remembering, recognizing, analyzing, evaluating and problem-solving. Affective objectives involve the learner's feelings, interests and attitudes. Psychomotor objectives involve the learner in various kinds of muscular activities and skills. Many objectives are a combination of cognitive, affective and psychomotor. For example, preparing a model or a graph may be taken as psychomotor objective, but it involves knowledge of the principles and conceptions about the model or a graph and also the attitude and interests of the learner. Of course, according to the importance of particular objective in a specific situation we designate the work as cognitive, affective or psychomotor and this categorisation helps us to recognise a given objective and treat it accordingly. Our decision about the emphasis lies in our teaching-learning system.

Hierarchy of Learning Objectives

In our existing conditions we lay more emphasis on cognitive objective and neglect affective and psychomotor objectives. Benjamin Bloom (1956), with his co-workers has produced two handbooks offering taxonomies of educational goals in the cognitive and affective categories or domains. In the cognitive domain, Bloom identified six levels of objectives: (i) Knowledge, (ii) Comprehension, (iii) Application, (iv) Analysis, (v) Synthesis, and (vi) Evaluation. In this hierarchy of objectives knowledge is the lowest level and evaluation the highest. In the affective domain, Bloom identified five levels: (i) Receiving/ attending, (ii) Responding, (iii) Valuing, (iv) Organisation and (v) Characterisation by a value or value complex.[1]

Benefits of Objectives

Now the question arises: What are the benefits of these behavioural objectives? According to Derek Rowntree (1974), there are mainly four kinds of benefits: communication, contact and structure, teaching and learning methods, evaluation and assessments. First of all, objectives enable us to communicate about the intentions of the teaching and learning. That is, the teacher can start communicating with his students, who learn faster and contribute more if they are aware of the goals. As Robert Mager, (1962), puts it, "If you do not know where you are going, you are liable to land up someplace else." Self-awareness of objectives leads to more purposeful teaching and insofar as the student is teaching himself, to more purposeful learning.

A second benefit of objectives is that they help us to select and structure the content of teaching. Thirdly, objectives help us decide on appropriate learning activities and teaching media. Different objectives will be realized through different learning activities and media. The fourth and final value of objectives is that they help us decide on appropriate means of evaluation and assessment, on ways of testing the effectiveness or teaching and on criteria of judging the success or failure of the course.

Different Kinds of Learning

The hierarchy of objectives makes it clear that learning is not all of the same type and the higher one climbs up, the more complex does the type of learning become. Robert Gagne (1965) in fact identifies eight types of learning, each of which results in different kinds of behaviour and each of which needs different conditions both media and materials to produce it. They are as follows:

1. *Signal learning:* involuntary conditioned behaviour, e.g., blinking of the eyes, withdrawal of hands from fire.
2. *Stimulus-response learning:* voluntary, selective responses stimuli, e.g., making pencil marks on paper, imitating pronunciation of a new word.
3. *Motor chain learning:* a sequence of physical acts carried out in a fixed order, e.g., tying a shoe lace, writing with a pencil, starting a car engine.
4. *V erbal association:* (verbal changing): verbal responses often useful in more complex learning, e.g., saying the alphabet, naming an object, giving English equivalents to foreign words.
5. *Multiple discrimination:* responding differently to similar stimuli, e.g., naming each members of a group, giving an appropriate English equivalent for each of a set of similar foreign words.
6. *Concept learning:* responding to new stimuli according to the abstract properties they share with previously encountered stimuli, e.g., saying which of two objects is nearer or further away, bigger or smaller, lighter or heavier, saying which of a group of animals are dogs or which are cats.
7. *Principle learning:* putting two or more concepts together in a relationship, e.g., using a rule like "hot air rises" or "area = length x width."
8. *Problem solving:* recalling previously learned principles and perhaps generating new higher order principles, to achieve some goal, e.g., writing an essay, planning a menu, making a medical diagnosis, tracing down the fault in motor car's electrical system, conversing in a foreign language or making a ceramic Jug.

John De Ceccoo (1968)[2], gives many examples and suggests how each type of learning can be brought about. Although we may aspire for higher type of learning, Gagne points out that 8 depends on 7 which depends on 6 which depends on 5 and so on. He is also of the belief that there may be higher or more than these learning types. According to Wilbur Schramm (1973), the taxonomy of Gagne's learning types is also hierarchical in nature. That is, (1) learning *Stimulus-Response*

Connections, (2) is prerequisite to learning *Chains*, (3) verbal Associations, (4) which are in turn prerequisite to learning *Discriminations*, (5) which must precede the learning of *Concepts*, (6) which are prerequisite to the learning of *Rules*, (7) which are required for *Problem-solving*.

Thus it is evident that one type of learning facilitates another and one prepares a base for the next. No learning is exclusive and free from the effects of another. Schramm (1973), has rightly observed, "Most learning is hierarchical. One step must be taken before another which can successfully be accomplished, and all the simpler types of learning are subsumed under the more complex forms. Instruction is designed that way."

Media Selection

Learning is modification of behaviour. So learning has to be translated into certain behavioural objectives which are observable as well as measurable. After translating the intents of the teaching-learning task into behavioural objectives relevant media have to be selected according to its nature and needs. The most direct attempt to tackle this problem was made by Briggs, Gange and May (1966), who suggested six steps in this context:

1. State the behavioural objectives for the course or unit of instruction in the sequence in which they should be taught.
2. For each objective, identify the types of learning involved.
3. Using the required conditions of learning as a guide, design a "media programme" for each objective which lists the instructional events, identifies the characteristics of required stimuli and states the media options which would be acceptable.
4. Prépare a summary of the media options for a group of objectives making up a sequence of instruction, and scan these to identify frequently occurred media options.
5. Assign the media in which the instruction should be packaged to achieve the best trade-off in respect to effective stimuli display, convenience in changing from medium to medium and economy in terms of size of unit which each sequence is to be prepared in the given media.
6. Write specifications for the preparation of the instruction for the various media producers.

Briggs, Gagne and May (1966), have also added, "Determining

appropriateness of media..... is a complex decision which cannot be done in cookbook fashion. For example, if the introductory portion of a course in Science requires the learning of a number of concepts.... the need for pictures (or actual objects) may be frequent. In such a case, an instructional sequence emphasizing picture might be an efficient way to present this part of the course. In practice, a sequence of slides or a film might be designed and might be the medium of choice provided it could include the other modes of presentation required (accompanying oral and printed speech)."[3] At the other end of the spectrum there will be portions of a course which need pictures to only a limited degree. For example, if the student already knows the required concepts, a presentation of the principles ... is simply not going to be helped by pictures, if any....

When a series of analyses of objectives indicates the need for a mixture of diagrams, still pictures, verbal descriptions and decisions to be made by the student, a format like programmed instruction would be appropriate. If the movements of objects in space and time relationships are involved as in understanding what causes night and day, motion pictures showing rotation of earth and its revolution around the sun, accompanied by sound narration of the principles involved would be relevant.

Thus, the selection of media is to be based chiefly on the way the different media can present physically the required stimuli for learning. In planning and designing media we should limit ourselves into one or two specific learning objectives. If we do not set any limitation, our media would be too complex and unmanageable. It might be better to develop a series of related media in order to cover more than one or two objectives.

Gagne has given three propositions about the selection of media:

(i) No medium is best for all purposes.

(ii) Most instructional functions can be performed by most media.

(iii) Media are not differentially effective for different people.

Rewriting these propositions for his purpose of considering small and big media, Schramm has said: (i) People can learn from *any* medium, big or little, (ii) More of the variance in learning effect can be explained *within* than *between* the media, (iii) It is commonsense to believe that one medium may be more effective than others for a *given* instructional task. It seems reasonable that a pictorial medium might be more effective in teaching concept of space or shape or time, that an audio-visual medium might be more effective in teaching concepts or principles that involve motion and change and physical relationships; that an auditory medium might be more effective in teaching chains and concepts that involve motion and change and physical relationships; that an auditory medium might be more effective in teaching chains and concepts that involve sound, that print might be swifter in teaching higher order learning such as rules or problem-solving, that a programmed medium might be most efficient for providing interactive practice when a teacher does not have time to give that much individual attention to every student; that a tape might be most efficient for providing models for language practice and so forth. Schramm has, however, remarked that "these distinctions are presently in the realm of the art of teaching and the experience of instruction rather than the realm of research and science."

Teaching-Learning: Two Sides of a Coin

It is a fact that whatever is taught is not learnt. Rather whatever is learnt may be taken as actually taught. Teaching and learning are two aspects of the same process. Teaching is transmission of some facts and figures, some values and attitudes to a group of students or clientele. In order to make such transmission effective and interesting, various methods are followed and different media and materials are utilised. Hence, teaching is a kind of communication of message (learning experiences) released by a source (teacher) and transmitted through a channel (medium or method) to reach the receivers (pupils). The teacher acts as a communicator for giving facts and ideas, skills and attitudes to the learners and good teaching requires interaction in the classroom or inter-communication between teacher and students. Teaching is a mutual sharing of experience and a continual feedback process. Such teaching or communication is meant for effective learning which is expected to change or modify the student's behaviour. Hence change in response or behavoiur is casued partly or wholly by experience. Learning is a process of modification of behaviour more or less permanently through the various experiences gained by inter-action with the people and the objects in the environment of the individual, as teaching becomes effective learning, creative and productive. Learning is therefore meaningful, purposeful and goal-oriented. It is an active process of behavioural changes taking place through classroom interaction.

Learning is thus a change in human disposition or capability which persists over a period of time. Learning is also called a process and a project. As a process it includes such factors as different types of learning, the nature of interaction between the learner and the teacher and other relevant matters. As a project it includes the outcomes of learning such as cognitive, affective and psychomotor learning. Outcomes of learning also not only include the types of achievement but also the level of achievement and various types of components attained by the learner. Learning comes only through experience and activites. The teacher has to provide different types of learning experience in the context of a particular curiculum or a course of study. Of course, there are different types of learning experiences. The teacher has to organise the teaching-learning process in the classroom environment and develop inter-personal skills. In this process the teacher through interaction gets feedback from the learners and accordingly, provides the learning experience as suitable and required for the purpose.

The learning environment at present has become multimedia or multi-channel and multi-dimensional which is very powerful. Of course there is a wide gap between learning environment and the learning systems. There are constraints and contradictions-resources, value system, and information delivery in and outside the school. Multi-channel learning environment is the product of new communication media and information technology. Multi-channel learning system is the product of various types of instructional materials, design and information, communication and management technologies. With the increasing democratisation of education, "The world comes into the classroom." Different social and political problems iike deprivation, hunger, caste and gender disparity and other community issues, social and psychological dynamics have their impact on instructional design and materials.

Pedagogy has given way to mathetics. That is, teaching has lost its priority and learning has gained its ground. Further "Learning to learn" has become more significant to sustain the onslaught of a fast changing world and the knowledge explosion. There are several taxonomies on the cognitive domain alone developed by Bloom, Merrill, Gagne and others. Knowledge is taken as the lowest level of taxonomy and there is a difference between information and knowledge. Information is a bit where as knowledge is a byte or the organised bits. Hence information comes as the lowest level of cognition. Previously evaluation was at the end of the taxonomy and it misses due to the highest form of cognition namely creativity. It is a cognitive process but triggered off with inspiration. A piece of good poetry or a good painting may be an outcome of a flash or a vision. Hence creativity deserves an important place in the taxonomy of cognitive process. Therefore, the classical statement of creativity i.e., 1% inspiration and 99% perspiration still holds good. It has also been proved by some research studies on the structure of the genius.

Modern educationists have laid great stress on value system in the affective domain, because it plays a critical role in human life. The values are the basis of an individual's behavioural changes and decisions. To a particular incident or issue different individuals behave differently due to their varying value system. Multiple choices are available in behaviour of individuals on account of the value system. One has to take a model of behaviour which is internalised. An individual may observe a behaviour pattern and imitate the same as a behavioural model. The individual internally assesses such behaviour and makes choice with alternative behaviours. Hence learning to learn is not only to learn knowledge and values but also skills. An individual has to learn or master the learning skills and gain mastery of content. Learning process is an instrument for mastery of content and gaining all kinds of learning experiences.

Learning through Classroom Interaction

Sustainability of learning is an index of its effectiveness. It is the ability to recollect, recall and apply the skills at appropriate time and place. From the memory we retrieve knowledge and skills. The various methods and media can contribute to the optimisation of human learning at various levels. The most important component or method of learning is behavioural modeling. Children learn mostly by immitation of the behaviour of adults. Parents and teachers influence such behaviour. Particularly behaviour modeling of the teacher needs special attention for facilitating learning. This is particularly necessary for value learning. The Gurukula system of education provided a bright example of behavioural modeling in which Guru's entire life was exposed to the disciple as an open book. The disciple saw the Guru in the various aspects of his life-as a teacher, as a human being, as a father, as the head of the family and as a good neighbour and so on. At present the disciple is exposed to the teacher's behaviour only in the classroom for a few hours in a day. Hence the impact of behaviour on students is getting less and less.

Research and exploration may be taken as another instructional strategy in which the child behaves as an explorer-frank and fearless.

Most of our learning experiences are therefore based on exploration and at the primary stage, children should be of learning for gaining various skills. Children do it natuɪally and sometimes skillfully. They consult with the people they confide and whom they feel are superior in knowledge and experience. Whenever a child asks a question to his or her parents or another adult, he or she is basically consulting. This question or consulting may be taken as an instructional strategy to develop the learning experience.

Co-operative learning is a significant method for children's learning. In this process they learn to be co-operate, to know each other and to share responsibilities. They recognise mutual talents and make use of their talents to create a synergy. Therefore, the ability to participate and co-operativive is an important learning skill. Related to co-operative learning is the interactive learning. Classroom interaction takes place among the teachers and students, they interact with environment, with teachers, with peer groups, with particular print or electronic media. Hence interactive learning is essential for achieving high levels of congnition and needs to be developed among children.

Behaviour modeling and classroom interaction depends heavily on Educational Technology. The optimization and sustainability of learning experience of the child depend on the effective use of technology. The competency of learning and articulation skills are essential for behaviour modeling and classroom interaction. The teaching learning process is made effective and efficient through various strategies and techniques and among them behaviour modeling and other learning skills are essential.

Programmed Learning

Programmed Learning/Instruction is a revolutionary strategy pertaining to the art and science of the teaching-learning process. It is not only a technique for effective learning, but also a successful mechanism of feedback device for the modification of teacher-behaviour. It nevertheless provides insight into the problem of teaching effectiveness through improved feedback and reinforcement mechanism. According to Schramm (1962) "By programmed instruction I mean the kind of learning experience in which a 'programme' takes the place of a tutor for the student and leads him through a set of behaviours designed and sequenced to make it more probable that he will behave in a given desired way in the future - In other words he will learn what the programmes designed to teach him."[4]

Programmed Learning is an educational innovation and auto-instructional device. It is a practice of breaking down a body of subject-matter into its constituent elements and requiring the pupil to master one step before proceeding to the next. It allows for more pupil involvement in the learning process. Since it is a self-instructional device, it is mostly individualised being adopted to individual differences. In this technique, learning is more rapid as well as interesting. It is directed towards specific objectives and retained better as well as longer.

Principles of Programmed Learning

Programmed Learning is based on the following principles:

1) A student learns by being active. If he has to perform in a certain manner after the learning session, he must be allowed to perform in that manner during the learning session itself.
2) A student learns better and is motivated to learn more, if he is told that he is right after he takes a step in the right direction, i.e., to say, if he is reinforced.
3) A student learns better if the task he has to learn is analysed into sub-tasks which are sequenced properly so that he can learn one step at a time beginning with a step which he already knows.
4) The sequences of these sub-tasks or the instructional events should be reproducible so that any person other than the designer himself can verify that the sequence leads to the effect, changes the behaviour of the acceptable students in the specified manner and that it does so consistently. This has to be specified in such a manner that its realisation can be measured.
5) For specific strategies in organising situations for learning and arranging their sequence, leads are provided by various principles of cognitive processes and motivation. These principles are derived from psychology of cognitive process, motivation and field theories.
6) No strategy can be considered to be effective unless it guarantees the learning of all students for whom it is designed. The designer may specify the prerequisites-relevant backgrounds necessary on the part of the learner. Those learners who have these prerequisites are then considered as acceptable students and it should be demonstrated that these acceptable students, learn through the programme.

These programmed learning principles may also be adopted to various media not only separately, but also to evolve, a common strategy so as to optimise students' learning. By 1967 when the United States National Society for the Study of Education published a year book on programmed instruction, there was general agreement among the experts that the process could be defined by the following steps:

1. formulation of objectives,
2. design and testing of a Propriate criterion measures to determine when the objectives have been achieved,
3. definition of the target population,
4. analysis of learning tasks,
5. preparation of prototype programme,
6. developmental testing programmes,
7. validation of programme.

In developmental testing, Mackenzie and others (1970) remark that the purpose is to improve the programme and in validation it is to obtain data to demonstrate the effectiveness of the programme.

Programme Types

The programmes are usually divided into two (i) linear and (ii) branching. Schramm (1962) mentioned the following salient characteristics of programmed learning meaning only linear programmes in this context. "To sum up, there are the essential elements of programmed instruction; (a) an ordered sequence of stimulus items, (b) to each of which a student responds in some specified way (c) his responses being reinforced by immediate knowledge of results, (d) so that he moves by small steps, (e) therefore making few errors and practising mostly correct responses, (f) from what he knows, by a process of successively closer approximation, toward what he is supposed to learn from the programme."

Again programmed learning is also divided into three distinct types (1) linear, (ii) branching and (iii) adjacent auto-instruction. Skinner (1961) invented and was in favour of the linear programme. As the name indicates there is a single line which all the students have to follow. This programme allows all the students to read and respond to the same frames. The student makes progress along a single line/tract from one frame to another irrespective of the answer. Most linear programmes use constructed responses. A few programmes also use both constructed and multiple choice responses. The linear programme is generally response-centred and in each frame only enough material is presented to evoke the correct response.

The branching programme allows the learner to take any number of different paths through the curriculum. In the programme the student proceeds to the next frame until he makes an error. Each response is evaluated and that evaluation determines where the student goes next. In case of wrong response given, the student is provided with help to avoid making that wrong again. A student who is able to do very well is given chance to go ahead, whereas anybody committing many mistakes is required to retrace his tesps or take an alternative route to resolve difficulties.

The well-known programme was developed by Crowder (1960) who called it intrinsic programming. It consists of rather long frames that often appear as pages in an ordinary book form. The student reads the page or frame and then responds by collecting the correct alternative in a multiple-choice item. The correct response directs the students to frame which confirms his response and introduces a segment of new materials. This system takes into account the individual difference and provides the necessary remedial material the student needs.

The supporters of the linear programme argue that in this system the students acquire the terminal behaviour with fewer errors, with greater interest and less time. Many branching programmes introduce very limited flexibility into sequencing of frames. Although there is controversy as to the advantages of either type, no research study has yet shown any significant gain in any. Rather it has been found that there is no real difference between the two.

Pressey (1964) advocates for the adjunct auto-instruction which requires little alteration in the learning situation than in the programmed instruction. According to him adjunct auto-instruction inserts programme or testing material that may be needed as supplementary material. In Pressey's opinion, the conventional instruction should carry the main burden of instruction and the programmed material should tackle only the material which is potentially difficult and confusing.

Programming Steps

(i) *Topic selection:* The programmer should select the most familiar topic, otherwise he has to take the help of a subject expert. He may confine himself to selecting a specified content or a small area of the subject matter.

(ii) *Content outlines:* After topic selection, its outlines may be prepared which should cover all the materials on plans to teach. For this the programme has to refer to and examine relevant books and materials.

(iii) *Instructional objectives:* Instructional objectives must be formulated which involve both task description and task analysis. The former is the description of terminal behaviours which the learner is expected to achieve and the later is the series of component behaviours that he is required to acquire in the process of achieving terminal behaviour. The instructional objectives should be written in behavioural outcomes.

(iv) *Entry skill:* The learner should have some prerequisite ability and skill to understand properly the new programme. This programme cannot be prepared without proper assessment of the entry skill. To prepare a programme adequately, target-oriented entry skill data should be utilised at this stage.

(v) *Presentation of the material:* Suitable format is to be decided for presenting the material from the educational point of view. Then the programmed material should be presented in a sequence of frames arranged as steps towards terminal behaviour.

(vi) *Student participation:* On analysis of the terminal behaviour one will find the critical responses of the students. Of course it is related to some part of the subject matter. The over-responses facilitate student learning. Students' participation is facilitated by presenting the programme in an interesting format.

(vii) *Terminal behaviour test:* The effect of programme can be ascertained by administering the terminal behaviour test, also known as performance assessment. This provides feedback to the programme and shows the effectiveness of the instructional materials. It may also serve as an entry skill data for the next programme on a related topic of higher level.

(viii) *Revision:* Lastly the programme may be revised on the basis of feedback. The instructional materials may be edited and modified according to the needs and requirements of the target-audience. Programmed Instruction is self-instructional material developed on the psychological principles of teaching-learning process.

A rapid learner can cover the material quickly and a slow learner may proceed at his own pace. This frees the learners from the same type of teaching materials delivered to the whole class at the same pace. The programmed learning material helps the learner to teach himself at any place and pace according to his convenience. Different types of programmes have their special advantages and facilitate learners' initiative, participation and involvement according to their interests and ability. They provide scientific teaching and learning for efficient and effective acquisition of knowledge and skills.

Teaching vis-a-vis Learning

Prior to the last century teaching was considered as a rigid, formal and stereotyped process of transmitting knowledge, facts and figures. Education was taken as a bipolar process with teachers at the giving end and students at the receiving end. Teachers were deemed to be the only source of knowledge, may be through manuscripts or printed materials. Schools were the knowledge shops and teachers are the information managers or vendors. Methods of teaching were logical, sequential and routine devoid of proper attention to the psychological needs and conditions of learners-their interests, curiosity, freedom and flexibility. Emphasis was laid on rigid discipline, blind memorization and hard reinforcement. Verbalism was enforced and no audio-visual aids or materials were utilised in the field of education.

The learner was always kept at the receiving end and was considered as an empty vessel to be filled with knowledge and information, facts and figures. At the advent of the 20th Century, a child is considered a tender plant whose growth is facilitated by the teacher as a gardener. The child is taught according to his abilities, attitude, interest and aptitude. He is helped to learn and to grow. New "to teach is to nourish." Cultivate the growing child or give him intellectual exercises or train him in the horizontal sense of directing or guiding his growth. Children are motivated to search and experiment, to gather facts and information. They learn by doing and learn how to learn both individually and in groups. Various media and materials are used for making learning more interesting and effective.

Recently, learning has assumed more importance than teaching. It has been rightly observed by the International Commission on the Development of Education. (1972, p.150) that there has been a change in the learning process which is tending to displace the teaching process. New theories of learning highlight the principle of contiguity and the importance of needs and motivation, of choice of content, of the hierarchic nature of learning, the inter-relationship between educational content and environment, etc. Multimedia systems have to now acquire more significance, and educational technology has been popularly used for effectiveness.

Now stress is on the mathetic principles of learning rather than on the traditional pedagogic principles of teaching. Mathetics, the science of the pupil's behaviour, has recently gained more importance than pedagogy, the science of the teacher's behaviour. The term "Mathetics" is derived from the Greek root signifying the learner and the process of learning is given high priority. The mathetic principle is now used for designing various programmes for individual learning by pupils.

References

1. Bloom, Benjamin, *et al. Taxonomy of Educational objectives: The Classification of Educational Goals*-Handbook 1-Cognitive Domain, New York, Mackgy, 1956
2. DeCeccoo, J. *The Psychology of Learning and Instruction;* Prentice Hall, New Jersy, 1968
3. Briggs, L.J. *et al. Instructional Media,* Pittesburg, America Institute of Research, 1966.
4. Schramm, W. *The Science of Human Communication,* Basic Books, New York, 1962.

6

Better Learning through Effective Communication

There has been rapid expansion of knowledge in almost all fields, and man is still discovering, classifying and recording new information at a phenomenal rate starting from the minutest particle of the atom to the farthest body of the universe. Application of this new knowledge in various disciplines has minimised the problems of time and space and facilitated the discovery of still newer knowledge in an endless cycle. Therefore it has been felt imperative on the part of teachers, to keep themselves abreast with the latest developments in their subjects and develop skills in applying criteria to assess the accuracy and validity. The development of new knowledge has resulted in the constant expansion of the school curriculum. As the curriculum expands, not only teachers fail to do justice to teach, but students too get very few opportunities and too little time to learn all objects in depth. On the other hand, student population is amazingly increasing year by year due to population growth and democratisation of education. Students come from varying experience, backgrounds and differing facilities. Their levels of motivation and aspiration are quite different from one group to another.

Even in the developing countries like India a large percentage of students are first generation learners who are deficient in background as well as motivation. Such heterogeneity and diversity among the pupils pose great problems in teaching as well as learning. In view of such problems and developments, special attempts are to be made for two types of instructional media, methods and materials: (i) those which are likely to prove effective for use with groups consisting of individuals of widely varying backgrounds and abilities and (ii) those which can be used advantageously for individualised instruction with only a minimum of teacher assistance. Fortunately, educational technology has come to our rescue with wide a range of hardware as well as software for tackling these problems. It is the development, application and evaluation of systems, techniques and aids in the field of human learning. The main objective of its use is to optimise learning processes and experience. Technology of education is intended to make learning effective as well as efficient. It facilitates learning through the systematic identification, development, organisation and utilization of a full range of learning resources, and through management of these processes. In brief, students are to be enabled to "learn more in less time" meaningfully and to remember longer what they learn without "watering down" or sacrificing quality.

Elements of Communication for Learning

According to Wilbur Schramm (1954, P.1)[1] the world famous expert in mass media and communication, there are at least four elements of communication (1) the source (2) the message (3) the channel and (4) the destination. This applies to both human and mechanical communication. But education is mainly concerned with personal or human communication. In this context either an organisation or a person can transmit a message which may be received by an individual or many. The message may be conveyed by verbal expressions, gestures, spoken or written symbols or by hand drawn or photographed pictures. The source is also called an encoder, the message a signal and destination a decoder. These terms indicate the need for common understanding of language and word-meanings based on similar experience background for making communication a success.

Mere presentation of a message or a lesson by the teacher may be a communication, but cannot be effective unless it leads to true learning. For example, a teacher teaches a new word. The child can repeat the spelling of the word correctly, but he should be able to use the word rightly on subsequent occasions. True learning has not taken place unless the teaching as an act of communication has succeeded in making a permanent and meaningful addition to the student's own communication skills. Brown (1964, P.9)[2] and others have therefore observed that classroom communication involves far more than the unilateral presentation by the teacher of new words or new facts or new ideas; it requires intercommunication between students and teachers, a mutual sharing of experiences and a continual feedback process.

Modification of Behaviour

Learning means modification of behaviour. Change in response or behaviour is caused partly or wholly by experience. Munn(1954) has rightly defined learning as "the process of being modified, more or less permanently, by what happens in the world around us, by what we do, or by what we observe." Geoch instead of giving a rigid definition of the learning process has made a general statement as following, "Learning, as we measure, is a change in performance which occurs under the conditions of practice." Thus learning depends on the following:

(i) Experience of the learner.

(ii) Capacity and motivation of the learner.

(iii) Methods in which the learning materials are presented to the learner.

(iv) Meaningful or difficulty of learning task; and

(v) Interaction between the above variables.

Sunitee Dutt(1960 pp. ll-12)[3] has enunciated the characteristics of learning as follows:

(i) Learning is purposive or goal-oriented. Human beings always learn to achieve something. Purposeless learning may not be effective. But when the goal is fixed and clear, the learning becomes more meaningful and effective.

(ii) Learning is an active process. There is no learning without self-activity. That is why, it is said, "whether or not you learn and what you learn depends upon what you yourself do, for learning an activity."

(iii) Learning is individual. Each learner has his own needs and interests, abilities and attitudes, hopes and aspirations. Some may learn quickly and some slowly. Thus the pace and depth of learning depends on that individual.

(iv) Learning is socially conditioned. It is not only individual but also social. It occurs in relation to social environment of the learner and a teacher has to take this into account.

(v) Learning is the response of the whole individual to the total situation. It is unitary as man learns as a whole being. So for effective teaching and learning, the physical, mental, social and emotional aspects of his whole being are to be taken note of and setting up the environment is very important

(vi) Learning is creative. It is not just an addition to the previous knowledge and experience of the learner. It is a creative synthesis of all the new and old knowledge and experience. True human learning aims at creative and critical thinking.

(vii) Learning is transferable. It is transferred to new tasks and the learner establishes relationship of the previous learning experiences with the new ones. Of course it is possible when there is identity of context, procedures and ideals and such transfer is necessary for economy as well as efficiency of learning.

Communication Vs Learning

There are different principles of learning like readiness, exercise, effect and insight which are useful for success of communication. Again there are various approaches to learning. The association theories of learning lay stress on the responses of the learner and bonds with stimuli and the behavioural changes of the learner. The field theories emphasize the learner's perception of the whole field of events. Skinner, Thorndike, Guthrie and Hall are the proponents of association theories. Lewin, Tolman and the gestalt psychologists are the advocates of the field theories. The association theories put emphas on the stimulus - response, environment and previous experiences and part elements in learning. On the contrary, field theories emphas perception and cognition of the learner, the whole rather than the parts and the relationship between parts.

Again, learning processes are classified into three: (i) enactive or learning by doing (ii) iconic learning by organisation of perception and (iii) symbolic, learning through symbols and language representations.

All these learning theories, principles and processes are of vital importance for successful communication which is equivalent to active learning. Participation, interaction, cooperation and different skills promote such lively learning experiences. Various media, materials and methods capitalise such principles and approaches for providing better learning experiences. That is why, educational technology consisting of all means, media and materials based on the psychological principles and precepts helps promoting learning as well as teaching.

The Report[4] of the Meeting of Chief Technical Advisers, National Directors and UNESCO specialists in Methods and Techniques, Paris, December, 1979 has said that. Educational Technology is a communication process resulting from the adaptation of the scientific method to the behavioural science of teaching/learning. It is a communication process which may or may not require the use of extending media (i.e., radio, television, film and other audio-visual media). The process contains essentially the following components.

(i) Specification of goals and behavioural objectives.

(ii) Analysis of the characteristics of the learners.

(iii) Selection and organisation of the content or subject matter to be learned.

(iv) Presentation of the content.

(v) Evaluation of the results.

(vi) Feedback. Feedback must be continuously interacting among all of the preceding five components. It is not just a final component, but it provides essential linkages among all the components.

All these components are also essential elements in learning. Unless all these points are taken into consideration, learning cannot be made effective. These are the basic needs for organisation of suitable media and materials in order to optimise learning outcomes. Modern communication methods, visual arts, classroom organisation and teaching techniques are to be made use of and geared to achieve the instructional objectives. Communication processes supported by technology of education intend to bring about effective and efficient learning.

Shift of Focus

Pedagogy, the science of teachers' behaviour, has now given place to mathetics, the science of learners' behaviour, that is there has been a shift in focus from the teacher to the pupil and learners' behaviour has been given more emphasis than teachers' behaviour. In other words, the learning process is replacing the teaching process. Learning to learn is essential and learning is more important than teaching. Learning is also a continuous process. It is lifelong. It is apt to be equivalent with education. Through education students learn how to learn, learn how to keep on learning, learn how to be creative and innovative, and learn how to contribute meaningfully and significantly to solving the new problems that are encountered in day to day world.

If learning is so important, what is the role of a teacher? Faure and others(1982 pp. 77-78) have rightly replied, "the teachers' duty is less and less to inculcate knowledge and more and more to encourage thinking; his formal functions apart, he will have to become more and more an adviser; a partner to talk to, someone who helps seek out conflicting arguments rather than reading out readymade truths. He will have to devote more time and energy to productive and creative activities such as interaction, discussion, stimulation, understanding and encouragement." The teacher is no longer the monopolistic purveyor of information and authoritative transmitter of knowledge. He is to inspire, motivate, guide and stimulate. His role is not merely to communicate the new knowledge, understanding and skills but to identify the pupils needs and provide facilities for promoting his cognitive, conative and affective development.

Communication is the master key to modern civilization. It has affected the entire world immensely as well as wonderfully. The whole world has been reduced to a close neighbourhood. The distance of time and space has been almost removed and all barriers of castes, communities, creeds and colours have given place to mutual fellow-feeling, inter-relationships and cooperative ventures. Robert M-Hutchines, a distinguished educationist has named it "a communication revolution." In fact, today it has exerted inevitable influence on millions and billions of people all over the globe through various means and media. It is informing, entertaining and inspiring individuals in many ways.

Defining Communication

The term "Communication" has been derived from the Latin word "Communis" meaning "Common." It implies common experiences, mutual sharing or give and take. It has different meanings for different people. Communication is defined as the sharing of ideas and feelings in a mood of mutuality. It involves interaction which encourages give and take. This provides feedback to individuals involved in the exchange of ideas. Effective communication is, therefore, a two-way process.

Communication assumes a democratic philosophy of life which implies the dignity and respect of all persons who enter into communication. It also assumes freedom to learn and criticize. John Dewey, an exponent of democracy has emphasized shared experience as a key element in communication and pointed out, "communication is a process of sharing experience till it becomes a common possession. It modifies the disposition of both the parties who partake of it"5. Willbur Schramm, an outstanding communication expert has said that it "is concerned with all the ways in which information and ideas are exchaged and shared. Thus we are talking about both mass and interpersonal communication. We are talking about the spoken word, signal, gesture, picture, visual display, print, broadcast, film-all the signs and symbols by which humans try to convey meaning and value to another."

Components of Communication

There are mainly four components of communication. They are (i) source or sender which is technically called "encoder", (ii) message or signal, (iii) channel or medium, and (iv) destination or receiver which is technically known as "decoder." In the communication process, the source or the sender has the correct information and transmits the same as accurately, clearly and speedily as possible. The content of transmission is called the message. It should be conveyed through the medium of words both written and verbal, gestures, pictures and so on. Thus the medium or channel may be either audio or visual or both. Every medium has its peculiar influence on the message to a great extent. That is why, it becomes, in a sense, an integral part the message and it is aptly called "medium is the message." The sender encodes the ideas or information as the message and channelises the same upto the receiver through medium or media. The receiver decodes or understands the message or interprets the information according to his background.

Since communication involves at least two or more persons, interaction is a "must" in order to make it effective. This ensures the mutual sharing or give and take of ideas and experiences. Such communication must also have a desired reaction called "feedback". Thus in any effective communication, in addition to the original four components, two more (i) interaction and (ii) feedback are also essential.

But interaction is so much inter-mingled with feedback that many communication experts like Harold D. Lasswell take both as one-feedback. The five essential elements of communication are: "who, says what, in which channel, to whom, with what effect?".

Modes of Communication

There are mainly three modes of communication. They are (i) Speaking-Listening, (ii) Visualising -Observing (iii) Writing -Reading. They may briefly be discussed as follows:

(i) Speaking-Listening : In this type of communication one speaks and another listens to it. This is mainly face-to-face as in the case of conversation or listening to a speech. In some cases, there may be gap or distance in between the sender and the receiver or the source and the destination like in radio broadcasting. But both the sender and the receiver of messages share the feelings and may interact with each other if they are in eye to eye contact.

(ii) Visualising-Observing : In this type of communication one visualises and another observes. There is usually a physical separation between the producer of the message and the audience to whom the message is conveyed as in the case of a television programme or a film. Dramatisation may also be included under this category in which facial expression and gestures produce an effective communication.

(iii) Writing-Reading : In this model of communication, the sender and the receiver are physically separated all the time, but both are able to share the experiences and feelings. An example of this model is the writing of a book by an author and reading of the same by a reader or a group of readers who can enjoy and appreciate the feelings and ideas of the writer properly.

The arrows moving both ways indicate that in all three kinds of communication, interaction and feedback are essential features in effective communication.

Theories of Communication

The basic communication theory indicates that there must be four elements - source, message, channel and destination, in the communication process. Any communicator sends message through a channel to the audience. In the technical jargon, the communicator is known as the encoder, the message whether words, pictures or signs is called symbol, the channel may be one of the media or means and the audience is called decoder.

In this process, an adept communicator knows what he wants to communicate as message, understands the characteristics of the channel and the social as well as psychological background of individuals constituting the audience.

Then it was found that feedback is essential for making communication effective. The communicator should know the reaction or response of the audience, so that it will be possible on his part to modify his message as well as the channel. There must be interaction between both the communicator and the audience.

Everybody has his own background, physical, social, psychological and sociological. He sends or understands a message from his own background. The physical and emotional conditions like health, mood, attitude and ego involvement influence his understanding or reception of the message. The audience provide their reaction to the message and the communicator modifies or revises his message and media according to such feedback effects. This classic model is again modified by some communication specialists like Willbur Schramm who advocated a circular diagram to represent the communication process. According to them both the parties - communicator as well as audience-should play the ideal roles as senders and receivers.

This is a kind of communication that occurs normally in conversation between two persons. But in order to ensure effectiveness in communication, it is felt imperative that there must be interaction and feedback continuously and mutual sharing or give and take of experiences and ideas. Another theory or model of communication is known as SMCR developed by David K. Berlo. This model emphasizes the psychological nature of communication and provides an analysis of messages and of sensory channels of communication. In this model, source is considered along with communication skills, attitudes, knowledge and socio-cultural context; message includes content, treatment and code; channel consists of eyes, ears, taste nose and touch and receiver comprises communication skills, attitudes, knowledge and socio-cultural context.

Berlo has rightly made it clear that encoding or decoding a message successfully will depend heavily on the communication skills. But the sender's as well as the receiver's attitude is of immense significance. For example, if the attitude of the recepient is favourable towards the source, reception of the message will be different, if it is otherwise. Similarly, knowledge and socio-cultural background of the source as well as of the receiver are equally significant for successful transmission and reception of the message. It is a fact that the message actually does not convey the meaning. The meaning is grasped according to the psychological, emotional and sociological background of the receiver. Berlo has aptly said, "Communication does not consist of the transmission of meaning. Meanings are not transmittable, not transferable, only messages are transmittable, and meanings are not in the message, they are in message - users."

Edgar Dale has corroborated Berlo's statement very strongly and clearly, when he observed that you can present stimuli to an individual, but his needs and background determine whether it will be accurately interpreted, and create the intended meanings. Furthermore, messages are also distorted by the receiver. They see what they want to see, hear what they want to hear, and distort messages unintentionally. Even there is selective perception; for example, heavy cigarette smokers do not quit smoking when they read about the harmful effects noted in research, rather they quit reading about cancer studies.

Even today the experience of Galileo about refusal of persons to see the truth holds good to a very great extent. Galileo wrote to his friend Kepler, "Here at Padua is the principal professor of philosophy, whom I have repeatedly and urgently requested to look at the moon and planets through my glass, which he pertinaciously refused to do ... what glorious folly!" In this context what can the communicator do? He may take the horse to the water, how can he make it drink? If the meaning lies with the receiver, neither with the message nor with the channel, what can the sender do to make the communication effective? These are the pertinent questions and an attempt will be made to answer them.

Communication and Social Progress

Democritus, the Greek philosopher has rightly said that you cannot live in the same society a second time. This is just as you cannot step into the same river twice (of course, in a particular place!) It means that change in the human society is continuous, perennial and pervading. Change takes place always, everywhere and in all aspects of the society. It may, therefore, be said that the only 'changeless' element in the society is the 'change' itself.

It is only through change that progress in the society is brought about. More are the changes, greater is the progress. Human civilisation has reached the present stage only due to social changes. The primitive society was comparatively less prone to change than the modern one and the lethargic, dull and backward people are more averse to changes than the energetic, ebullient and advanced persons. Thus the social change is the key to social progress.

Social Change

Social changes are mainly of two kinds. One is structural and the other is functional. When the entire structure of the society is changed by means of a political movement or national struggle, it is a structural social change and when a change take place in man's behaviour, ways of living, dress and food habits through education and culture, it is functional. The American War of Independence the French Revolution, the Russian Revolution and the Struggle of Indian Independence come under the first category and change over from wearing the untailored dhoti to putting on a pair of suit, from using the bullock-drawn plough to a power driven tractor, from squatting on a mat for eating to dining at a table are the examples of the latter. Both structural and functional changes have almost the same degree of difference as between the major and minor operations. Thus in the struggle parlance 'operation' and in the social science "social change" have both the broad and narrow connotations and have immense significance for physiological and sociological life.

Dynamics of Change

According to Ottaway (1962) social change is the result of interaction of both techniques and values. It is of little use to desire social change either in terms of technical progress or in terms of a change in values when one is considered independently of the other. The state of society depends on both and they are inseparable. It is also not easy to say which influence is dominant or takes the lead in any particular social change. It is said by some social scientists that new inventions and discoveries are a primary cause of social change. But any invention or discovery alone is not adequate to explain the social change. Its use depends on the prevailing set of values in the society. The aims and objectives, life styles and philosophy of a community determine how its techniques will be used. The same technical invention can be used differently in different societies or its use may be delayed if the existing conditions of the society are not favourable or it may be accelerated if the society is amply prepared for the same.

On the other hand, some sociologists believe that the value-systems, ideas and aspirations play a dominant part in changing the society. We must, of course, recognize the force of technology, which brings about changes in our habits of work, thought and belief. Thus we have to deal with the problems of social change by considering a number of variables, each influencing the other. Mac Iver and Page(1950) in their important work "Society" have distinguished between the technological factors and the cultural factors in bringing about social change. These two factors may be compared with techniques and values given by Ottaway. All these three authors also equally believe in interaction between the two sets of factors and reject all theories which place the technical and cultural factors in opposition to each other and stress the dominance of the one or the other in determining social change. Ogburn (1947) has also used the terms material culture and non-material culture and described the "cultural lag" When the former comes first, it is more rapid and more effective in determining the social change. That is, non-material factors likes values lag behind the material factors or conditions like techniques. Marx and Engels had earlier put forth their extreme views of economic or material determinism in the change.

Recently, Thorstein Veblin has developed a thesis that the kind of work and leisure which men do determine the social structure. Here he has stressed the importance of adjustment to changing techniques. It may thus be concluded that both material and non-material aspects of culture are simultaneously involved in any social change and that neither is necessarily dominant. The relative significance of these factors will be different on different occasions. The cultural lag or social leeway however often comes into being when a man's values cannot keep pace with his technical development and a cycle of interaction always revolves involving both techniques and values simultaneously, but not equally.

Communication is the powerful means of bringing about social change. Mac Luhan has developed a thesis of technological determinism which says that changes in the technology of communication brings about social changes. The revolution in the media of communication has helped accelerate the pace of social change during these few decades. Radio, television, newspapers and other mass-media have not only made this world "shrunk" but also have revolutionised the values, attitudes, interests and social milieus.

An important task of communication is to promote development and without its support no project can be made successful. Balcomb (1975) has aptly mentioned that many ambitions projects have failed because of poor all round communications.[6] From his own experience he has clearly pointed out that the UNICEF and other agencies had supplied a considerable amount of audio-visual equipment to various projects but much of this equipment was being poorly used. The hardware was there, but the software had very often been left to take care of itself. That is, proper dovetailing and adequate coordination as well as integration of the technical equipments used for communication puposes and the messages or information that are to be transmitted through these mechanisms are essential for effective communication. Thus for implementing projects in every field whether health or agriculture or education, the building of such overall communication systems is technically called the "Project Support Communication."

It may be mentioned in this connection that at least four elements are required for communication: (I) a source (II) message (III) channel and (IV) destination, (Schramm, 1954). These involve both human and mechanical segments of communication. There must be person(s) to initiate at one end and receive at the other end and a message to be conveyed by expressions, gestures, spoken or written symbols or by drama or photographed pictures. This process emphasizes the need for common understanding of language and word meaning based on similarity of experience background for effective communication.

The source must have the correct message to be transmitted clearly to the receiver. It is also to be ensured that the receiver is understanding the message accurately and producing a desired response. Thus the communication must be a two way process resulting in intercommunication and based on mutual sharing of experiences and a continual feedback.

Making Communication Effective

With a view to making communication effective, motivation of the persons concerned is to be generated. The people should think for themselves and on their own initiative. They must do whatever they think right and desirable for them, not as they are told to do. They are to function as project participants, not merely as project's beneficiaries. Without the needs being felt by the beneficiaries themselves the project howsoever need based and useful, cannot be implemented successfully. A small example may be cited here. In a tribal village women had to go to distant hilltops to fetch drinking water. Under the Community Development Project in that village a well was sunk and sweet water was also available. But alas! the tribal women were so much used to bringing water from a high altitude and not oriented to draw water from a well nearby that the well turned to be a big dustbin!

Another interesting incident of this nature has been narrated by Matheson (1975). Many years back a big project was started in the vicinity of Rome to clear the Pontine Marshes for eliminating mosquitoes and the diseases from the city and at the same time to create more arable land for cultivation of vegetables and fruits. But fishermen living in the swampy places and earning their livelihood from fishing grew irate at the prospect of swamps being drained. As a matter of fact they broke the walls of the water tanks that had been created to lead off the water and soon the ambitious drainage project was completely wrecked. These phenomena clearly indicate the communication gap as the tribals and fishermen were not explained about these projects which were meant for a better and happier life. Matheson has therefore remarked that unfortunately although the tools of technology are available today to help improve the lives of people throughout the developing world, too many projects are failing to achieve their goals because communication experts and development planners often do not communicate effectively with each other or with the people they are trying to help. Unless the people themselves are made ready for the changes and feel the needs, no project can be a success.

We may use various kinds of mass media and audio-visual aids but our message must be clear at first and communicated as effectively as possible. In order'to facilitate this, audience have to be motivated through various means, most important of which is felt to be interpersonal communication. Matheson has again hammered this point when he says that finding the right message for the right medium for a specific audience is a constant challenge to communication experts and development planners and workers. Much has been claimed for the power of the mass media and it has certainly achieved wonders in bringing people instant information and in shaping lifestyles and beliefs. But when it comes to rural societies especially where literacy levels are low and traditions deep-rooted, the effectiveness of mass media in bringing about change is very limited. Experience has shown that probably the single most effective means of communication is the interpersonal one - dialogue between two or more people.

Every medium of communication has its own limitations. So it has to be selected according to the socio-cultural conditions of the clientele and be used in appropriate time and place with much caution. Nevertheless communication elements should be built into a project in the initial planning stage. They must be integrated with the whole system and not just tagged on as an after thought.

References

1. Schramm, W. *The Science of Human Communication,* Basic Books, New York, 1954, p.1
2. Brown J. *et. al. Instruction Materials and Methods,* McGraw Hills Book Company, New York, 1964, p. 9.
3. Dutt. S. *Learning Process,* NCERT, New Delhi, 1960, pp. 11-12
4. UNESCO. Report of Meeting of Chief Technical Advisors, National Directors and UNESCO specialists in Methods and Techniques, Paris, 1979.
5. Dewey, J. *Democracy and Education,* Macmillan, New York, 1963.
6. Balcomb, J. *Communication for Development: From Propaganda to Dialogue and Entertainment,* in the UNICEF News issue 84/75/2

7

Educational Broadcasting

The importance of educational broadcasting is quite significant in developing countries like India where the socio-economic condition is yet to reach a take-off stage and universalization of elementary education is still to be realized as per the Constitutional Directive. Therefore, there has been an imperative need for furthering national development in all facets of life and for providing increased access to education, both through formal and non-formal systems and reducing the massive wastage and stagnation at all stages of education. Educational broadcasting is required to be a potential instrument of educational advancement and an integral component of educational inputs in traditional as well as distance or other alternative learning systems for different categories of learners.

International Level Efforts

The Asian Programme of Educational Innovation for Development (APEID) technical working group in its draft final report in the context of formulating guidelines for the development of educational broadcasting services has laid down the following for consideration:

(i) Guidelines should have application to the universalization of education and the special needs of rural communities.

(ii) There is a great variety of administrative patterns and in the stages of development in educational broadcasting among member countries.

(iii) Advice should be practical of implementation, and should have a proper regard for limits of financial and other resources.

(iv) Radio is a cheaper form of broadcasting than television, both in the production and transmission of programmes and in the facilities required for reception. It has the advantage of greater penetration of the general population.

(v) Notwithstanding the previous statement, television is a powerful educational tool and must be given full consideration by governments and ministry policy-makers when determining priorities for the allocation of resources.

At the National Level

In view of the above considerations, the APEID group was rightly conscious of its limitations and has aptly observed that the guidelines that were laid down by it are not either general principles or specific statements that are not applicable to any one country or educational system. Therefore, it was felt necessary to discuss and spell out these guidelines in further detail of specificity in national seminars or workshops of various Asian countries. In India, such a national workshop was held at New Delhi from 1 to 6 December 1980 under the joint collaboration of the Ministry of Education and Culture as well as the UNESCO's APEID. This workshop in the fitness of things specifically viewed educational broadcasting including both radio and TV programmes:

(i) as a means of motivation by informing and encouraging people to participate in national development,

(ii) as a major component of the non-formal education system by providing an alternative approach to the education of out-of-school children, youth and adults,

(iii) as a direct instructional medium dispensing with the need for an intermediary,

(iv) as an enrichment of the formal system of education where it can fill instruction gaps, up-to-date knowledge and bring in new learning experiences,

(v) as a training component for teachers (instructors) and supervisors,

(vi) as a means of imparting vocational (agricultural and industrial) and professional (medical and engineering) skills.

The national workshop thus wished that educational broadcasting would be multipurpose and sought to make multi-pronged efforts for educational advancement. It would not only move away from narrow syllabus-based approaches, but also would try to reach the learners directly. It would aim at reduction of load and drudgery in the classroom and make teaching-learning process interesting and effective. Both radio and TV programmes would serve all categories of learners and provide all kinds of learning experiences-knowledge, understanding, appreciation, attitude and skills. The new curriculum with emphasis on SUPW, citizenship training and national integration could be better realized with the help of educational broadcasting.

Our Priorities

In planning and production of programmes both the media-radio and television-would emphasize the following national priorities.

(i) Universalization of elementary education, both formal and non-formal,

(ii) Non-formal education for adults, linking education to economic and social tasks,

(iii) Development of vocational and professional skills,

(iv) Training for citizenship,

(v) Popularizing science with a view to developing a scientific outlook,

(vi) Promoting national integration, and

(vii) Providing information about themes of national importance-population education, energy conservation, preservation of wild life, environmental sanitation, nutrition and health.

Training and Management

With a view to realizing the above national objectives and priorities, it has been decided that educational broadcasting should form an integral part of the total educational system. It means that the responsibility of policy and management of educational broadcasting should be with the educational authority. It has been suggested that advisory bodies and educational technology institutes should be set up at the national and state levels for extending advice from time to time and taking up the management. These advisory and executive bodies should take up responsibility for all kinds of educational media. This responsibility must include formulation of policy, programme planning, production, utilization, evaluation and feedback, training of personnel, providing support materials and publicity. This must also comprise administration and accounting of the organization. Although these institutions should be part of the educational infrastructure, they should have operational freedom.

Educational broadcasting by its very nature must address itself to mass audience. It must also serve the national interests and goals. But it is also necessary that it should take cognizance of local needs, language differences, cultural variety and other similar factors. Therefore, besides national framework within which the priorities, broad areas, themes, objectives, utilization and evaluation procedures of educational broadcasting should be spelt out, similar action should also be taken up at regional, State and even local levels. Planning, production and evaluation should be a collaborative venture involving curriculum developers, subject experts, teachers, scriptwriters, social scientists and producers. Even audience would be involved in planning, production and evaluation for ensuring credo and reality in programmes.

Feedback and Utilization

In order to ensure optimum and effective utilization of educational broadcasts, the national workshop suggested that all schools and learning centres should be adequately equipped with listening and viewing facilities. Although the government should take up the main responsibility for this, public funding, participation of the community and national as well as international voluntary agencies may also be explored. Adequate steps should be taken for maintenance and operation of the receivers. Even necessary incentives may be made available to teachers for bringing their own radio sets. Educational broadcasting should also form an integral part of teacher education programme. Besides, in-service training courses should be organized for orienting the teachers and supervisors media; various kinds of support materials should also be provided to teachers and students by the educational authorities. Research and evaluation should form a significant part of the total process of educational broadcasting. Both short-term as well as long-term, formative and summative research studies should be conducted for better utilization, evaluation and feedback.

Radio Broadcasting

Gone are the days when education was the luxury of a few. Now education is the necessity of many, rather of all. Previously, its main objective was to impart some knowledge and skills required for the white-collared jobs or other few vocations. But now it is necessary for all kinds of jobs that are available in any part of the world. Education is regarded as a potential instrument of social change that is thought desirable at a particular point in time. It is intended to bring about social upliftment, political awareness and promoting economic growth of the masses in general. Governments of different countries have, therefore, taken up the responsibility of universalising school education and widening the access to tertiary and technical education. It has been ensured not only in the Constitution of most of the countries, but also in the International Charters of UNO and UNESCO.

Education is not limited to the classroom teaching only. It is broad-based and multi-dimensional. It is lifelong, universal, free and open. Education is learning and learning is life. Learning, living and working should go together. Education is not only lifelong, but also life-wide. Hence, there is no end to learning and no frontiers of learning. School is not the only institution of learning. It has ceased to monopolise the sources of learning. Schooling is not the only education or education is not the only schooling. The traditional curricula, methods, organization and examination are found irrelevant to the modern age. Therefore, flexibility and multiplicity of media and materials are to be encouraged. Since the children of today are the citizens of tomorrow, they have to be provided with all kinds of facilities and techniques for effective as well as efficient learning.

Radio Programmes for Education

In this context, radio has been playing an important role for promoting relevant and interesting education. It brings the outside world into classrooms and makes the educational programme very attractive and useful. It not only informs, but also inspires the audience. It incullcates values, develops virtues and encourages imagination. Therefore, radio has been used as a potential medium for helping in realization of educational objectives most efficiently. Being an inexpensive medium, it has reached villages and is now available in the nook and corner of the society. Radio is, at present, not only one of popular mass media, but also a potential instructional tool in the formal, informal and non-formal education.

Although All India Radio (now *Akashvani*) introduced programme for children from the Bombay station as early as in 1929 and from Madras station in 1930, the pioneering school broadcast programme started in 1932. The other stations followed suit and have been broadcasting educational programmes quite successfully. Educational broadcasts are now a little over 70 years old. The educational broadcasts for secondary schools are mostly syllabus-based and the subjects covered in these programmes are English, modern Indian Language, Science, Social Studies, Sanskrit etc. Secondary school broadcasts aim at helping students and teachers by giving upto-date content-knowledge, providing new approaches and methods of teaching and filling curricular gaps. A few non-syllabus programmes are, however, broadcast in order to break away from the stereotyped formal education, for doing away with monotony in the curricular topics and also to stimulate awarness and curiosity about the modern world dealing with themes ranging from popular science to current affairs.

Besides secondary school broadcasts, primary school programmes have recently assumed greater importance. This has been done in order to reduce wastage and stgnation at the primary school stage by making the school situation attractive and interesting. Dullness of the classroom, irrelevance of curriculum and rigidity of school timing are the reasons for the high percentage of drop-outs. Hence along with the various attempts of the Governments at the State and the centre, the AIR has shifted the emphasis of educational broadcasting towards the primary stage. Besides introducing primary school programmes with the existing school broadcasts, priority is being given to the primary school service. The AIR has given preference to tribal and interior areas for expansion of instructional broadcasts. The personnel incharge of these services are being recruited from among those who are familiar with the tribal culture and languages. The programmes are being related to their education, health, hygiene, nutrition etc., with a stress on bringing the audience into the mainstream of national life.

There are also broadcasts for tertiary or university students which are of two kinds. One is a general and enrichment service which mainly constitutes the Youth Programme. These broadcasts are not syllabus-oriented and topics of general interest are discussed therein. The second category is the radio support to correspondence or Distance Education. These broadcasts are related to the course of studies and are planned in consultation with the Correspondence Education authorities of the respective univerisities.

Since it is not possible to cover all the students under formal educational system, efforts are being made to provide facilities to the drop-outs and those who have not entered into the schools so far, through non-formal educational system. The AIR has not lagged behind to support this system through its educational programmes. As such non-formal education broadcasts were started from 5 stations since 1976 on an experiemental basis. These programmes were broadcast to non-formal education centres where rural workers assemble to study in the evening between 7 or 8 P.M. and 9 or 10 P.M.

The National Adult Educaton Project was implemented on massive scale by the Government of India in order to remove illiteracy from the country since October 2, 1978. The AIR also has committed itself to supporting the project with suitable programmes for publicity motivation and training of instructors/ helpers. Since learning directly from the teacher is minimal and there is more emphasis on learning through various mass media, educational broadcasts are expected to play an important role in non-formal system. Farm Schools of the AIR is another example of non-formal education through the AIR. It was inaugurated in the year 1973 and thousands of farmers have been registering for different courses under this service. A series of lessons on selected agricultural topics are planned and produced according to local needs.

The AIR is now laying more emphasis on the planning and production of science programmes in both the formal and non-formal spheres of educational broadcasts. Special Science Cells have been set up in most of the major stations of the country to improve the quantity and quality of science programmes. There are also special programmes for teachers and teacher-educators in most of the stations. These are intended to familiarise the teachers with methods of teaching, curricular changes, advanced content and so on. This service has been more necessitated in recent years on account of large changes in school curriculum and methodology particularly in subjects like science, mathematics, social studies and English, Teachers have to be oriented to these changes and their knowledge in content and methodology needs to be updated. Hence teachers programmes have assumed more importance today than before.

A Pilot Project for teaching of mother-tongue as a first language through radio was started in Jaipur, Rajasthan during July, 1979. The project was organised by the Centre for Educational Technology, NCERT. This project aims at teaching Hindi to children in the first years of their schooling. Evaluation of this innovation showed substantial improvement in the achievement of children. During the SITE experiment in 1975-76, in-service training in science was organised with the help of a multimedia package consisting of radio programmes as an important component. This package was developed by the Centre for Educational Technology, NCERT and the training programme was implemented by the CET and ET Cells of 6 SITE States. About 43,000 teachers of primary schools and M.E.schools benefitted from the programme and experience was quite interesting. Besides this, a few other innovations are being tried out both in rural and urban schools.

Infrastructure

Every radio station with school broadcasting service has a unit with only three persons - a producer, scriptwriter and a production assistant with a general assistant to help. There is a consultative panel for school broadcasts comprising usually 6eminent heads of schools and experts who monitor the broadcasts and advise the station. As spokesmen of the programme-users they point out the deficiencies as well as useful features and suggest measures for better planning and utilisation of the educational broadcasts. Planning of programmes is done in consultation with the Education Department. There are advisory bodies for various subjects who help the station in choice of subjects and in drawing the broadcast schedule. This help is provided through the State Institute of Education, State Council of Educational Research and Training, State Institute of Languages and State Institute of Science Education depending on institutions available in a particular State at the time.

With the establishment of Educational Technology Cells in many States since the year 1974 the collaborative efforts between the AIR and the Education Department have been promoted satisfactorily. The E.T. Cells have been taking an active interest in educational broadcasting - provision of radio sets, planning programmes, producing and distributing teacher's notes, training teachers in the use of media and scriptwriting. The State Governments have been actively participating in various training programmes, particularly in the Radio-cum-Correspondence courses by funding and organising workshops and seminars and producing support materials. Most of the personnel in charge of Akash Vani educational broadcasts are recruited from among experienced trained teachers and educationists who have a favourable aptitude and positive attitude towards the medium. They are also trained in the Akash Vani Staff Training Institute at the centre and subsequently updating is provided there or at the two Regional Centres of the Institute or at specially organised workshops. The training is both in-service or on the job as well as formal. Exchange of ideas and mutual sharing of experiences are facilitated at the periodical seminars, workshops and conferences held at the regional and national levels. With a view to sorting out the problems and devising ways and means for overcoming them, the Director of Public Instruction, Directors of SCERT and Educational Technology Officers are invited to participate in these seminars and workshops. Most of the producers are also deputed for training abroad and get exposures from BBC, NKH, ABC or AIRD (Kualalumpur) which improve their expertise and outlook in the filed.

Since quality of educational programmes depends on the quality of scripts, now-a-days a number of scriptwriters are being trained at the national as well as state levels. The Centre for Educational Technology, NCERT has been organising training courses for radio scriptwriters from various parts of the country. The E.T.Cells also are organising scriptwriters workshops in collobration with Akash Vani and CET experts. Akash Vani also occasionally organises training of teachers in properly using radio and writing scripts in special workshops. This is mostly done on requests from the State educational authorities. Although Akash Vani Staff Training Institutes are mainly intended for Akash Vani personnel, they and individual stations organise such workshops for outsiders on special grounds.

Television Broadcasting

The American author James S.Kinder has aptly remarked, "Television has literally captured the country. Its expansion has been much more dramatic than of radio or the automobile. It has become an important part of our way of life, so much so that it is difficult to say whether it is a luxury or a necessity."[1] This is the state of affairs not only of America, but also in most of the developed as well as developing countries. Its glamour has caught the attention of all irrespective of economic and political or religious affiliation of the country.

John Baird was able to transmit a visual across a few meters for the first time in 1924. Marconi also succeeded in starting experimental television. The BBC initiated its television service in 1936 with only 300 TV sets. But in 1939 it closed down this service and could not muster its strength till 1946 for starting the same again. It, however, flourished in the developed countries particularly in the Western world during nineteen sixties.

Early Efforts

In 1956, the General Conference of UNESCO was held in New Delhi and it was decided therein that a pilot project should be implemented in India to study the use of television as a medium of education and community development. In 1959 an agreement was signed between AIR and UNESCO for starting the project on experimental basis. This was inaugurated in Delhi by the erstwhile president of India Dr.Rajendra Prasad on the 15th September, 1959. Thus the experimental television service was started with the objectives of "experimentation, training and evaluation" as a part of the UNESCO project. It was experimentation with the new medium, training of the personnel for running it and evaluation of the new medium as a vehicle of communication and education.

Television sets were installed at first only at 21 community centres of adult education and social welfare services. A tele-club was formed at each centre and was expected to promote organised viewing, conduct post-telecast discussions and convey the viewers' reactions and comments as feedback to the All India Radio. A convener was appointed at each club for this pupose and the programmes were telecast for one hour every Tuesday and Friday. TV programmes were educative and informative and of various formats like talks, plays, ballets, interviews, discussions, music and documentary films. Besides, important occasions like Independence Day, Republic Day, State visits of foreign dignitaries, Holi and Diwali festivals also had their coverage. This TV service was operated from the Akash Vani Bhavan in New Delhi and the area of coverage was within 12 to 15 miles. About 150 to 200 persons were viewing the programmes at each of the 21 centres. During 1960-61 a series of social education programmes were telecast in collaboration with UNESCO. As many as twenty such programmes were telecast from December, 1960 to May, 1961. The topics covered were, for example, traffic and road sense, community health, good manners and rights and duties of citizens. After the completion of these programmes another series of twenty programmes were telecast. The nature as well as impact of these programmes was evaluated by the National Fundamental Education Centre and Indian Adult Education Association, New Delhi. The findings of the experiment were quite encouraging and significantly beneficial.

Television into Classrooms

The first move towards educational television was made by AIR in January-March, 1960 and an experimental programme was telecast for schoolchildren of New Delhi every Tuesday from 3 to 4 P.M. in lieu of the evening programmes. Although a number of difficulties were experienced in assembling batches of students at nearby community centres with TV sets, the experiment, on the whole, was inspiring.

A Ford Foundation Project, in fact, laid the foundation stone of educational television service. A four-year agreement was made with the Ford Foundation for launching a regular TV programme for schools in Delhi. According to this Agreement 600 TV sets were installed in secondary schools by 1965. This service was inagurated on the 23rd October, 1961. Eight E.TV programmes of 20 minutes each were telecast every week for the students of secondary schools. These programmes were also repeated in the afternoon in order to make them available to students of the second shift. The subjects covered by these programmes were Physics, Chemistry, Hindi, English, Geography and current affairs.

The agreement also provided for the supply of technical equipment, deputing AIR personnel abroad for training and making experts on educational TV from America available to the AIR. Initially, 250 TV sets were installed in secondary schools having AC Electricity supply and it was proposed to cover all the high schools in Delhi. As the number of schools equipped with TV sets increased, benefits of ETV programmes were extended to 36,000 students of science and 96,000 students of English. After four years of execution, the project was evaluated by Dr. Paul Neurath, a New York City University Professor of Sociology. The overall impact of the ETV programmes was quite satisfactory. G.C. Awasthy on the basis of his personal contacts with schools, reports from the viewing schools, discussions with teachers and AIR personnel has observed that the results of the projects were very encouraging. AIR has also claimed that as a result of TV programmes, academic performance of students viewing ETV programmes had improved, interest in science has increased and standards of teaching had improved.

Regular TV service was inagurated in Delhi on the 15th August, 1965 and a landmark was made in early 1966 with launching of the Krishi Darshan Programme for farmers. The AIR was organising this project in collaboration with the Institute of Agricultural Research, the Delhi Administration, and the Atomic Energy Commission. The experiences of this project were quite enlightening and interesting.

SITE Project

The famous Satellite Instructional Television Experiment (SITE) was implemented during the year 1975-76. This project however, originated during the year 1965-the year of International Cooperation and initiative was taken by the UNESCO. In a meeting of the UNESCO on Space Communication, an Advisory Panel was set up and an International Committee of Media Experts submitted a report after carefully examining the issue. It was decided to take up a pilot project in India on TV programmes through satellite. It was felt that the project would help India in solving her problems of food scarcity, mass illiteracy and ignorance about developmental strategies.

The SITE was inagurated by Smt. Indira Gandhi, the Prime Minister of India at Ahmedabad on the 1st August, 1975. The TV programmes could be telecast with the help of a satellite called ATS-F loaned by the National Aeronautics and Space Administration USA. The TV programmes related to Education, Agriculture, Health, Family Planning, National Integration and so on. The telecast was for four hours a day out of which one and half hour in the morning were meant for primary school children and two and half hours in the evening for adults. The total time was equally divided into three segments for six States of India in view of the capacity of satellite for telecasting on video with two audio channels.

The project was intended to cater to the development needs of the rural community and with this in view, about 2,400 direct reception television sets were deployed in different cultural, linguistic and agricultural regions located in 6 States-Andhra Pradesh, Bihar, Karnataka, Madhya Pradesh, Orissa and Rajasthan. The ETV programmes were produced by the TV Base Production Centre, Doordarshan and Indian Space Research Organisation (ISRO). Besides students programmes, a number of ETV programmes were also telecast for teachers who participated in the in-service training courses in science. A few organisations at the State and national levels like ISRO, NCERT, Ministry of Education, E.T. Cell and universities were engaged in conducting research studies on impact of TV programmes on the rural audience. The findings of these studies were, on the whole quite inspiring and useful.

Terrestrial TV Programmes

After the SITE, the Government of India decided to provide TV viewing facility in 40 percent of the SITE-served villages by setting up terrestrial transmitters in the six SITE States. As the infrastructure and studio facilities already existed in these States, it was easier for the Doordarshan authorities to take up the SITE continuity programme in these areas by setting up low-power terrestrial TV transmitters.

With a view to utilise the INSAT capability for educational development, the Ministry of Education initiated action for preparing plans of operation as early as in July 1979. In view of the experience and involvement of the Space Application Centre, Ahmedabad in different aspects of TV, it was decided to elicit their cooperation in preparing a basic document for consideration and discussion. It was expected that the document would provide, inter alia, an outline of the institutional, human, technical and financial resources available and those that could be developed in the country and were necessary for a national system of utilisation of television for education. In response to the Ministry's request, the SAC prepared a background paper entitled "INSAT." The paper outlined the INSAT capability, the ground segment requirements for TV, the possible hardware for satellite utilisation and an approach for developmental communication.

A meeting was convened by the Ministry of Education on the 30th January, 1980 to disuss the background paper and all connected issues involved in the satellite utilisation for radio and television programmes. The Education Secretary presided over and representatives from SAC, NCERT, A.I.R., Doordarshan, Planning Commission, UGC and Ministary of Education attended the meeting. It was decided that urgent steps should be taken for planning software in connection with INSAT' utilisation by all the user Ministries in general and by Education Ministry in particular.

The Ministry of Information and broadcasting set up a Working Group under the Chairmanship of the Secretary, Information and Broadcasting on the February 2,1980 in order to draw up a software plan for INSAT utilisation. The Group consisted of members from various affiliated organisations and different user ministries. The Working Group finalised its report in September, 1980 and mainly recommended that the concerned Ministries should develop programme production capability and take upon themselves specific responsibility for producing programmes. The Ministry of Education after due consideration took the decision that educational authories would be entrusted with programme production and indicated to the Working Group that the major educational objectives of a satellite television would be to promote alternative approaches to education for children, youth and adults. The thrust of the specific programmes would be to emphasize direct teaching, moving away from curriculum-oriented approach and aim at reduction of load in the classroom, and improvement of the quality of programmes through training of manpower.

Another Study Group set up by the Ministry of Education under the Charirmanship of Shri S.Sathyam, Jt. Secretary, Education in May also developed a policy for the use of TV, identified approaches, priorities, target audences and themes for programmes, considered in detail the implications arising out of the decision that the educational authority shall be responsible for the production of educational televsion programmes in terms of an infrastructure and manpower requirements, identified key areas of infrastructure and manpower requirements, identified key areas for training and developed training courses in detail and suggested lines for further action. In April, 1980, the Government of India was invited by the UNESCO Regional Office for Education in Asia and Oceania, Bangkok to participate in their Asian Programme of Educational Innovation for Development (APEID) in the field of educational technology. As the participating countries were required to orgnise national workshops, the Ministry of Education, Government of India, in collaboration with UNESCO convened National Workshop on Educational Broadcasting from December 1 to 6, 1980 at New Delhi. The basic reference document for the National Workshop was the Draft Guidelines on Educational Broadcasting which was developed at a Technical Working Group Meeting on Educational Broadcasting organised by the UNESCO during 1979 in Malaysia. The NCERT, AIR and Doordarshan authorities extended necessary cooperation in organising the National workshop.

The National Workshop was attended by 41 participants representing various media and educational interests from all over the country and consisting of media practitioners, media experts, planners, administrators, teachers, trainers, educationists, researchers and social scientists. The workshop assumed special significance on account of the nations's renewed emphasis on educational broadcasting on the eve of putting INSAT in the orbit. The main highlights of the workshop were as follows:

1. Recognition of Educational Broadcasting. New priority role to move away from syllabus-oriented approaches into non-formal systems and lesser dependence on intermediaries.
2. Stressing team mode of production, making the planning and production of educational broadcasts a collaborative effort of the producers, educators and social scientists.
3. Calling for an integration of educational broadcasting within the total educational system and for the pupose recommending autonomy to the Centre for Educational Technology at the national level and creating autonomous State Institues of Educational Technology at the State level which will be necessary professional and technical structures for Educational Broadcasting.
4. Laying more emphasis on research and evaluation as an essential component of Edicational Broadcasting at all stages of planning, production and utilisation.
5. Evolving a national framework spelling out the priorities, broad areas, themes and objectives of the programmes.
6. Entrusting the responsibility of planning production and use of educational broadcasting to the educational authority.
7. Urging immediate action on all fronts to prepare for the utilisation of the television facilities under INSAT.

The Report of the National Workshop has rightly mentioned that the participants representing a cross-section of varied professional background and interests were able "to take collective look at the problem of educational broadcasting, share their individual and group experiences and to pool their expertise in the creation of new approaches towards making broadcasting a meaningful educational tool, the free spirit of which came out across the barriers of syllabii, age-groups, and traditional restrictive educational philosophies. It is to be hoped that the liberal thinking that permeated the workshop will be instrumental in shaping Educational Broadcasting and pave the way for exciting educational horizon behind and beyond INSAT."

Evaluation and Feedback

With a view to bringing about improvement in the educational broadcasts, it is imperative to evaluate them and get feedback from the audience. This is done through so many techniques. The immediate antenna for sensing the reactions of the listeners is the value of letters received by the station. A format for Setting immediate feedback is printed on the Data-Schedule of programmes or any teachers' note supplied to teachers who are requested to furnish data in the same. The filled in proforma are sent back to the station. Some stations send printed proforma in bulk to the radio user schools and get them back every week for processing and reporting. These reports provide immediate feedback from the field. At times, producers also pay visits to school, and listen to the programmes with the students there. The reactions collected from students are of immense use to the producers for their guidance.

In most of the stations there are Audience Research Units which undertake surveys and studies for assessment of individual programmes in various subjects like drama, farm programmes educational broadcasts and so on. Since these units have a small staffing pattern, they are not able to take up many research studies. Usually they conduct surveys of programmes in a series. A number of external agencies like State Institute of Education, SCERT, Educational Technology Cells, Centre for Educational Technology and some other organisations also have started undertaking studies in this area. Even some scholars, for their Ph.D., M.A and M.Ed. degrees, are taking up research studies in educational radio programmes.

The findings of these studies are largely revealing as well as useful. They are found quite necessary for planning, producing and utilising the educational broadcasting. Akash Vani as well as the Education Departments should take adequate note of them.

Problems and Prospects

Since radio is one of the popular mass media, there are pressing demands for other services like drama, music, women, workers programmes and so on. At the time it is felt that more time chunks should be made available for adult education, workers education, open universities or distance education and teacher education. In order to partly tackle this demand, the Akash Vani authorities are trying to fit these developmental ideas into the already existing special as well as general audience programmes.

Provision of radio listening sets in the schools and centres for non-formal education is not at all adequate. Another problem likely to be faced is that educational broadcasting would lose its initial glamour and might get into rut. But in the changing society it has to be accepted as a universal reality and attempts should rather be made to recreate new attraction and novelty in the medium through various innovations and experiments. For example, radio-vision or audio-vision with the help of slides, filmstrips, graphics etc., can make the radio programme interesting and attractive. Nevertheless, from cost-effectiveness consideration and due to relative convenience in production and utilisation, radio broadcasts can be appreciated and preferred to TV programmes.

The educational planners and administrators are yet to realize the importance of educational technology in general and educational broadcasting in particular. Although resources are available, they are not properly utilised for provision of radio sets and other media in the schools. Whatever media are available they are not suitably used in the teaching-learning process. An initial orientation towards the media is, therefore, felt imperative for heads of institutions and educational supervisors. Adequate cooperation and coordination among the producers, user teachers, educationists, evaluators and planners are not yet forthcoming in our country. Whatever attempts have been made in this connection are quite enlightening, but they are very occasional and fragmentetary. Such collaborative efforts are therefore necessary in all aspects of educational broadcasting-from planning and designing to production and evaluation in a very systematic and inter-disciplinary manner. Systems approach and cost-effectiveness should be taken into account for planning optimum or mastery learning and achieving excellence through educational broadcasting.

Satellite Experiment in Education

A manmade machine called satellite revolves very far away in the sky and works wonders in the field of communication. It is highly powerful and with its large antenna (the eyes, ears, and tongues of the machine) the satellite is able to send strong signals which are picked up even by a small and cheap antenna connected to the television set in a village. This type of TV broadcasting is an experimental project covering a very vast area which is not normally possible by any ground system.

SITE: A Grand Experiment

As long back as in 1969 a memorandum of understanding was signed between India and U.S.A for conducting an epoch-making experiment called "Satellite Instructional Television Experiment" (SITE) by means of the Applications Technology Satellite F(ATS-6). This ATS-6 was described as "the most complex, versatile and powerful communication satellite ever developed." In this context Dr. Wernher Von Braun has been quoted to have said, "ATS-6 could turn to be the most important advance since movable type as a means of reaching people separated by vast geographical, economic and cultural barriers."

Mr. P.V.Krishnamurthy rightly assertd, "Time is of essence, India cannot afford to wait. We cannot think of slow processes like bullock carts.... The satellite route is the only way to go if India is to develop quickly." The satellite was thus regarded as the most potential instrument for accelarating the pace of national development. Accodingly on May 30,1974, the satellite was sucessfully launced from Cape Canaveral and located over the U.S.A for making various experiments. It was orbiting the earth at the height of about 36,000 kms. and its movement was so matched with the earths movement that for all practical puposes, it remained, stationary at any one given point over the earth. The telecast via this satellite began in India from August 1,1975 which is taken as a red-letter day in the annals of mass communication.

The satellite was loaned to India by the National Aeronautics and Space Administration (NASA) of LJ.S.A and the Indian Space Research Organisation (ISRO) jointly with All India Radio(AIR) took the responsibility of broadcasting ITV Programmes to all selected villages in the six States-Andhra Pradesh, Bihar, Karnataka, Orissa, Madhya Pradesh and Rajasthan.

The experiment continued for a year from August 1975 to July 1976. The instructional objectives of SITE were in the fields of Education, Agriculture, Health and Family Planning, National Integration and so on. Television broadcasts via satellite were made for four hours a day and out of these four hours, one and a half hours a day would be in the morning and two and half hours in the evening. The morning time was utilised for broadcasting programmes for children and the evening hours devoted to broadcasting programmes for adults. This total time available was equally divided into three segements for the six States of India and in doing so the capacity of satellite for telecasting one video with two audio channel was fully exploited.

SITE was designed as a communication experiment which would provide vital inputs in planning and executing a Nationwide Television System. With this in view, about 2400 Direct Reception Television Sets deployed for SITE were located in different cultural, linguistic and agricultural regions of the country. Different socio-economic environments were also chosen for the purpose. The television programmes would be oriented to local needs for providing effective support to developmental endeavours.

The Educational Goals

Since the SITE was basically directed at the rural audience, the television programme was an unprecedented phenomenon for the villagers so far not exposed to such experiences. The major goal of the SITE programmes was to help people in their developmental endeavours. As children's morning programme formed an important component of the SITE, educational advancement was emphasized more than anything else. It was expected that the education television programmes would bring about improvement both in quality and quantity of education. The following outcomes were envisaged through this by the Ministry of Education, Government of India.

(i) There would be more enrolment, more regular attendance and less dropouts as the children would feel attracted to the school through this programme;

(ii) Children would develop receptivity to the new ideas and activities as they get exposed to various external stimuli of the immediate and distant environment.

(iii) They would form good health habits as a result of understanding the merits of such habits through practical demonstration;

(iv) They would develop proper attitudes, interests and values that were conducive to social harmony and democratic growth;

(v) Children would realise the factors in pollution of air, water, and noise and could help maintain environmental sanitation;

(vi) They would develop interest for living objects and be conscious of the need for conservation of wildlife and forests;

(vii) Children would develop scientific attitude as a result of observing natural phenomenon, doing experiments themselves skillfully questioning and analysing facts and figures;

(viii) They would develop awareness about different communicy development programmes so that their participation in them would be promoted;

(ix) Children's interest and awareness in proper utilization of natural resources would be increased as a result of their understanding;

(x) They would develop skills and ability of free discussion in proper organisation of various meetings, seminars and conferences;

(xi) They would have better achievements in school subjects like Mother Tongue, Mathematics, Social Studies, General Science and Crafts;

(xii) They would be able to participate in group activities in the line of their perception and experiences;

(xiii) They would develop the ability of coordination between the visuals and auditory reception;

(xiv) Children would develop feelings of national and international understanding.

Administration and Management of ETV

The Educational Television Programmes were mainly intended for the children of the age group 5 to 12 years. But they were so designed as the children under and above that age group could enjoy and benefit from them. Hence these programmes were not merely for classroom teaching. They were rather enrichment and supplementary materials for children. An important objective of these programmes was to involve children in group activities and discussion. Therefore an informal and congenial atmosphere was created and maintained in the classrooms so that all children irrespective of their age, sex, ability and interests felt motivated to participate and show initiative. The role of teacher in this situation was to introduce, guide and direct chidren's participation and activities.

Several programmes were tagged together for each day's children's programmes which was of twenty two and half minute duration. Thus every day's integrated programme was called a capsule consisting of two or three components on entertainment, scientific exploration, visits to places of historical and geographical importance, learning through doing and so on. Each capsule was designed as a magazine with a variety of materials.

The TV programmes were transmitted in the morning and in the evening. The morning transmissions were educational in character and intended to cater to the needs ofschoolchildren and information for development. The morning programmes were transmitted daily except on Sundays and school holidays for 22-1/2 minutes from 10.22-1/2 A.M. to 10.45 AM. The morning educational programmes were produced by the Upgrah Doordarshan Kendras. The Education Technology Cell took the entire responsibility of administration and management of ETV service in the State. One custodian and one additional custodian were appointed for each TV Centre from among local school teachers. They were also called TV User Teachers who were trained in properly operating the TV sets, conducting pre and post-broadcast discussion and providing feedback to the producer for improvement of programmes. Besides, TV User Teachers' Training, teachers were also trained in science with the help of a multimedia package for improving their competence.

Evaluation Studies

With a view to ascertain the influence of ETV Programmes in particular and ensuring the effectiveness of the SITE in general a number of studies were designed and conducted at the State as well as the national level. Both formative and summative studies were undertaken by different agencies to evaluate ETV Programmes. Rao, (1974) has aptly observed, "Feasibility and problems involved in producing such programmes need to be explored and studied. Finally, audience research and evaluation of the programmes is an integral part of any broadcasing system. To avoid costly mistakes, research and evaluation should be given high priority along with hard and software development." According to a clause in the Memorandum of Understanding social scientists were appointed by the ISRO to conduct evaluative studies and the following were the findings.

(i) Children exposed to TV in the classroom showed significant increase in their language development;

(ii) The presence of TV in the school had no impact on enrolment and attendance because of poor economic conditions and need for children to help their parents in the household/farming activities;

(iii) TV School teachers were excited about TV as a classroom aid, but they found "enrichment" programme unrelated to their syllabus.

An evaluation of the Sciences TV Programmes produced by the Centre for Educational Technology, NCERT., New Delhi for teachers training revealed the following:

(i) Dubbing of ETV programmes from Hindi to the regional language was not appreciated as there was overlapping of both the languages and lack of synchronization.

(ii) Students' participation in most of the ETV Programmes was not upto the mark.

(iii) Most of the programmes were not presented in problem-solving, demonstration and discussion method;

A comprehensive study of ETV Programmes conducted by the Ministry of Education, Government of India reported as follows:-

(i) There was high degree of liking for the programmes among children and teachers;

(ii) The most important factor governing favourable assessment are familiarity of subject matter and its satisfactory treatment;

(iii) There was close connection between liking and comprehension.

(iv) Dialogue was not found to be a successful method of purveying information particularly in a dubbed version of programmes;

(v) High comprehension is closely related to visually effective and conceptually well structured communication;

This study has established the considerable success of the Educational Television Programmes and more importantly, the acceptance of TV as an educational force in our rural primary schools. It also revealed the great potential for communicating directly to children and as such, recommended for stimulating their interest and curiosity to learn from ETV Programmes. The study has concluded "Television is too great a medium to be allowed to remain as an aid in the hands of an indifferent teaching community and arid educational system. Our search must be for the means whereby the potential of television can be realised".

A Study to measure the impact of SITE ETV Programmes on attendance and enrolment reported the following findings:

(i) Taking the total average attendance of 1974 - 75, 1975 - 76 (SITE Years) and 1976 - 77 into consideration, it was found that there was 5 per cent increase of attendance during SITE period in comparison to Pre-SITE and decreased by 2 per cent during post-SITE period in comparison to SITE Years.

(ii) Total average enrolment in the month of June increased by 5 per cent during SITE Year in comparison with pre-SITE year and by 2 per cent in post-SITE year in comparison to SITE period.

(iii) During July, enrolment increased by 8 per cent during SITE year in comparison with pre-SITE Year and by 7 per cent during post-SITE period in comparison to SITE Year.

(iv) The total average enrolment in August increased by 5 per cent during SITE period in comparison with pre-SITE and by 7 per cent during post - SITE period in comparison with SITE period.

INSAT Project

The national workshop held at New Delhi from December 01, to 06, 1980 under the joint collaboration of the Ministry of Education & Culture as well as the UNESCO's Asian Programme of Educational Innovation for Development (APEID) decided the following priorities for educational broadcasting (1981, p.21).

(i) Universalisation of elementary education both formal and non-formal;

(ii) Non-formal education for adults, linking education to economic and social tasks;

(iii) Development of vocational and professional skills;

(iv) Training for citizenship;

(v) Popularising science with a view to developing a scientific outlook;

(vi) Promoting national integration;

(vii) Providing information about theme of national importancce, energy conservation, preservation of wildlife, environmental sanitation, nutrition and health.

ETV Programmes under INSAT

The Indian National Satellite (INSAT) is a multipurpose communication project of great national importance. The INSAT -IA was launched on April 19, 1982 by means of which TV Service was provided in the States of Andhra Pradesh, Orissa, Bihar, Maharashtra, Gujarat and Uttar Pradesh. However due to ceratain mechanical snags it failed in September 1982 and TV Service was continued through terrestrial transmission.

The INSAT - IB was launched on August 30, 1983 and was made operative from October 15, 1983. Since then educational television service is being provided with the help of this satellite with great success. The total duration of TV transmission by INSAT was one hour and 25 minutes - for 45 minutes in the morning and for 40 minutes in the evening besides 90 minutes for National Programmes. The morning 45 minutes were devoted to school education from 10.30 AM to 11. 15 AM - 20 minutes for children between 5-8 years and 20 minutes for 9-11 years with 5 minutes for change over from one lesson to another. Besides, a specific programme for teachers was telecast every Saturday from 10.30 AM to 10.50 AM with a duration of 20 minutes. The Educational TV Programmes were not broadcast on Sundays and holidays.

The ETV Programmes are produced by two agencies (i) Doordarshan Kendras, and (ii) Centre for Educational Technology, NCERT, New Delhi. The programmes for the primary school teachers are exclusively produced by the latter. The attributes of these programmes are :

(i) to motivate children towards learning and attending school or instructional centres;

(ii) to develop desirable attitudes and habits;

(iii) to create awareness of the community;

(iv) to contribute to the improvement of skills;

(v) to lead children to expoire and to do;

(vi) to create awareness of the immediate and surrounding environment;

vii. to generate awareness of the prevailing evils of society and efforts being made to eradicate them.

Research Studies

With a view to obtaining feedback on the quality of the ETV Programmes and getting information about the position of their utilization, early steps were taken by the Centre for Educational Technology, NCERT in collaboration with the Department of Educational Techology, SCERT for conducting a few studies and suveys in the TV cluster areas. Subsequently, some individuals either in fulfilment of their M.A., M.ED., degree examination or their academic interests, undertook some studies. Although these studies had some limitation, thier findings could throw light on the quality and utilization of ETV Programmes.

A few findings of an initial study(CET., NCERT., 1983 pp. 6-7)[2] conducted by the Centre for Educational Techology, NCERT may be mentioned as follows:

(i) A large number of TV sets were not in working order or working poorly. As high as 62% of TV User Teachers reported that on account of the above reason they were not able to watch all the ETV Prgorammes and from 30% to 40% of teachers reported that though their sets functioned, either the quality of the majority(85%) of the sets were old ones and repairs were not undertaken despite requests made to Doordarshan;

(ii) Another major reason for under-utilization of ETV programmes was the failure of electricity which was a common problem in the area. Other resons were lack of awareness and non-paymentof remuneration to the custodians in time;

(iii) The time for telecast of the ETV Programmes from 9.45 A.M. to 10.30 A.M. was not favoured by the teachers. They preferred the earlier timing from 10.30 A.M. onwards;

(iv) The teachers 1 iked the arrangement of putting the programmes for the younger children first;

(v) In most of the cases the children of the two age groups watched the ETV Programmes together;

(vi) The teacher generally had a favourable attitude towards the ETV Programme produced by the CET., New Delhi. However, some teachers felt that the content of certain programmes series was a little above the level of the target audience, "the language used was somewhat difficult, the speed of presentation not very interesting."

(vii) One important suggestion for improving the ETV Programmes was to include lives of locally popular leaders in the programmes series "National Leaders" and some other local topics of interest.

According to a study(CET, NCERT., 1983, pp 52-59)[3] the following are the findings:-

(i) Some TV User Teachers opined that language used in the programme was a strong barrier in thier fuller understanding.

(ii) Another difficulty in understanding programmes was pointed out to be the dubbing programmes of the CET.

(iii) A few teachers reported that the programmes were not always interesting and able to hold the attention of the children. Those might be an impediment in creating fuller impact on children. One of the causes as pointed by them was that there was repetition of the same programmes over and over again.

(iv) Since TV sets operated under various handicaps and limitations, the children gained only to the extent of 3.2% as a result of watching the ETV Programmes regularly.

(v) Quite a few teacherrs suggested that the ETV Programmes should be supplementary to the classroom teaching rather than of enrichment type.

(vi) According to 23% of teachers, TV functioned on all the school days and 77% of teachers, it functioned most of the days.

(vii) It was also suggested that proper orientation of the TV custodians and suitable remuneration were necessary for effective utilization of ETV Programmes.

Besides the Central Institute of Educational Technology some researchers also undertook evaluative studies on ETV Programmes under 1NSAT. The following has been reported on the quality of ETV Programmes:

(i) In most of the programmes the visuals and/or voice/were clear.

(ii) Pronunciation and standard of language were found to be defective.

(iii) A few programmes were too loaded with content or teaching points resulting in loss of interest and attenion of learners;

(iv) Adequate care has not been taken in making the ETV Programmes methodological as well as psychological.

(v) In most of the dubbed programmes of the CET., NCERT., New Delhi verbal synchronization and action synchronization were found to be lacking with the visuals.

Excepting ETV Programmes for children of primary schools a specific series is telecast on every Saturday from 10.30 A.M. to 10.50 A.M. with a view to improving the competency of teachers. A study on critical appraisal of such Teacher Education Programmes reported that -

(i) Since all the teacher education programmes were dubbed from Hindi there was lack of synchronization of voice with visuals.

(ii) Since too many facts were presented in some programmes, the TV lessons were overcrowded and occasionally confusing to the teachers.

(iii) In some science programmes the visuals were not shown for a reasonable time in order to enable the viewers to observe the various factors and sequencess minutely and clearly.

In another similar study besides the above comments, the following observation have been made:

(i) In 60% of the TV Programmes emphasis was laid on technology of teaching and educational innovation and the remaining 40% have dealt with geography;

(ii) In 60% of cases the formats used are narration-cum-demonstration and the rest 40% were lecture based;

(iii) In 100% of programmes the objective of knowledge, in 50% comprehension and skill, in 40% attitude and in 70% interest were likely to be realised to a great extent.

Reviewing the Scenario

Television no doubt is an expensive aid to education. Satellite is far mor expensive in a developing country like India. Some economists and politicians raised their eyebrows at the huge expenditure incurred on the INSAT Project. But it is argued that in view of its far fetching importance for the national development such an expenditure has to be regarded as an investment which is likely to bring about very rich dividends in the long run.

Satellites like SITE and INSAT are not euphoria or illusions. They do not merely provide glamour and glory to our national status. They are utilised as potential instruments of social change and effective media for communication of messages of national development. Television services which is the main objective of these satellites, immensely affected the various aspects of development education, industry, agriculture, health, sanitation, environment and so on. The research findings have confirmed the effectiveness and efficiency of television as a medium of education and learning. It has been rightly observed/ 'By means of the satellite it became possible to take television to the villages of India before it reached the metropolitan centres covered under normal expansion programmes of television. The areas selected for the Experiment (SITE) were remote and poorly served by modern media of communication for national development. The backward areas are covered by these satellites with a view to accelerate the speed of development in its various aspects for bringing the same at par with the mainstream.

In the context of education, it must be agreed that the existing school situations and the supporting infrastructure are inadequate for making such expensive media educationally useful and meaningful. The planners, administrators and inspectors, even teachers have not been mentally prepared to accept the medium as a useful means of education. Maintenance of TV sets is a prerequisite for effective utilization of ETV Programmes. But due to want of proper maintenance about 50% of sets were out of order most of the time. Though some sets functioned, the quality ofvisuals/sounds was unsatisfactory. Further repair work was not taken, up quickly. Inconsistency and unsatisfactoriness in functioning of TV sets has resulted in loss of interest and lack of attention in watching the ETV Programmes.

Most of the primary schools did not have good accommodation. Although ETV Programmes were telecast for two age groups to be watched by the junior and senior students separately, usually they viewed both the programmes together. Consequently, small rooms were packed with students and satisfcatory viewing conditions were not available. Eventhough, both the groups were separated due to want of separate rooms, no fruitful pupose was served by depriving one group from watching the programmes. Thus due to inadeuacies in the viewing conditions, effectiveness of ETV Programmes was undermined to a great extent. There is an Advisory Committee consisting of media men, teachers, inspecting officers and administrators for suggesting suitable topics for production of programmes and previewing samples of them, if possible, for enabling the members to give their comments. But very often the administrative problems take much time and adequate attention is not paid to this important aspect of the committee's responsibility. Sometimes programmes are repeated as a result of which students and teachers are not interested in viewing them.

References

1. Kinder, J.S. *Audio-Visual Materials and Techniques*, American Book Co., New York, 1959
2. Centre for Educational Technology, NCERT, Study Report, 1983, pp. 6-7
3. *Ibid.*, pp. 52-59

8

Technology in Distance Education

The system of formal education has been perpetuating the disparities and imbalanced growth in the society. It has been realised that this system cannot make universalization of education successful due to its inadequacy. Therefore, other systems and innovative approaches like non-formal education, correspondence courses, open universiy, open school, off-campus courses etc., have been implemented and popularised both in the developed and developing countries of the world. With a view to widening the horizons of education, opening new frontiers of knowledge and democratizing the teaching-learning process in general, such non-formal systems have to be utilized for supplementing and enriching the traditional as well as formal educational system. It goes without saying that formal system of education has contributed significantly to the expansion of education as a whole. But such expansion has been lop-sided and undemocratic in the sense that the aristocratic and affluent people have benefitted by the tradional system more than the poor and lower classes.

There is, therefore, a glaring disparity and discrimination between rich and poor people, high and low classes, and developed and undeveloped countries. This gulf instead of being bridged, is becoming widened day by day and unless such imbalanced position is removed or reduced to the minimum, peace, prosperity and progress of the mankind cannot be achieved to the desired extent. Education has to be made accessible to all irrespective of financial, social and psychological conditions. Lifelong education is also emphasized not only for all but also for all stages of life. People engaged in various vocations or deprived of education at any stage of their life may like to get education of their choice. Thus equalization of educational opportunity shoud be ensured through diversified sources and multi-point entries and democracy can transcend the entire educational system throughout the world.

Understanding the Concept

Non-formal education is not entirely new. Correspondence education also added another dimension to the facilities of education starting from school to tertiary level. It is called instruction or education through correspondence. It is also known as home study or postal tuition which is popularly called Distance Learning or Distance Education. All these concepts more or less mean the same system and is found as an effective alternative to present-day education, non-formal system to formal education. The educationists and researchers were attracted to this non-formal approach and felt that it could help in diffusion of education and equalization of educational opportunity. Moreover, cost of such correspondence course would be less in comparison to the formal system and its standard would not be lower in any way.

Self-Learning

Distance education or learning is primarily a self-learning method. The student has to depend more on his own initiative and motivation than anything else. Classroom teaching is absent in the system and instruction is imparted to distant or off-campus students. Distance education is quite innovative, flexible and less expensive. The learner is to make progress according to his own capacity. Nothing is imposed from outside and everything is achieved by himself. That is why, this system is psychologically as well as sociologically sound and effective. Since millions of people the world over are able to fulfil their academic aspirations and satisfy their unfulfilled desires of knowledge through this system, it is also called democratic. Now that distance learning has been able to equalise educational opportunities among the people irrespective of their status and conditions, it is assuming socialistic dimensions.

The Kothari Commission (1966)[1] has pointed out the special features of this system and aptly said that the home study or correspondence method, no doubt, lacks the inspiring contact with the teacher, but inspiring teachers are rare, and in correspondence study the adult has a strong motivation to learn. The method also establishes a personal and private relationship with the teachers which encourages discussion and understanding through written and verbal communication thereby ensuring relevance and precision. It is a fact that distance education, in order to be effective, must provide for a kind of close relationship between the teacher and the taught for discussion and clarification of doubts. There are, therefore, contact classes and study centres provided in the correspondence education. Some may contend that these personal contacts are very rare and far between. But can we ensure this in most of our present-day schools where classes are crowded and teachers are overburdened and indifferent? The driving force behind the distance education is the self-motivation of learners and in their efforts some guidance and supervision of experienced teachers would be very useful.

Mere exchange of assignments and written instructions, therefore, cannot be all important. Besides, personal contacts and discussions in science and technical subjects, the learners are required to conduct practicals in the workshops during week-ends and vacation. These students may themselves form study groups or discussion groups and help one another individually as well as collectively. The Commission has rightly suggested that they should be attached to some colleges and allowed the benefit of the use of the library and such other amenities as viewing educational films, listening to recorded speeches of distinguished scholars and guest speakers. Another feature of distance learning is that its courses are sequenced according to the principles of programmed instruction which are beneficial to the learner to grasp the fundamentals and make progress according to his own pace. The distance learning system must be well supported with suitable radio and television programmes in different areas of study. The British Open University is a bright illustration in this respect and distace learning system in our country as well as other developing countries is yet to reach the standard and status of these facilities.

Distance learning should not be confined merely to help students secure university degrees or diplomas. The Kothari Commission has rightly felt that important programmes can be taken up in the fields of industry, commerce and agriculture to help the workers improve their competence and increase productivity. A large number of such courses with practical significance have been suggested by the Commssion. They are, for example, electronics, radio and TV servicing, commercial arts and dress making, business and secretarial practice, air conditioning, heating, refrigeration and so on. The Commission has rightly observed, "Good correspondence courses in thoughtfully identified fields of service will create demand for themselves and can help participation by the people in introducing better methods of production."[2]

Distance learning courses should be available to those who desire to enrich their lives by studying subjects of cultural and aesthetic value like art, appreciation, literary criticism, philosophy, languages and so on. These courses not only help economically but must help culturally and intellectually. In this way, distance education can promote the aesthetic, cultural and intellectual standards of the people.

Universal Experience

The growth of correspondence instruction can be better traced back to the middle of the 19th Century and a number of European countries like Germany, England and Sweden were pioneers in starting correspondence education. Then US and USSR developed this system of education in a big way by the middle of the 20th century. Subsequently, this educationai model was accorded high priority in New Zealand, Japan, Australia and many other countries.

This non-formal system of education was in course of time crowned with great success in many countries of the world. At first, only written or printed materials were made available to students. Educationists, curriculum planners and researchers, however, made their combined effort and utilised various media, methods and materials to supplement the printed word or the course materials. These are now called, in general, educational technology which consists of radio programmes, television programmes, slides, film strips, tape recording, counselling contacts, study centres,video tapes, experimental kits and so on.

The Open University in the UK is the most successful innovation of non-formal education and the greatest achievement of educational technology. Within a decade of its existsence, the Open University claimed to be one of the greatest universities of the world. Study is primarily done at home through correspondence, talks, radio, printed books, specially produced radio and TV programmes and so on. There is also scope for inter-personal communication at local study centres and summer schools. The students' main sources of personal tuition is through correspondence tutor. The courses are designed by teams of academics, BBC producers, educational technologists, artists, teachers, photographers, librarians and others. The course team decides the policy for the use of different media and methods. The Open University courses have earned universal reputation for their high standards. The Open University course materials and media programmes are of such high academi quality that even traditional universities in England, US, and other countries model their material for their students, after this model. Countries like US, Germany, Canada, Australia, Israel and Pakistan have developed open univeristies, off-campus and open campus courses with great success.

Indian Scene

After Independence, India faced the colossal problem of educating teeming millions of students at all levels. Although a large number of schools and colleges were set up to cope with the ever increasing demands, it was not possible to provide adequate facilities for education in the formal system. The Planning Commission, the Union Ministry of Education and the University Grants Commission made some loud thinking about the problem and appointed an expert committee under the chairmanship of Dr.D.S. Kothari to explore the possibility of starting correspondence courses in a few selected universities. Delhi University, in pursuance of this recommendation, started B.A. and B.Corn correspondence courses as a pilot project in 1962 and Punjabi University, Patiala introduced correspondence courses at the pre-university level and B.A. level in 1963. At present more than 30 universities and organizations are providing correspondence courses at the undergraduate level and some univerisities even at the postgraduate level in social sciences, life sciences, physical sciences, commerce and languages. A few univerisities and institutions are also providing B.Ed., M.Ed and some other educational courses through correspondence.

The Indian Education Commission 1964-66 discussed the issue in detail and has made some useful observations. It has rightly said, "There must also be a method of taking education to the millions who depend upon their own effort to study whenever they can find time to do so. We consider that correspondence or home study courses provide the right answer for these situations." The Commission has also opined that there is hardly any ground for the apprehension that correspondence courses are an inferior form of education than what is given in regular schools and colleges. There are ample evidences for widespread expansion of correspondence education in our country. The Patrachar Vidyalaya of the Directorate of Education, Delhi Administration, took initiative in starting correspondence course for the secondary school level examinations. A number of Boards of Secondary Education have already started correspondence education for high school examinations and secondary teachers training examiniations. The latest innovation in this direction is the establishment of Open School at Delhi under the auspices of the Central Board of Secondary Education. The Open School at Delhi started its activities in July 1979 and since then it has been preparing students for the Central Board of Secondary Education through its specially prepared instructional materials, students' assignments, face to face contacts and other multimedia programmes. Thus, correspondence education or distance learning is becoming popular and being accepted as an alternative and economical approach to our formal education.

Distance education, although launched in sixties, has not so far made a dent particularly in the field of higher education. It practically took roots in the seventies when more and more universities started institutes for correspondence courses. So far as the demand for higher education is concerned, the formal system is unable to meet it. That is why, a very large number of students take to distance education or private appearance. In areas, where strong and viable distance education institutes have developed, the number of students taking recourse to private appearance has declined. But the areas devoid of good distance education facilities have a very large number of private coaching centres. Non-availability of seats in the formal system leads to such private coaching centres. If distance education facilities are available, they are made use of but in their absence, people make use of the provisions of private appearance to satisfy their demand for higher education.

It may, thus, be concluded that the more facilities for distance education available, the more the demand is evident. Constraints on such facilities are still operating in the field of higher education.

Alternative to Formal Education

Distance education is an effective alternative to the formal education. It has immense significance for the emerging learning society in general and educationally undeveloped or developing society in particular. It has its message both for lifelong education as well as for universalization of education. It is necessary not only for eradicating mass illiteracy, but also for meeting the ever increasing demand for higher education. It is a potential means of equalization of educational opportunities and a useful medium for promoting deversified as well as vocational education. It is a source of inspiration for the disappointed and a providence for the deprived. It is, therefore, democratic as well as socialistic in nature. In India, an emerging model of distance learning has taken shape as the Open School that has opened a new frontier of hope in education. It has been rightly said, "The Open School should be a pilot project taken up at the national level by the Central Board of Secondary Education (CBSE) which has all India jurisdiction. The experience gained through this pilot project may be disseminated to the other State Boards to help them evolve their own distance teaching system through Central Board of Secondary Education" (1979, 80, p.2).[3] This Open School can show new light and hope in non-formal education if it proves its worth and achieves its objectives.

The International Commission on Education has also strongly supported distance learning system in provision of lifelong education and in adoption of learning as a process of human growth towards fulfilment in individual as well as members of many groups in the society. Education is concerned with the total man for his creative living. The Eduational Planning Commission in Alberta Province in Canada spearheading an interesting educational reform says that education should develop ability in the learner to learn under a variety of circumstances and conditions, on a part-time basis at home using a variety of media and in informal setting. All this eloquently pleads for distance learning and shows the special feature and significance of this innovation. The Programme of Action (1986) in the context of implementing the National Policy on Education has rightly observed, "The Open University system augments opportunities for higher education, ensure access, is cost-effective and promotes as a flexible and innovative system of education. The Indira Gandhi National Open University has been established with these objectives and assigned the responsibility to coordinate the distance learning system in the country and determine its standard."[4]

Distance education has assumed immense significance as a viable alternative to conventional system of education all over the world. This is mainly due to the efforts for increasing accessibility for promoting equality of educational opportunity and for ensuring continuing education. The scope and strength of distance education has been further widened and heightened with the revolution of electronic media in communication. In our country distance education has also expanded faster than formal education at the tertiary level. Thus, the distance education system has to go a long way and has a very bright future with rich possibilities.

Role of Audio Electronic Media

We are in the midst of a Revolution of Electronic Media consisting of radio, television, audio/video cassettes, computers, films etc. Radio is found to be a powerful medium. Without electricity, we can listen to radio programmes with the help of transistors. Production of educational radio and audio programmes is also comparatively easier and cheaper.

Hence, the role of radio/ audio programmes in education is very significant.

Herein we propose to explain the role of radio broadcast and audio cassettes in education with special reference to distance education. On going through this you will be able to understand these:

(i) know the importance of radio broadcasts as well as audio cassettes in the field of education.

(ii) get an idea about the achievement of educational radio broadcasts and audio tapes in and outside the country.

(iii) identify the various advantges of educational radio/audio programmes.

(iv) appraise the disadvantages/limitations of the media in the educational context.

(v) acquaint yourself with the ways and means of overcoming the limitations of educational broadcasting.

(vi) acquire certain knowledge skills for effective utilisation of educational broadcasts and audio cassettes.

(vii) develop competence for properly evaluating the school broadcast/ audio cassettes for improvement.

(viii) utilise the findings and feedback of the evaluation studies for improving the quality of the radio/audio programmes.

Utility of Audio Media

Radio is an effective medium. It is also comparatively inexpensive. It has occupied a significant place in distance education. It is playing an important role in providing effective education. It not only informs, but also inspires. It not only inculcates values and virtues, but also creates attitudes, and interests. It can cover a very wide area at the same time. There is already a well-developed infrastructure, a background of long exprience to its advantage.

Similarly, educational audio cassettes/tapes can easily be utilised by means of cassette players and tape recorders which are now easily available and can be procured with reasonable amount. Handling these machines, even recording and playing of the cassettes/tapes are not difficult. Hence in classroom teaching, tape/cassette recorders are useful aids. Educational broadcasting and audio cassettes/tapes have therefore, immense patentialities and possibilities. Particularly in a developing country like India where we are experiencing constraints of finance, efficient teachers, suitable equipment and appliances, radio and audio cassettes/tapes are to play a significant part in expansion as well as qualitative improvement of education. India is still having some inaccessible areas where educational institutions are not feasible and expansion of education has faced serious difficulties. To a large number of socially disadvantaged children, education is not meaningful and interesting. There has been a growing awareness about the inadequacy of the traditional formal system of education not only for expansion, but also for improving the standards of education. The need for alternatives in the shape of non-formal education, distance learning and correspondence courses is gradually felt imperative. Both for improvement of quality and quantity of education, use of radio/audio programmes has great significance.

Accomplishments of the Educational Radio

Throughout the world, educational radio programme has become popular and in certain countries it has worked wonders. These countries also represent both developed and developing world and the radio programmes have been found effective both in formal and non-formal systems of education.[5] Wilbur Schramm and others in their research work "The New Media: Memo to Educational Planners" have elaborately discussed the achievements of various media in the field of education and training. Especially the use of radio is quite remarkable in Algeria for meeting the post-Independence emergency in the shortage of teachers by providing pre-service and in-service training, in Australia for extending the school facilities to far-flung sparsely populated areas situated hundreds of kilometres away from the nearest schools, in New Zealand for providing educational opportunities to remote families, in Niger, Toge Honduras for providing literacy and adult education and in Thailand for teaching teachers.

Besides Schramm and others, Godman, UNESCO expert in sound broadcasting in his paper "Educational Radio: Some Notes on its Potential and its Utilisation" has narrated the successful stories of educational radio in three countries. In the Australian State of Tasmania, a new form of handwriting was introduced with massive preparation and cooperative efforts. In Papua New Guinea with 700 linguistic groups, English was taken to be the common medium of communication by utilising various well-designed print materials and other techniques. In Indonesia, radio was able to provide in service teacher-education through an extensive pilot project. In Kerala, teachers' competence in English and during SITE, teachers' efficiency in science was improved and upgraded with the help of suitable radio programmes planned, produced and broadcast in a particular time in six States of India - Andhra Pradesh, Bihar, Karanataka, Madhya Pradesh, Orissa and Rajasthan. Thus we have ample evidence of the achievements of educational radio in different countries of the world. Educatoinal broadcasting has also been used for enrichment purposes, for non-formal education, for open school and open university systems.

Limitations of Radio

Radio has a number of inherent limitations. It is a medium dependent on sound only. It demands a habit of constant listening which is not ordinarily available with many. Radio may broadcast a well developed lesson, but cannot develop a lesson with the audience. No intervention on control over the broadcast is possible to suit the special need and interest of any group.

In radio programmes there is no scope for interpersonal contacts and interaction between the artist (here radio teacher) and the audience. So the elements of notivation and inspiration are usually lacking in the sound broadcasting. Audience cannot see the performers directly, nor are the artists or performers able to see the audience. It therefore makes a lot of difference in the approach and techniques. Sole dependence on sound and complete absence of any visuals make this medium quite different from television or film. G.C. Awasthy has aptly said, "In radio, the aritist and his audience are nowhere near each other. In the physical sense they are non-existent to each other. The basic fact about radio art and this is the over-riding fact is that it is entirely an aural art with a complete absence of visual components. This is at once the weakness and the strength of radio as an art form."

To most of us, listening is very exacting and to some it is taxing also Since radio calls for listening only from its audience, it has to perform a difficult task. Donald McWhinnie discussing the true nature of radio has observed that we are used to seeing and listening simultaneously and listening only proves inadequate or the effect demanded too exacting. Asking for imagining a piece of conversation in a dark room. McWhinnie has added "The words acquire a compulsion of meaning they did not have before, they develop a richness of texture through being isolated and you focus your sensibility and imagination on them as you rarely do in daylight. That is why, radio as a medium makes the heaviest demand on the listener's imagination and sensibility. The listener has to make the experience gained from the radio his own, by relating it to his own terms of references on his own background."

How to Overcome the Limitations?

With a view to overcoming the limitations in radio broadcasting, the following steps should be taken up.

(i) Since sound is the only means of communicating the message in the radio broadcast, it has to be supported with printed materials, illustrations, posters, slides, film-strips etc., as well as discussions.

(ii) As the programme is on the air we listen to anything only once for all and every thing changes from moment to moment. In order to make an impact, it must draw attention right from start and continue to sustain the interest of audience. This will be possible only by adopting certain attention-drawing and interest-sustaining techniques.

(iii) Sound being the only medium in radio-broadcasts, it has to be enriched by variety and reality in music and sound effects. By this the absence of visuals is mitigated and the deficiency made up giving ample scope for audience's imagination.

(iv) Suitable script should be developed as framework of the radio programme giving adequate scope for generating interests, sustaining suspense or curiosity throughout, and she sing new light and sound.

(v) Scripts are also to be properly handled by the producer in producing prcgrammes. Awasthy has nicely observed, "A radio script, no matter how well it is written, is but the bare bones of a programme. What counts is how well it is put across. Between the script and its broadcast lies the whole technique of production and the success or otherwise of the producer."

Lastly, it may be pointed out that educational radio has to utilise selected subject areas for clearly defined puposes. It should have emotional appeal, power to stimulate the imaginatian to bring the external or distant world to the classroom and to recreate an event or episode from the past life or history. Thus the choice of material and formal optimum use of sound and musical effects, utilisation of suitable techniques and treatment would ensure success of educational broadcasting.

Advantages and Disadvantages of Audio Cassettes/Tapes

The advantages and disadvantages of audio cassettes and tapes are mentioned as follows:

Advantages

i) Tape recorders and cassette recorders are not expensive in comparison to other electronic media.

ii) Even without electricity, tape/cassette recorders can be used with the help of battery sets.

iii) These recorders can play back cassettes/tapes according to convenience of the learners. That is, these materials can be utilised for repetition, drilling, practising and illustrating some specific teaching points.

iv) Tape/cassette recorders are comparatively handy and quite portable, and as such can be used easily at various places.

v) Production of educational cassettes/tapes is quite easy and does not require much technicality.

vi) Production cost of educational audio cassette/tapes is quite reasonable.

vii) Tapes/cassettes are produced according to educational needs and conditions of special groups of learners.

Disadvantages

i) Like radio, audio cassette/tape programmes are only sound-based and have no visuals. Hence, these programmes are boring.

ii) Audio cassettes/tapes are generally developed locally, even institutionally. So professional quality is often sacrificed.

iii) Like radio programmes, in the audio cassettes/tapes there is no scope for interaction and feedback. Hence these are one-sided/one-way communication and miss the personal touch.

Limiting the Limitations of Audio Cassettes/Tapes

With a view to overcome the limitations of the audio programmes, the following steps should be taken:

i) Sound being the only or the main medium, it has to be supported by printed materials, posters, slides, pictures etc.

ii) As listening is very exacting for many, appropriate attention-drawing and interesting techniques need to be adopted in the audio programme.

iii) In these programmes, there should be adequate and appropriate use of music and sound effects.

iv) Scripts being the backbone of these programmes should be prepared taking pedagogic and psychological needs and conditions of the clientele into consideration.

v) In educational audio programmes there should be imaginative use of humour, elasticity, suspense, curiosity etc.

vi) In order to make audio programmes effective, teachers should conduct pre, during and post audio discussions and other follow-up activities.

Optimum Utilization of Radio/Audio Programmes

In order to ensure optimum utilization of educational radio/ audio programmes the following factors are to be taken into account:

(i) Provision and maintenance of radio sets/audio/tape recorder.

(ii) Organisation of radio/audio listening in class.

(iii) Pre-broadcast/play back discussion.

(iv) Post-broadcast/play back discussion.

(v) Use of support materials

(vi) Follow-up activities.

Provision of Radio Sets and Audio Tape Recorder

The primary requisite of utilization is the provision of a radio set and tape recorder in the school. Since at present these sets and equipment are of different varieties and of various makes, the schools should not go for very costly sets or for very cheap ones. If the Headmaster or Headmistress likes to have one for the school, these can easily be done by purchasing from the funds of the school.

The sets belonging to the school can be kept under the custody of either the Headmaster or the User Teacher. Small battery sets are preferable if they are portable and can be taken to different classes without any difficulty. However, if the school is electrified and plug points are there in different rooms, an electricity operated set will serve the pupose. Sets with both these facilities would be better. The radio and tape recorder should be properly maintained in the schools.

Organisation of Radio Listening

User Teachers are generally the subject teachers or teachers who are interested in the media and remain in charge of the same. There are different subject teachers in different classes. Since a topic relating to one subject for one class is broadcast in one day for 20 mts., the User Teacher may not find any difficulty in organising the broadcast activities in the class. The problem of the presence of subject teacher in all the classrooms may arise if there are more sections in a class. If a tape recorder or two-in-one is purchased, it can be utilised for recording the school broadcast programmes and played back at different times in the remaining sections.

Before switching on the radio it is the responsibility of the User Teacher to create proper atmosphere in the class for listening to the school broadcasts. The receiving set should be kept in a central position so that every student of the class could listen to the programme without any difficulty. Since radio is an audio equipment, every care should be taken for its clarity in listening by each and everyone in the class.

Pre-Broadcast Discussions

After maintaining proper listening atmosphere in the class the User Teacher will ask certain questions preferably three to five relating to the broadcast topic in order to arrest the attention of the pupils towards the radio lesson. This will help students listen to the programmes attentively and the very purpose of the broadcasting would be achieved. Before a radio lesson, the User Teacher should be aware of the specific objectives of that particular lesson.

Let us take the example of the lesson "Duties of Students" topic in the language book for class-VIII. In this lesson the specific aims are two-fold.

1) To make the children aware of their duties towards the country.

2) To encourage them to do their duties.

There should be some introductory questions which would be asked to the students prior to the broadcast. The questions may take the form as given below. The duration may be fixed for about 10 mts.

1) What is meant by Independence?

2) When did our country get Independence?

3) Who were ruling our country before Independence?

4) Who are the citizens of our country?

5) When will they be citizens?

Then he may say, "Now let us listen to to-day's radio/audio programme on Duties of Students."

During Broadcast

During the broadcast or play back the User Teacher will silently observe the reaction of the students and will make a note of the difficult concepts, words, phrases etc., and any unusual reaction of the students. At the same time he may listen to the programme and give his own opinion and suggestions to the concerned authority and also to All India Radio for the improvement of the programme.

Post-Broadcast Discussions

After the programme is over, the User Teacher may invite questions from the students in order to clarify their doubts on the programme. He may try to explain the difficult ideas, words, phrases etc., and ask certain questions which he feels relevant and useful and not covered by the students and to give reply in case of failure on the part of the students. The User Teacher will try to clarify the words and concepts found difficult for students. This activity may take about 10 minutes.

Use of Support Materials

The support materials sent by the Education Department and AIR to the radio schools from time to time may be consulted for effective discussion with the students. The support materials are prepared on the basis of the radio scripts scheduled for broadcast on different subjects and for different grades. It is not necessary that only the questions, the support materials contain, will be asked by the teacher. He may ask questions which he deems fit on the lines suggested in the support materials.

Follow-up

After this is done, when the teacher is satisfied with the activities, he may give some practical assignments to the students to do by themselves in order to bring out the creativity in them. They can write an essay or a story or a poem according to their ability and interest. In the above lesson the children may be asked to write what they learnt from the lesson. This will help the students to exercise their brain and to recollect the information they got in the lesson. They will also help them to enter into a healthy competition. Again, the spelling errors of the students, if any, will be rectified when the same would be seen by the subject teacher.

All these activities when properly organised result in joyful and effective learning. Thus the teacher concerned should take active interest in the audio/radio programme and present himself throughout the period with keen interest and close attention to the listening of the programmes from the begining to the end and organise all relevant activites in a very planned and meaningful way. All this is essential for ensuring efficient learning through radio/audio programmes.

Role of Teachers

We all know that radio is a potential medium and it is within the easy reach of most of us. Its programmes can reach out people not only in a vast area, but also in the interior and isolated parts of our country.

Radio programmes can inform, instruct, entertain, advice and inspire. That is why, educational broadcasting can effectively communicate new knowledge, attitudes and interests to the learners in the schools and colleges. Educational radio programmes can easily enrich and supplement the learning experiences that are provided by teachers in the classrooms. In spite of the dazzling effects and attractive features of TV programmes, radio has its own advantages particularly in the developing countries like India. But it is the irony of fact that radio is not adequaiely used and thousands of rupees spent on production and transmission of educational programmes are utilised only to a very limited extent.

Importance of Evaluation

Evaluation and feedback are essential not only for generating awareness and getting information about the listening conditions, but also for bringing about improvement in the radio programmes.Therfore, they are found useful both for utilisation as well as production of educational broadcasting. A large number of short-term and long-term studies are to be conducted for evaluating the radio programmes and getting feedback from the user teachers and students concerned. But it is our experience that these audience are not sensitive to the medium and found quite indifferent to the radio programmes with paricular reference to their reactions to be made available to their own department or All India Radio. Unless regular and adequate feedback is made available from the filed, the Education Department will be in dark about the problems at the consumption end and the All India Radio is unable to ascertain the extent of effectiveness and reception of their programmes for effecting improvement in their production strategies.

Means of Evaluation

Teachers and students listening to a particular radio programme can write to the concerned authorities about their reactions in a letter even on the body of a postcard. In order to ensure regular receipt of this feedback, prepaid reply cards may be sent to the radio user teachers. A sample proforma may be given for the pupose which may take only a few minutes to fill up and despatch. A little more detailed proforma in the cyclostyled or printed form may be supplied to the supervisors and user teachers earlier to fill up and send back after listening to the radio programmes. This will furnish more data as a feedback on the radio programmes. Questionnaire is a more detailed form of collecting data on various aspects of radio programmes like language, content, format, sound, difficulty level, problems in reception and so on. This is used in comparatively long-term research projects with a view to study specific objectives. Since it is more comprehensive and lengthy, responses may not be forthcoming as we usually expect through prepaid postcards on short proforma. Attempts should however be made to make it as precise and relevant as possible. Another technique of getting feedback is through setting up monitoring panels in various parts of the State. Enthusiastic and interested teachers are usually entrusted with responsibility of listening to a series of programmes regularly and furnishing data in prescribed proforma or questionnaire. Since a team of teachers are engaged/appointed to provide feedback on a series of programmes in a particular subject/subjects after listening to them purposely, they are called monitoring panels.

A more sophisticated research study may be taken up by an individual or institution on a programme series or programmes broadcast over a particular span of time. A controlled group and an experimental group is taken for the purpose and data is collected before and after experiment. The end results may be statistically interpreted and scientifically reported, so that the findings and conclusions will have necessary validity and reliability.

Interview and observation are utilised as suitable techniques of collecting data for enlisting reactions and feedback from the field. Individual or group discussions as well as personal interests are conducted with teachers, pupils, supervisors and managements. Predesigned information sheets and interview schedules should be used for the purpose. The points dealt therein will be as regards theme and quality of programmes, reception, teachers preparation, pupils' participation and reaction, difficulties faced, attitude and suggestions of the teacher and follow-up activities.

Here we have no scope for going into the details of these studies and for discussing the data collection and findings. But it is the general conclusion that school broadcast programmes were utilised only to a little extent (10%) and separate periods have not been kept in the majority of schools (85%) for listening to the radio broadcasting. There was inadequacy of funds and non-receipt of circulars from the Inspectors of Schools. Only in 10% of high schools pre and post broadcast discussions were being conducted. Most of the school broadcast programmes were syllabus-based and no follow-up activities were organised by teachers. On the whole, it is found that in those schools where teachers, particularly heads are interested in the school broadcasting, there has been satisfactory utilisation of educational radio. In the National Workshop on Educational Broadcasting held at Delhi from December 1-6, 1980 and Regional Seminar-cum-Workshop on Educational Broadcasts held at Trivandrum from the 17th January to 31 st January, 1981, it was resolved that different techniques of evaluation both short-term and long-term formative and summative should be undertaken internally by the All India Radio, and externally by the Education Department, Universities and other agencies. The departments of State Institutes of Educational Technology have been utilising questionnaire and information sheets for collecting data, and has set up monitoring panels in a few selected districts. In this method a good number of enthusiastic teachers have been involved and they have been provided with a set of printed proforma on various subjects. Unless teachers get interested in this medium, however potential it may have, we cannot take advantage of radio programmes for improvement of education. We should realize that it is there to help us, not to hinder us. Educational broadcasting can be improved upon and made suitable for our purpose only with whole-hearted co-operation and keen interest of teachers.

Similarly, audio cassettes and tape programmes produced either professionally or by commercial firms or institutionally, should be properly evaluated for bringing about improvement in their quality relevance and accessibility, so that learning experiences can be made joyful and efficient. On the basis of the findings and feedback from the learners, students, teachers, supervisors and planners of the Education Department, we can modify and improve the existing programmes and produce some useful and relevant programmes and media materials for the benefit of the target audience.

Having been in the midst of the Revolution of Electronic Media, we cannot underestimate the role of radio and audio programmes for improving the quality and quantity of education at all stages. Radio and audio cassette/tape recorder are potential media. These are also not so costly to procure and difficult to handle in the classrooms. Radio service has established a wide network and infrastructure throughout the country. Similarly tape recorders, two-in-one, cassette recorders have been introduced in our education system with great profit in the educational institutions. Educational radio has already achieved wonders in upgrading the teachers' efficiency in various subjects and expansion of education in different countries. Particularly, radio and audio programmes would be utilised for improving the quality of education at all levels.

There are however, a few limitations in radio and audio programmes which can be overcome to a great extent. Particularly the materials, slides, pictures etc. Interesting scripts need to be prepared and adequate music and sound effects can be utilized in these programmes. Pre, during and post broadcast/playback activities would go a long way in making them interesting and effective. With a view to ensuring effective utilisation of radio/audio programmes we have to provide and maintain radio and audio sets, organise radio/audio listening in the classroom, hold pre-during and post broadcast discussions, use various support materials and organise follow-up activities among students.

Role of teachers in evaluation of educational radio/audio programme is of crucial importance. Evaluation of these programmes is essential for improving their quality, economy and receptivity and teachers with different means and techniques should evaluate these programmes with the help of supervisors and students, so that the findings and feedback of these studies can help improve the quality and utility of these programmes as well as produce more relevant ones for promoting quality and quantity of education at all levels.

Role of Video Electronic Media

Now, we intend to explain the concept of telecasting and video cassettes, and their role and functions, the ways and means of overcoming the limitations of telecasting and video cassettes, effective steps for utilisation of educational TV and programmes for their improvement. Let us now focus on the objectives that we have in mind to help you.

- acquaint yourself with the need and importance of distance education and the use of electronic media for its effectiveness.
- know the significance of educational TV and video cassettes.
- identify the strengths and weaknesses of telecasting and video cassettes.
- acquire suitable knowledge and skills for overcoming their limitations.
- develop competence for effective utilisation of telecasting and video cassettes in education.
- acquire some expertise in evaluating educational television and video cassettes.

Place of Telecast and Video Cassettes

Distance education is the most democratic and socialistic pattern of education. It is very democratic in the sense that deprived and under privileged people get the benefit of education under this pattern. It is socialistic in the sense that the government controls and provides this system of education mostly for the benefit of the weaker sections of the community. The International Commission on the Development of Education (Learning To Be, 1972) has aptly remarked, "The future of our societies lies in democracy, development and change. Our societies must accordingly train men for democracy, humanistic development and change. Democracy has to blaze a path through a mass of obstacles and snares. Technical progress, the relative abundance of goods already available in some places and the plethora likely in the future, all hold out great promise lor justice. But the progress is also a source of inequity, alienation and new tyrannies." (p. 101.)

It has therefore been observed, "The formal and traditional system of education has been playing an elitist role through ages. It has been perpetuating the disparities and imbalanced growth in the society". We have also seen that inspite of the Constitutional Directive, universalisation of elementary education has not yet been realized on account of the inadequacies of the formal system of education. School and higher education has not been made available to a large number of individuals inspite of their interest, due to various constraints. Therefore, other alternatives and innovative strategies like non-formal education, correspondence education and distance education have been introduced and are rather found more effective and useful for democratization and socialization of education.

Utility of Media

Distance education has been utilising the electronic equipment like the radio, television and audio/video recorder more than any other systems of education. In this context, the Open University (OU) of the United Kingdom has set the model and earned the credit of making the innovative use of various media besides printed and spoken words. It is worth mentioning here that the OU was first suggested by Harold Wilson, the then leader of the Labour Party in 1963. He announced a plan called "University of the Air" on educational innovation which would utilise the TV, the radio, etc., along with its correspondence courses.

The first educational radio and television programmes of the O.U. were broadcast in January, 1971 as part of its courses. The radio and TV Programmes were specially produced and broadcast by the BBC in order to supplement the correspondence materials, standard textbooks, contact course etc. The BBC producers and educational technologists were associated in planning or designing the curriculum along with the academics and subject experts from the very beginning. A supporting staff of artists, photographers, librarians and other technical persons are required to help implement or organise the course/curriculum plans. The course teams make the policy decisions for the use of various media and materials, but production of a radio or television programme is the joint responsibility of an academician and producer.

It may be pointed out here that O.U. lays great emphasis on research and feedback for improving the system. As early as in 1970 the OU set up an Institute of Educational Technology for the purpose. The educational experts of this institute provide guidance at the planning stage, extend advice for preparing suitable materials and for producing the required radio and television programmes, and work hard for assessing the students performance and evaluting various components of the course including the radio and TV programmes. It is also interesting to note that BBC producers are found to be very keen in getting feedback reports from the educational technologists on their programmes in order to improve their further production. In India, unfortunately, electronic media have not assumed adequate importance in the sphere of correspondence education. The National Policy on Education, 1986 has however, enunciated (p-22) that "modern educational technology must reach out to the most distant areas and the most deprived sections of the beneficiaries, simultaneously with the areas of comparative affluence and ready availability."

In the context of distance learning the National Policy has also specifically pointed out "The Open University system has been initiated in order to augment opportunities for higher education and as an instrument of democratising education." (p-15). The Indira Gandhi National Open University set up in 1985 has now been strengthened with massive infrastructure at the headquarters in Delhi and its regional centres in various other States. It has developed various courses of studies under the distance education system which means a student joining one Open University can take courses from another open university. Besides, the system will offer a wide variety of academic programmes supported by various media.

Although distance education is mainly meant for the deprived and underprivileged, the quality of such education is in no way inferior to the formal system of education. Rather it should be richer, better and more effective with the help of various modern media, methods and materials, which constitute educational technology in true sense of the term and ensure the optimization of learning experiences. Both quality and quantity of education can very well be reconciled, safeguarded and promoted by this system, which would be really democratic as well as socialistic in nature and spirit.

Pre-SITE ETV Programmes

Television as the most powerful medium of communication has revolutioned the lifestyle of many people in the world. It has remarkable versatility in treatment of themes and an outstanding impact on the various aspects of modern life. It can reach an enromous cross-section of population with simultaneous presentations. It combines all kinds of audio-visual aids and equipment. It is capable of helping learners and viewers to overcome the cultural barriers and social deprivations or deficiencies. On the whole, television has immense attraction and enormous potentiality in moulding characters, forming attitudes and shaping values and vision of life.

Educational Television was first produced and telecast by AIR in January-March, 1960. According to an agreeement with the Ford Foundation, 6 thousand TV sets were installed in secondary schools by 1965. This service was inaugurated on the 23rd October, 1961. The agreement also provided for the supply of technical equipment, training of AIR personnel and so on. After 4 years of experiment the project was evaluated and the overall impact of the ETV programmes was found quite satisfactory. The regular TV service was inaugurated in Delhi on 15th August, 1965.

The SITE Experiment

The Satellite Instructional Television Experiment (SITE) was implemented during the year 1975-76. The TV programmes produced by Doordarshan and Space Application Centre (SAC) were telecast for primary school children since the 1st August, 1975. The ATS-F loaned by NASA., U.S.A., was utilised for telecasting the programmes. The six States of Andhra Pradesh, Bihar, Karnataka, Madhya Pradesh, Orissa and Rajasthan were covered under this project and about 2400 villages were served by this service. The Educational Technology Cells organised training courses for the Television User teachers and provided teachers' notes and other support materials with the help of NCERT, New Delhi.

Since the impact of ETV programmes was found to be quite useful, the Government of India decided to provide TV viewing facilities in 40% of the SITE-covered villages by means of terrestrial transmitters. In the aforesaid 6 States, the project was popularly called as Community-

Viewing Scheme and besides education other subjects like agriculture, health, family planning etc., were provided through the TV programmes. Subsequently, the ETV service has been made available in most of the important cities of the country.

INSAT ETV Programmes

The Educational Television Programmes were telecast through Indian National Satellite (INSAT-IA) for some months during 1982 and then through INSAT-IB from 15th October, 1983. The ETV Programmes produced by Doordarshan and Centres for Educational Technology/ Central Institute of Educational Technology were telecast by Doordarshan for rural primary school children. The States like Andhra Pradesh, Bihar, Gujarat, Maharashtra, Orissa, Uttar Pradesh were covered under the INSAT project.

Pluses and Minuses of Educational Telecast and Video Cassettes

All educational systems and educational materials are consciously and carefully designed to help pupils learn and grow towards certain pre-stated educational objectives. Most of the television programmes are also an education of a kind, because they inform, instruct, entertain and thus educate. When used as a teaching tool in an educational situation - formal or non-formal-television may well be labelled as "the queen of audio-visual aids." It can effectively combine a multitude of teaching aids-films, slides, tapes, charts and other graphics. As a teaching aid, television has several advantages and can play a very important role in making learning effective and joyful.

The Pluses

Some of the advantages television has over other media are:

i) Television can bring the whole world into the classroom

ii) It combines both sound and pictures, moving and still, grips the attention of viewers and has great motivating power.

iii) It makes the past alive.

iv) It can bring distant objects, places, people, events and processes to the classroom.

v) It is a mass medium and can reach vast number of viewers simultaneously and at distant places.

vi) It can magnify small objects which can be seen by several students at a time.

vii) It can also show events in slow and fast motion.

viii) Live and dramatised situations presented through television can be used to educate the viewers.

ix) Equipment and materials not generally available in school laboratories, can be shown on television.

x) In teaching foreign languages, the native speaker can be brought in the classroom for ideal demonstration of speech.

xi) TV can also cut down the cost of education to some extent, if more and more pupils are allowed to have access to television programmes.

xii) As a corrolary to above, unit cost will come down and cost effectiveness of education will increase.

The Minuses

Television, however, suffers from a few serious drawbacks also. These are:

i) Television is a one-way medium. Once it starts, it goes on and on. It can't stop to answer the questions or remove doubts, if any, arising in the minds of viewers. That means you cannot turn the page back and information retrieval is nil.

ii) Television is a very expensive medium; and to bring down cost, it should cater to a large number of learners, making effective programmes and using interesting formats capable of being repeated.

iii) TV tends to make the viewers inactive and, as some modern researches have pointed, it damages the brain temporarily.

iv) It surely is a dissociative medium and turns one off.

v) TV cannot cater to individual differences and can at best cater to the average group.

vi) Steps for Overcoming the Limitations of Telecast and Video Cassettes

With a view to overcome the limitations of telecasting and videocassettes, the following steps need to be taken:

i) Television being a one-way medium should be supported by interaction of teachers with students, once prior to and another, after the telecast for generating curiosity, preparing students for reception of the ETV programmes and video cassettes and clearing doubts, if any in the language and content transmitted therein.

ii) Since television is an expensive device, it is desirable that more care is taken for production and utilisation of suitable ETV programme, so that more students would be benefitted and cost effectiveness would increase.

iii) There is no conclusive evidence that viewers become inactive and their brain is temporarily damaged. Besides, viewing the ETV/video cassette programmes intermittently, not at a stretch, cannot do any harm to the mental or psychological make up and conditions.

iv) ETV/video cassette should be made interesting and relevant to the needs of the curriculum, so that these can be made useful and the individual differences taken care of.

v) With the imaginative use of various visuals, music and electronic effects, the ETV/video cassette programmes could be made pleasant and educationally efficient.

For promoting effective utilisation of ETV and video-cassette programmes, the following strategies need be taken:

i) Procuring and maintenance of TV/VCR sets.

ii) Organisation of efficient viewing of ETV and video cassette programmes.

iii) Pre-telecast/playback discussion.

iv) Post-telecast/playback video discussion.

v) Use of support materials.

vi) Follow-up activities.

Procuring and Maintenance of TV/VCR Sets

Procuring TV/VCR sets is prerequisite to the utilisation of programmes. It could be done with the help of unutilised funds. UGC is also making adequate funds available to the university departments and affiliated colleges for purchase of these A-V aids. Maintenance of these valuable equipment is very important and it should be done from the funds available for the purpose. But skilled and well-trained technicians should be available for properly repairing and handling these aids.

Useful Viewing Sessions

Appropriate accommodation for installation and safe-custody of these valuable equipment is essential and teachers who are interested in as well as committed to these programmes should be kept in charge of these instruments, so that they would like to organise the viewing sessions of ETV/video-cassette programmes properly. Appropriate sitting arrangment of students and placement of TV/VCR sets at the right place while telecasting or playing back is necessary for proper viewing.

Pre-telecast/Playback of Discussions

Students should be made curious and motivated to know what is coming in the programme, briefly told by the teacher about the caption, content and a few highlights of telecast/playback to take place.

During-Viewing Session Activity

Sometimes students are left alone in the viewing session and teachers go out of classroom for other activity. But it is felt necessary that the teacher should remain for viewing the programme and take note of the reactions of the viewers, the difficult concepts and words not intelligible to them.

Post-telecast/Playback Video Programmes

As soon as the watching session is over, it is desirable that students are asked certain questions to test how far they have been able to grasp the programme. Teachers should explain the difficult concepts and words, so that it would be easier for them to clearly understand the content and message of the programme.

Use of Support Materials

Printed materials should be provided adequately for going through the content and teaching points minutely and leisurely which is usually missed in course of watching the telecast/video programmes.

Follow-up

After all the activities are properly orrganised, students would be satisfied with the learning experiences and be in a position to express their own ideas about the programme creatively. Teachers need to give some assignment to students with adequate freedom and flexibility to write a poem or a story or an essay as they like. This would be a joyful learning experience as well as a relevant educational exercise.

At this stage video cassettes have special significance as these can be played back to show the teaching points, the visuals, and actions minutely which might have been missed while telecasting or playing back for the first time, so that difficulties could be explained by the teachers for easy comprehension.

Importance of Evaluation and Research

Any educational programme aims at changes in the human behaviour. It is designed to produce specific changes in the behaviour of the individuals who are exposed to such a programme. The basic purpose of evaluation is to produce information that can be used in educational decision-making. Thus evaluation provides data to frame appropriate policies for an educational media system. It also increases knowledge of how to integrate media most effectively into an overall teaching context. It not only provides information on the success or failure of educational objectives, but also gives explanations for the same. On the whole, findings of evaluation throw light on the effectiveness of planning and management elements for best utilisation of media.

Formative and Summative Evaluation

Evaluation is divided mainly into two kinds: (I) Formative and (II) Summative. The former is conducted in connection with new educational programmes and the latter is used to assess the effectiveness of the existing or ongoing ETV/video programmes. Formative evaluation attempts for collection of the data on the student's learning needs, his readiness for learning and problems he faces in the learning situations. It helps teachers and pupils to bring about desired modifications in the teaching and learning programmes. Summative evaluation on the other hand, is required to assess how far the existing programme has been effective in the teaching-learning situations. It is conducted at the end of a course or a programme for certification or validation.

During the development of a TV/video programme, data are also collected for making revisions in order to improve its functioning and effectiveness. Formative evaluation is necessary to diagnose the problem and indicate the corrective steps warranted under the circumstances. The results of formative studies are useful in designing other programmes of similar nature and planning media policy. Teachers' notes and students' workbooks are also revised on the basis of findings of such studies.

Types of Formative Evaluation

Tony Bates (1978) has described various kinds of formative evaluation as follows:

1) *Piloting:* It consists of showing a programme to experts, subject matter specialists and curriculum specialists. Expert opinion is thus obtained for making the programme more effective and meaningful.
2) *Pretesting or developmental testing:* The programme or material either in rough draft or in finished format is shown to representatives of the target audience.

Responses so collected are helpful in making suitable modifications in the programme/material.

Audience reaction is obtained by the following ways:

i) Observing and noting the audience behaviour (e.g. attention, facial expressions, laughter, exclamations, verbal participation, etc.) on a work-sheet.

ii) Discussing with the audience individually or in groups about the programme.

iii) Administering a questionnaire/opinionnaire regarding various aspects of the programme.

iv) Recalling the programme over a period of time.

v) Testing the change in behaviour of the audience.

Due to certain constraints, major changes in the programme may not be possible, but developmental testing might be useful for the preparation of appropriate support materials. Decision to use formative research should be made from the very beginning and producers as well as researchers should be involed in such decisions.

Summative Evaluation

It mainly differs from formative one in time perspective and both kinds of evaluation overlap each other in many ways. Summative evaluation, however, is primarily concerned with assessment of the finished product. The techniques and methods of study in formative evaluation, are also followed in summative one. The need for immediate information to guide short-range decisions justifies formative evaluation, whereas the need for long-range decisions and policy-making require summative evaluation of the impact of ETV/video programmes. Due to its long-term effects and importance, data in summative evaluation are gathered in more systematic and scientific manner.

When a TV/video programme is of repetitive value and formative evaluation has not been possible at the initial stage, summative evaluation is more justified to be conducted for bringing about necessary revision in the programme. Nevertheless, it is wise as well as economical to undertake formative evaluation and improve upon the programme/project in the process of its production on the basis of its findings.

Feedback Methods

Wilbur Schramm (1972) has similarly enunciated the following feedback methods which may be taken as formative as well as summative evaluation.

Pretesting programmes

Prior to the transmission of educational television programmes to the entire school system, they are shown to a representative sample of target audience. This try-out is felt necessary as a teleteacher cannot be confident of the all-out success of the programme unless it is pretested on students. But producers and teleteachers do not accept such try-out because of limited time and resources.

Teaching pupils in the studio

By teaching a group of students in the studio itself, the teleteacher can get as much information from the pupils as he would get in a normal classroom situation. This feedback helps him to modify or improve upon his lesson-plan. Studio-classes may be off-camera or on camera according to convenience and help teleteachers particularly in conducting experiments or demonstrations.

Immediate electronic feedback

It is a kind of "talk-back" system installed for enabling pupils to raise a point or ask a question through a classroom microphone. These comments and questions would go on the air and furnish some feedback to the tele-teachers.

Testing at frequent intervals

All classes are administered tests at the same time on programme content using television and results of the tests are also made known through television. These results help in reviewing the subject matter or to introduce new approaches to teaching.

Obtaining comments from classroom

Class-teachers are requested to fill up a report proforma and send it to teleteacher/producer once in a week or fortnight. Such feedback is generaly received on various aspects of television programme including content design and presentation style.

Making regular observations of classroom activity

Supervisors/Education Officers are required to observe classroom situations regularly and collect information in respect of teachers' and students' reactions to TV teaching. Teleteachers themselves can also observe classes during television lessons and get feedback.

Getting regular reports on attitude of pupils and teachers

By adopting the above methods or by administering attitude scales, feedback is obtained as to whether they like television lessons, what they like or dislike in it, whether teachers are receptive or aggressive and so on.

Getting reports on specific problems

With a view to getting feedback on certain problems, both questionnaire and interview techniques are required and the supervisor entrusted with responsibility of looking into the problems gets suggestions for solving them from these reports.

Expert reviews

At the time of decision-making for revising the programme/ materials, specialists consisting of poducers, teleteachers, supervisors, teachers, subject and media experts are required to give their views. As every programme usually has a scope for improvement, various methods of feedback have to be adopted. But there are constraints of time and resources in the matter and as such, some selected methods most suitable and economical, have to be put into operation according to the local needs and conditions. Thus evaluation, both formative and summative can be applied, action-oriented, decision-directed, short-term, programme specific and project-based.

Evaluation of ETV/video programmes needs collaborative and interdisciplinary approach and sympathetic understanding of the processes involved in the system. It has also been rightly said, "We might add that educational television opens up a new area for research for which our existing tools and techniques are not adequate. It will be necessary to develop appropriate concepts, techniques and methodology that would be sensitive to the child audience and provide insight into the complex manner in which he gains from or accepts television."

References

1. Kothari D.S. *et al.* The Report of Indian Education Commission, 1964-66, New Delhi, Ministry of Education, Government of India.
2. *Ibid.*
3. Central Board of Secondary Education, Annual Report: Open School, New Delhi, 1979-80, p.2.
4. Government of India, *The Programme of Action, (MHRD), Education, 1986.*
5. Schramm, W. *et. al., The New Media: Memo to Education Planners*, UNESCO, 1967.

9

Instructional Materials and Teaching Aids

To impart instruction we need a number of materials. Our senses eyes, ears, tongue, nose and skin are the gateways to knowledge. We acquire all knowledge through instructions. The senses are used for instruction. More the senses are used, better is the instruction. Most of our experiences are gained through hearing and seeing. It is said that about 85% of the total experiences/knowledge are gained through eyes and ears. The materials that are used for imparting are audio-visual aids or materials. After going through the module, you will be able to

- know the role and importance of instructional materials.
- classify the instructional materials on the basis of their characteristics.
- acquaint yourself with the various uses and applications of these materials.
- enlist a number of guidelines for ensuring effectiveness of learning experiences.
- integrate the instructional materials with teaching aids.

As mentioned above, instructional materials are used to enable the learner to achieve the learning objectives effectively and interestingly. You are familiar with common audio-visual aids/ materials such as books, blackboards, maps, charts, globes, pictures etc., which are traditional in nature. Now-a-days electronic media like programme learning materials (PLM), computer, audio and video programmes have come in a big way and are apt to influence not only communication and education but also the manner and behaviour, lifestyle attitudes and interests of the clientele. These media and materials provide direct as well as vicarious or improvised learning experiences to the students at all levels of education. These include traditional aids as well as electronic media, emerged from time to time in large variety and great novelty.

Learning becomes effective when students are actively involved in the process. To the extent his different senses are related, his learning becomes successful to that extent. For using various senses in the teaching-learning process, different materials are utilised in the classrooms. The learning experiences are thus made quite relevant, meaningful and effective. That is why, the materials are also called 'multi-sensory materials' 'multimedia' or 'instructional aids' or 'instructional materials.' These materials mainly being of two kinds, audio and visual, they are known as 'audio-visual aids' or A-V materials. Similarly the learning materials may be divided into printed and non-printed or projected and non-projected materials/aids. As these materials are to be used as an integral part of the entire learning situation and are not just ancilliary or supplementary, many educators are not happy with the term 'aids.' Therefore, the term 'material' is safely used and sometimes the term, 'technique' is also used to mean how these materials can be used. Thus instructional aids/materials have various connotations.

The main features about instructional materials are summerised below:

i) Instructional materials, particularly printing should be written in the language and style, easily intelligible and quite interesting to the target groups.

ii) Content or thematic as well as linguistic aspects/factors must be flawless and correct.

iii) The materials must meet the curricular needs and mental/ psychological conditions of learners.

iv) Adequate illustrations and visuals should be used in the learning materials. But these should be relevant and meaningful, not merely beautiful.

v) Attempts should be made to explain the difficult concepts and reinforce teaching points in course of description or at the end.

vi) Instructional materials should not try to deal with too much content in limited time.

vii) Exercises/practices should be provided in between, so that learning experiences can be tested and important points can be reinforced.

viii) As far as possible, programmed learning principles, should be followed in the development of learning materials.

ix) In case of non-print or projected learning materials, the target audience/audience profile should be kept in mind by the scriptwriter and producer.

x) The language and format used in the materials should be informal and interesting.

Different Instructional Materials

According to the sense-stimulation the instructional aids or the audio-visual materials may be divided into three categories: (i) Visual (ii) Audio and (ii) Audio-visual. The materials which appeal only to the sight are of the first category. Examples of these materials are slides, filmstrips, transparencies, silent motion pictures etc. Other materials traditionally used in the schools are textbook illustrations, photographs, prints, graphs, charts, maps, globes, etc., which may be taken as visual aids. The chalkboard, felt board and bulletin board are also visual materials appealing only to the sense of'sight.' Displays and exhibits like specimens, mock-ups, electric maps and some dramatisations like pageants, pantomimes, puppetry and dancing are regarded as successful visual materials.

Radio, gramophone, tape recorders and different magnetic recordings provide audio materials which appeal to the sense of hearing only. The television programmes, tape slide programme, video tape recordings and films are materials which appeal to both sight and sound and are very effective audio-visual materials, Dramatic plays, role-playing, socio-drama, verse choirs etc., are a few types of dramatization that can be used with satisfying results.

These three types of materials audio or visual or audio-visual cannot be exclusively categorised. There is no distinct compartmentalisation and the list of such materials is not exhaustive. Imaginative and resourceful teachers can invent, explore and discover various sources collecting and developing these materials. It has rightly been remarked by J.S. Kinder (1950) "Any device which can be used to make the learning experience more concrete, more dynamic can be considered audio-visual material.'

According to projection facilities available audio-visual aids are also divided into (i) Projected, (ii) Non-projected and (iii) Activity aids. When aids are projected on screens or even against white-washed walls to give an enlarged image of the material they are called projected aids. Projected aids include slides, film-strips, films, transparencies which bring about better results and are more effective. The darkened room reduces distractions and the bright image on the screen secures the attention of learners. By the use of different colours, the aids become more attractive and impressive.

Non-projected aids are generally still materials including maps, charts, globes, models, display boards, bulletin boards etc. These aids are not so costly and no sophisticated aids are required for their use. Therefore non-projected aids can be easily used with good results.

Lastly, the activity aids include field trips, excursions, exhibitions, museums, demonstrations and dramatisation. Organisation of various activities in and outside the campus make the programmes effective as well as interesting. Planning, execution and evaluation of those activities ensure better effects and help improve these aids to bring about quality in education.

Instructional aids can be classified *on the basis of the kinds of experiences* they provide: The cone of experience has a broad base of direct meaningful or purposeful experience which can be provided mostly through instructional aids consisting of real objects, specimens and methods or activities like field visits, observations, experimentations etc. As we move away from the base towards abstractions (viz. verbal messages) we come across many instructional aids which provide indirect or vicarious experiences. T.V. programmes, video cassettes, and case studies provide more life-related meaningful experiences whereas audio cassettes, radio etc., tend to provide only verbal experiences.

According to the learners' control aids can be classified not in categories, but are continuous. For example, while using textbook or an audio tape, the learner can use and learn from them at his or her own pace, he/she may go back and read the paragraph or listen to a portion of the programme according to his need and convenience. Hence these aids are learner-controlled. On the other hand, a T.V./radio programme when listened to by a learner, the message is transmitted at a stretch without his intervention, even though it may not be according to his pace or interest. Thus mass media like radio or TV cannot be controlled by the learner who may of course switch it off if he is not interested in it. Therefore various aids can be arranged in a continuum ranging from no control to high control by the learner.

According to their reach, instructional aids can be classified *on the basis of the size of the group of learners* or an individual learner for whom they are meant and utilised. Take an example of a Programmed

Lesson or a Computer-Assisted Instructional(CA) programme which is prepared for individualized learning. It takes into account the difficulties usually encountered by an individual learner who is learning on his or her own without any help from others. Non-projected aids like maps, charts and models are used for a small group of learners. A class consisting of about 50 students can take advantage of these aids. Projected aids, however, like films, film-strips and slides, can be shown to about 80-100 students sitting at a place. Mass media like radio, T.V. and newspapers can reach thousands of audience at a time.

Textbooks

In education, textbooks are the oldest type of learning materials that are being used at present also. These are books prescribed for study in educational institutions. According to some, a textbook is a manual of instruction or a book containing a presentation of the principles of the subject used as a basis of instruction. The famous English essayist Bacon has aptly defined the textbook as 'a book designed for classroom use, carefully prepared by experts in the field and equipped with usual teaching devices.' All this indicates that textbook is meticulously used by students as learning material over the years.

The Dictionary of Education has defined a textbook as a teacher's tool. But the Encyclopaedia of Educational Research has given a comprehensive difinition of the textbook both from thematic as well as physical point of view. It says, in the modern sense, and as commonly understood, the textbook is a learning instrument usually employed in schools and colleges to support a programme of instruction. In ordinary usage the textbook is printed, it is non-consumable, it is hard bound in the hands of the learner. Textbooks indicate the standard of education, specially the standard of the subject concerned. A textbook helps a teacher to know the curricular needs in vivid and concrete manner. It supplements the teacher's teaching in the classroom. It also shows and suggests the methods of teaching and evaluating students.

Characteristics of Textbooks

i) The textbook must be prescribed or approved by the competent authority.

ii) It is normally printed and illustrated as well as bound with suitable get up for the intended age-group.

iii) It is a standard book in a particular branch of study containing a body of well-organised and carefully selected materials. Suitable to a particular class or classes.

iv) It is a manual of instructions for teachers and students in a particular branch of study.

v) It reflects the principles of teaching and approach in order and has a status of a tool of teaching and learning.

vi) It is prepared by one or a group of subject experts or specialists in the field of subject with a view to making it free from all factual flaws and thematic errors.

vii) It is meant for a particular group of learners with a common chronological age and background of knowledge and experiences.

viii) It is not only learning material, but also a teaching device.

ix) It is a common measuring rod both for teachers and taught indicating to the former what they are required to teach and to the latter what they are supposed to learn.

x) It also reflects the changing concept of education, emerging social needs and aspirations.

xi) It is an educational thermometer or barometer to point out the warmth or pressure of various forces and philosophies.

xii) Sometimes it leads and sometimes it follows the educational activities-methods and practices.

Utility of Textbooks

i) The textbook is used both in formal and informal situations of instructions.

ii) It is used in situations of classroom teaching or self-study.

iii) It furnishes the scattered bits of knowledge in a concentrated form and systematic as well as sequential units.

iv) The modem idea of providing a "core curriculum" or general knowledge/education in a well-synthesized and compact manner is possibly better realized through quality text-books specially designed for the purpose.

v) Since the textbook presents the content of a discipline in an embroynic form, its quick and repeated references give ample opportunities for reinforcement of learning.

vi) The textbook gives a visual impression of the subject matter read by pupils from time to time which ensures better retention.

vii) Like films, television/radio programmes and other electronic media, textbooks do not provide only "instantaneous communication", but constant flow of information, allowing sufficient time for reading at one's speed and interest.

Limitations

i) Textbooks are traditional and stereotyped learning materials which do not allow free thinking, innovative ideas and refreshing presentation.

ii) As a corollary to the above, textbooks become dry, dreary and drab lacking interest and motivation of learners.

iii) Very often textbooks become outdated and superflous due to explosion of knowledge and information.

Handbooks

The handbook is mainly meant for teachers and its importance is not yet realised adequately. Its need becomes imperative when teachers' competency is grossly inadequate and under changed educational system, textbooks are found quite deficient as a learning material. The teachers' pedagogic training also very often effects the transaction of textbooks. It is desirable that teachers' handbooks should accompany textbooks for effective teaching-learning process.

Characteristics of Handbooks

i) The teacher's handbooks should contain general objectives of teaching the subject, specific objectives, and learning outcomes to be achieved.

ii) There must be a content analysis with teaching/learning points.

iii) Every teaching/learning point must be presented in meaningful situations/activities.

iv) The methods of teaching different topics/lessons must be suggested therein.

v) Hints for audio-visual aids/activities must be given for their utilisation in the classes.

vi) Various important skills should be mentioned and exercises/ activities be described for training.

vii) Tests/questions must be given for evaluating the students performance/teaching-learning process.

Utility of Handbooks

Handbooks are desirable instructional materials. But these are felt essential, when higher content topics are introduced or new methods are asked to be followed in the classrooms. Sometimes new philosophy or general objectives with consequential changes in specific objectives are visualised. Unless these are explained to the teachers through training and handbooks, the very prupose will be defeated. For example, teachers' handbooks in English should have the syllabus/curricular requirements, teaching objectives, outlines of each topic to be dealt with, various teaching points and main structures to be mentioned and the procedures/methods for treating them should be explained, with appropriate oral and aural training strategies, audio-visual materials/ media and situations/activities for transaction and evaluations.

Teachers' Handbooks are to be prepared in such a way that they can be "friend, philosopher and guide" to the teacher. That is why, some handbooks are named as "Guidebooks." These are essential for effective use of textbooks and proper transaction of the curricula.

Limitations

Handbooks due to their very nature and functions of helping teachers are criticised to be "spoon feeding." These are to be developed by experts with adequate subject knowledge, necessary pedagogical training and good teaching experience. They must also have creative ability for improving situations/activities. Hence they are rare persons and not available so easily.

In the handbooks, guidance is given to teachers. No attempts are made for providing the same to students who need such material badly. That is why, workbooks are suggested and developed for students who are required to learn through sufficient drills/practices and exercises given therein. Workbook is regarded as a supplementary learning material giving details for students practices and responses. Hence, handbooks should be prepared with the detailed suggestions for organising various activities as well as for helping students for proper practices and exercises.

Programmed Learning (PL) Materials

Programmed Learning (PL) is a technique of self-instruction. The pupil can learn by himself with the help of the programme. The programmes can be in the form of a printed book or a recorded tape or cassettee fed into machines which are called PL materials. No teacher is required to teach students. In PLM, knowledge or information is given in small steps and students are required to respond to stimulate its different steps. The PLM is developed in such a way that students can easily understand and make correct responses. It can also be verified in the PLM itself whether the students' responses are correct or not. After making correct responses, the student can go ahead step by step. In case of mistakes or incorrect responses, he is required to read again and try to understand the mistake himself. Thus PLM enables students to learn themselves according to their own ability.

Characteristics of PLM

PLM has the following characteristics.

i) *Small steps:* The new knowledge or information is divided into small parts, or steps are arranged in a sequence in such a way that the student can give the correct response to a step and go ahead in learning himself. In case he fails to make correct response, he can repeat the step and get correct response. It is presumed that in at least 90 per cent of steps students will be able to make correct responses. If a large percentage of students cannot respond correctly, it is taken that the steps have not been prepared properly and need to be rewritten.

ii) *Student's Responses:* The student is required to give his response to each step. In the book form of PLM he is to write a word or a phrase or a sentence. In the machine he indicates his response by pressing the correct button. If his response is correct, he can go to the next step and in case of incorrect response he has to reapeat the process and learn.

iii) *Self-pacing:* The student can make progress in learning according to his own pace based on his ability and interest. The teacher does not regulate the pace of learning which is completely individualised.

iv) *Immediate Feedback:* As soon as the student makes response to a step, he is able to know immediately whether his response is correct or not. This enables him to make progress in learning quickly.

v) *Reinforcement:* Thorndike's Law says that if a response to a stimulus is followed or accompanied with satisfying experience, the response is reinforced. If it is followed or accompanied with dissatisfying experience, the response is not strengthened. The former is called positive reinforcement and the latter is known as negative reinforcement. In PLM, positive responses are mostly forthcoming and accordingly learning is reinforced and promoted adequately.

vi) *Evaluation:* PLM provides for recording the student's responses at every step. It is therefore possible to go through the record and ascertain his progress of learning. After successfully completing one step, he can go further. Thus, evaluation of a student's learning takes place and he is given green signal i.e., to go the next step, may be a difficult one. If his evaluation result is not satisfactory he is to repeat and relearn the step. Thus speedy evaluation helps the learner to make progress according to his own pace, and to revise the material if it is not found suitable.

Types of PLM

There are mainly five types of PLM as given below:

i) Linear or extrinsic
ii) Branching or intrinsic
iii) Computer-Assisted Instruction (CAI)
iv) Mathetics
v) Learner-controlled

i) Linear or Extrinsic: This type of PLM is developed according to the Skinner's principles of operant conditioning. As the name implies, in a linear PLM all the learners advance in a single series of short steps which are designed to ensure a high rate of correct response to the frame. Irrespective of their back-ground, all learners have to pass through the same fixed sequence of frames determined by the programmer. The learner starts from his initial behaviour to the terminal behaviour following the straightline sequence. A diagram of the linear PLM is given below.

1 2 3 4 5 6 7 8 9 10

The responses are controlled by the programmer and the learner must respond to each and every frame for learning. Feedback to the responses is readily available. Sometimes an additional stimulus is given as prompts or hints or cues. Linear type involves active participation. Every learner proceeds at his own pace. This type is also extrinsic as it depends heavily on external factors like computer.

ii) Branching of Intrinsic: Crowder who originated this type of PLM believes that learning is communication and it takes place during the student's exposure to new materials. In branching type, multiple-choice questions are asked. If the learner selects the correct response, his response is confirmed. If he selects the wrong response, he is led to a material explaining as to why he is wrong. The format of this type is given below.

For example, Information.

Answer.

i) .... page 34
ii) .... page 2
iii) .... page 31
iv) .... page 18

The learner enjoys freedom to choose his own path in the light of his background of the subject matter. He also knows where lies the mistake if committed. This kind of PLM is therefore more challenging.

iii) Computer-Assisted Instruction: It is a natural growth of application of the principles of programmed learning. The first major attempt in Computer Assisted Instruction (CAI) was the Programmed Logic for Automatic Teaching Operations (PLATO). CAI has two main components (i) hardware (machine like computer) and (ii) software (the programme or book). Programme is stored in the computer and utilised for learning. CAI is used at all stages of education from schools to universities.

iv) Mathetics: Mathetics comes from the Greek word 'Mathein' which means to learn and this kind of PLM was developed for the first time by Gilbert. It is a job-oriented technique of teaching most specifically suited to skills training. It utilises the principles of motivation. Mathetical programmes have been developed in the areas of psychomotor skills but attempts have also been made in the filed of congnitive and affective domains.

Utility of PLM

It has been universally realised that PLM is a very useful aid to teaching-learning process and for achievement of educational objectives. Both the developed and developing countries have made use of PLM at various stages of education. A good number of intellectual abilities can easily be taught through the utilisation of PLM.

PLM. can effectively be used for inspiring students to creative thinking judgement. Good teachers can be freed from the humdrum of routine classroom activity, with the help of PLM. The introduction of PLM in the western classrooms has revolutionised education by solving many social and emotional problems.

PLM has given new thrust in the direction of individualised instruction which caters to the needs of individual students of the class. Besides, PLM as self-learning device makes learning more interesting and effective. Students therefore learn faster through the PLM and understand the concepts very well and their achievement is found better.

Students are motivated and interested to learn with PLM as it meets individual difference, and instructional objectives are better realised through PLM uses. Due to better comprehension, the knowledge and skills are retained for a longer period.

Limitations of PLM

i) The student's behaviour is very much restricted as PLM does not provide for his free activities/learning. This also kills his creativity.

ii) As the students do not need the teacher nor the company of other classmates, they feel dehumanised.

iii) Learning through PLM becomes dull, drab and monotonous. The learner fails to sustain his interest and attention as the process is time-consuming.

iv) The student does not get any scope for novelty and discovery as he is required only to stick to the rigid line of the programme.

v) On the other hand, branching type of PLM provides a lot of responses, and students without understanding the subject can guess one of them.

vi) For small children, this device is also not suitable and they may find difficulty in locating the right response.

vii) Sometimes no sequence is maintained in branching type of PLM and it adversely affects the teaching-learning process.

Modules

According to the International Encyclopaedia of Education (1994p.3886). A Module is a unit of curricular material, complete in itself, to which further units may be added for the achievement of larger tasks or more long-term goals."[1] Originally this term was used in architecture as a standared of unit of measurement, a unit of size for construction of building. The Encyclopaedia Britannica (1964 p.647) says "Most of architects and producers of buildings materials continue to use modules based on their own special needs and interests without coordination."[2]

Modules are now commonly used in education, particularly in Distance Education such as IGNOU, Kota and some other Open Universities. The module had its origin in short, credit-awarding course in higher and further education in the foreign countries. Subsequently, the system has spread in a variety of formats worldwide to all sectors of education and training. There are two approaches to module development. The first one begins with the established subject matter which is broken down into smaller units that are used as sequential stepping stones towards clear understanding of the content. The second approach takes the pupils (as its starting point) who are given modules from which a wide range of programmes are constructed to meet individual needs. As an example of such modules the "Self-Instruction Modules for Teacher Education through Distance Education Mode" produced by NCTE-1997 may be mentioned here.

Characteristics of Modules

i) Module is a well designed self-instructional or self-learning material.

ii) It has enormous flexibity to accommodate and for appealing to students as well as teachers.

iii) It provides ample motivation to students.

iv) It can be "banked upon" for repetitive uses.

v) It has adequate relevance for the course.

vi) It suggests a series of activities.

vii) Its course content is presented step by step in order to reach the goal.

viii) There are tests for self-assessment.

ix) The modular construction of curricular material is sequential in nature.

x) It is a specific and small instructional unit.

xi) It is self-paced employing various types of media having specific steps ranging from objectives to evaluation.

xii) Modules are a comprehensive strategy of instruction.

Utility of Modules

A module is now popular learning material developed on the principles of self-instructional methods. Its origin and development is not far too seek. Hence its uses of late are multiplied and getting popular. In 1976 at Tagaytaj City in the Philippines, a workshop was organised for developing and application of learning materials. It reported "a module is a learning opportunity organised around a well-defined topic which contains the element of instruction, specific objectives, teaching activities and evaluation".[3]

Gabriel (1981) observed, "Module is a learning strategy, of a system with a set of definite objectives to meet the divergent learning styles and individual differences by personalised instruction using multisensory approach and built in evaluation schemes." NCERT (1979) in the context of Comprehensive Access to Primary Education (CAPE)

Programme metioned that "Module is a self-contained unit with a definite set of expected behavioural outcomes, providing an experience of series of experiences resulting into learning or problem-solving."4 Modules were developed byNCERT for involving teachers in the universalisation of primary education. The steps are (i) module statement (ii) prospectus (iii) pretest (iv) pre-requisities (v) resources (vi) objectives (vii) learning experiences or activities (viii) self-checks and assignments (ix) post-test and (x) model answers to self-checks.

Sansanwala (1988) mentioned the following presentation of activities like reading a book, watching a film, discussing in a group, working in a laboratory, writing some assignments etc.. The style of presentation in a module takes care of individual differences in interests, potentiality, tastes and attitudes of learners. A great number of opportunities is provided to the learner to understand the prescribed subject matter. Limited studies so far conducted in this field such as Mukhopadhyay and Balguruswamy (1981) and Sharma (1982) indicated that teaching college students with modules was found significantly more effective than teaching in traditional methods.

Limitations of Modules

Modules are not entirely free from shortcomings and the limitations found therein are as follows:

i) Both students and teachers may be fully motivated, but an adequate system of monitoring the progress and recording achievement is necessary for ensuring effectiveness.

ii) If the module organisation is complex and most of the students are not able to understand the same, its use may not be effective.

iii) It is complained that curriculum developed through modules is apt to be fragmented in the process.

iv) Hence utmost care is to be taken for tight control and close coordination for development and utilisation of the modules.

Steps of Development of Materials

Students admitted into distance education such as Kota Open University are to be provided with inter alia, instructional materials that enable students to learn themselves with or without others' interventions. These are mostly self-learning materials developed according to the principles of PLM and as per certain guidelines or steps, which are discussed as follows:

Writing Instructional Objectives

For writing any materials for students who are required to cover a prescribed course of studies, the first step is to identify and state the instructional objectives. The instructional objectives have to be specified in term of the expected learners' behaviour. The subject matter has to be analysed into small units so that they can be organised in a meaningful sequence with reference to the expected learners behaviour.

An instructional objective is a desire or aim expressed through a statement to bring about a proposed specific change in the learner. The proposed change in the learner should be laid down in terms of specific behaviour of the learner. Such behaviour can be expected from a learner after he has read the material. It should also be expressd in terms of end behaviour which can be observed and evaluated. The writing or statement of instructional objectives should be such that evaluation tools based on these objectives can be constructed and used to determine if the objectives have been achieved. In the meantime, content of the material is determined through content analysis and then it is to be made clear that the statements of objectives should be clear-cut, pin-pointed and specific.

The first step is to specify the behaviour that is to be accepted as evidence that the learner has achieved the objective. Each objective should indicate one particuir kind of end behaviour and as such there should be separate objectives for various end-behaviours expected of the learner at the end of the lesson/ programme. Then it is necessary to specify the acceptable level of learner's performance. It should also outline the conditions under which the desired behaviour can be expected to occur.

Content Analysis

Content analysis is a kind of task analysis in which the content or subject matter is analysed into subtopics and subtopics into elements and these are arranged into a logical sequence. This is purely academic or educational in nature. According to I.K.Davies, "It is the analysis of topic or content unit to be taught, into its constituents or elements and arrange them in a logical sequence". That is, a content is broken down into its elements. Each element may be performed by using specific tactics and the specific objectives can be realised. The elements are arragned in a logical sequence, so that learning can be facilitated and the teacher with imagination and insight can synthesis the elements of the content.

The teacher makes use of different sources for a content analysis and is able to present the correct structure of the content. He should have the mastery over the content. The sources essential for content analysis are as follows:

i) Study of standard textbooks
ii) Considering the needs of the learners
iii) Keeping in view the objectives of teaching learning.
iv) Considering the examination system.
vi) Use of teaching aids
vii) Teacher's own skills of teaching.

Content analysis is based on the needs of students of particular grade or age-group. Content is taught according to the student's ability and background. The teacher should consult the best books avilable on that content and determine the appropriate content structure. He can review the answer/examination papers. The objective type tests require specific but less elements, whereas essay type questions call for elaborate and more elements of content. Hence, examination system influences the content structure. Important characteristics of the content element are the following:

i) The student can show through his behaviour that he can understand the element.
ii) The comprehension of an element can be evaluated by a test/ question.
iii) The level of the element can be examined by behaviour of the student.
iv) The level can be knowledge, comprehension, application etc.
v) The understanding of different elements can be tested with the help of students' behaviour.
vi) The response received on an element can indicate the change in behaviour.

Writing the Text

The content elements have to be arranged in a logical sequence for writing the text. The sequence principles are as follows:

i) From known to unknown
ii) From simple to difficult
iii) From concrete to abstract
iv) From observation to logical thinking
v) From parts to whole.

The arrangement of elements according to the above principles can ensure psychological validity. Content elements on a particular aspect or topic can form a unit or step. Each unit is meaningful and quite different from one another. For writing the effective text, the writer has to keep the following points in view. Text must be written primarily for the purpose of helping students. The students must be of more or less specific and more or less uniform group of persons. They are to be imparted some prescribed body of knowledge, understanding, application, attitude, skill etc.. This implies the following considerations.

Firstly, the text is to be written with specific objectives. Secondly, it is meant for a uniform group of learners of similar age-group and experience. Thirdly, it should not be regarded as the sole means of gaining learning experiences. Fourthly, as a corollary to the above, the text writer has to select subject matter with care and expertise. Taking into consideration the learners' needs and instructional objectives, the writer must try to give the latest ideas on the topic. Otherwise the text may be out-dated soon. The author must be conscious of certain criteria which state (a) what must be known (b) what should be known and (c) what could be done.

The presentation of the subject matter in an effective order with sufficient pedagogical and mathetic skills is a great task for the writer. Since easy assimilation of content elements is essential for modification of behaviour, all this should be presented in a psychological order. Both completeness and coherence of the subject matter are desirable. Uniformity should be maintained throughout the presentation. The content material to be given in the text are mainly of six types (a) introducing material presenting new learning experiences on the basis of existing experiences of the learners (b) augmenting materials-new materials intended for learning (c) integrating material-new knowledge to be integrated with previous one (d) generalisation material-summary of the new learning experiences in a precise and sufficient manner (f) application material-applying new data and skills in graded exercises.

Language is the next important point for consideration. It should be intelligible as well as interesting. Students' vocabulary or language level must be kept in mind. The length of sentences and paragraphs, reading and comprehension rate of students etc. are to be taken into account. On the whole, in writing the text, the principles of PLM are to be adopted for facilitating self-study.

Validity

Validity, as we know, is a characteristic of the material that serves the purpose for which it is meant. In other words it refers to the extent to which the material developed for a particular pupose serves the same purpose. Of course, we have discussed so far, more in the context of a test than in connection with the material. For example, Garrott says, "The validity of a test depends upon the fidelity which it measures what it purports to measure." According to Stanley and Hopkins "The validity of a measure is how well it fulfills the functions for which it is being used the degree to which it is capable of achieving certain aims. That is, validity of the material can be measured in the context of the objectives which are set for realisation." As regards the nature of validity, it is said that validity refers to the results or outcomes of the material. Validity is also a matter of degree. That is, we cannot say accurately a material is valid or invalid. We therefore have to describe validity in terms of degrees such as high validity, moderate validity and low validity. Validity is also considered in relation to the specific purpose, because it is found that an instructional material may have high validity for a particular purpose, but the same material is found to have low validity for another pupose.

In educational measurement, three important types of validity are used, viz (a) content validity (b) criterion-related validity and (c) construct validity.

For our purpose of validation of instructional materials, content validity is of great use and relevance. A teacher makes use of achievement tests to measure/assess the knowledge of his pupils in different content areas. Such tests are designed to know how well a pupil has mastered specific knowledge or skill in a course of study. While developing material, the writer has to see whether all the instructional objectives have been taken care of, in the treatment of the content. All objectives need to be covered in the material. It may not be possible to measure all conjectives for validation purpose. The essence of content validity is, therefore sampling. According to Gronlend "Content validity is the extent to which a test measures a representative sample of the main tasks under consideration." In this context, content validity refers to the extent to which the material is representative of the entire content areas and instructional objectives. That is why, content validity is also known as curricular validity.

With a view to ensuring adequacy of content validity, the writer of the instructional material should adhere carefully to course outlines or the objectives set for the purpose. As the content validity is based upon rational judgement of specialists and subject experts, it is, therefore called rational validity or logical validity. Validation thus seeks to ensure that the entire course content is covered as per the instructional objectives set for the material.

Integration with Teaching Aids

Instructional materials have to be properly integrated with suitable teaching aids for promoting effectiveness of the teaching-learning process. Illustrations, maps, charts and other print materials can be used in texts/discussions/narration methods. Demonstration method can make use of instructional material with slides/transparencies. There are no hard and fast rules for integration of instructional materials with teaching aids. The teacher, according to the resources available, can utilise the aids in integration of instructional materials.

Audio cassettes, radio lessons, video lessons, ETV programmes and Computer Assisted Instruction are often produced and made available to the students of distance education for their utilisation alongwith the self-instructional materials developed and distributed to them earlier. A bright model of such integration is evident in the British Open University in which learners after their enrolment/admission to the courses are provided with appropriate kit boxes, slides, charts, transparencies etc., alongwith printed self-instructional materials and a copy of the schedule of radio and TV programmes that are produced and broadcast in time for their information and utilisation. There is a wide range of instructional materials starting from print materials like textbooks, handbooks to programme learning materials including modules which are produced with specific objectives to deal with a fixed quantum of content knowledge, comprehension skills etc. Generally the self-instructional methods/ strategies are adopted for developing the instructional materials. Different types of materials have various purposes as well as limitations which need be taken care of while developing the materials.

Teaching Aids

Teaching aids are used to enable the learners to achieve the learning objectives effectively and interestingly. There are audio-visual aids such as blackboard, maps, charts, globes, pictures etc., which are traditional in nature. Now-a-days electronic media have come in a big way and are apt to influence not only communication and education, but also the manner and behaviour, lifestyle, attitudes, and interests of the clientele. These media and materials provide direct as well as vicarious or improivised learning experiences to the students at all levels of education. These include traditional aids as well as electronic media evolved from time to time in large variety and great novelty.

Learning becomes effective when students are actively involved in the process. To the extent his different senses are related, his learning becomes successful to that extent. For using various senses in the teaching-learning process, different materials are utilised in the classrooms. The learning experiences are thus made quite relevant, meaningful and effective. That is why, these aids are called 'multi-sensory materials', or 'instructional aids' or 'instructional materials.' These materials mainly being of two kinds, audio and visual, they are known as 'audio-visual aids' or A-V materials. As these aids are to be used as an integral part of the entire learning situation and are not just ancillary or supplementary, many educatros are not happy with the term 'aids.' Therefore, the term 'material' is safely used and sometimes the term, 'technique' is also used to mean how these materials can be used.

Objectives

After going through the module, you will be able to

- know the role and importance of audio-visual teaching aids
- classify teaching aids on the basis of their characteristics
- acquaint yourself with the various uses and applications of these aids
- enlist a number of guidelines for preparation of some selected teaching aids viz - charts, models, slides, transparencies and cartoons.

Types of Teaching Aids

According to the Sense-Stimulation:

The teaching aids or the audio-visual materials may be divided into three categories: (I) visual (II) audio and (III) both audio-visual. The materials which appeal only to the sight are of the first category. Examples of these materials are slides, film strips, transparencies, silent motion pictures and projections with the opaque, the techistoscope and the over-head projector. Other materials trditionally used in the schools are textbook, illustrations, photographs, prints, graphs, charts, maps, globes etc., which may be taken as visual aids. The chalkboard, felt board and bulletin board are also visual materials appealing only to the sense of 'sight.' Displays and exhibits like specimens, mock-ups, electric maps, diagrams and some dramatisations like pageants, pantomimes, puppetry and dancing are regarded as successful visual materials.

Secondly, radio, gramophone, tape recorders and different magnetic recordings provide audio materials which are appealing to the sense of hearing only. Thirdly, television programmes, tape slide programmes video tape recordings and films are materials which appeal to both eyes and ears and are very effective audio-visual materials. Dramatic plays, role-playing, socio-drama, verse choirs etc., are a few types of dramatization that can be used with satisfying results.

These three types of materials either audio or visual or both audio-visual cannot be exclusively categorised. There is no distinct compartmentalisation and the list of such materials is not exhaustive. Imaginative and resourceful teachers can invent, explore and discover various sources collecting and developing these materials.

According to Projection Facilities Available:

Audio-visual aids are also divided into (I) Projected, (II) Non-projected and (III)Activity aids. When aids are projected on screens or even against white-washed walls to give an enlarged image of the material, they are called projected aids. Projected aids include slides, film-strips, films, and transparencies which bring about better results and are more effective. The darkened room reduces distractions and the bright image on the screen secures the attention of learners. By the use of different colours, the aids become more attractive and impressive.

Non-projected aids are generally still materials including maps, charts, globes, models, display boards, bulletin boards etc., These aids are not so costly, and no sophisticated aids are required for their use. Therefore non-projected aids can be easily used with good results.

Lastly, the activity aids include filed trips, excursions, exhibitions, museums, demontrations and dramatisation. Organisation of various activities in and out of the campus make the programmes effective as well as interesting. Planning, execution and evaluation of those activities ensure better effects and help in improving these aids to bring about quality in education.

According to the Learner's Control:

Aids can be cissified not in categories, but in a continuum. For example, while using textbook or an audio tape, the learner can use and learn from them at his or her own pace, he/she may go back and read the paragraph or listen to a portion of the programme according to his need and convenience. Hence these aids are learner-controlled. On the other hand, a TV/radio programme when listened to by a learner, the message is transmitted at a stretch without his intervention, even though it may not be according to his pace or interests. Thus mass media like radio or T.V. cannot be controlled by the learner who may of course switch it off if he is not interested in it. Therefore various aids can be arranged in a continuum ranging from no control to high control by the learner.

According to learner's reach:

Teaching aids can be classified on the basis of the size of the group of learners or an individual learner for whom they are meant and utilised. Take an example of a programmed lesson on a Computer-Assisted Instructional (CAI) programme which is prepared for individualized learning. It takes into account the difficulties usually encountered by an individual learner who is learning on his or her own without any help from others. Non-projected aids like maps, charts, models are used for a small group of learners. A class consisting of about 50 students can take advantage of these aids.

Projected aids, however, like films, film-strips, slides, can be shown to about 80-100 students sitting at a place. Mass media like radio, T.V., newspapers can reach thousands of audience at a time.

Charts

Chart is either or both graphic and pictorial representation designed for the orderly and logical visualisation of relationship between facts or information and ideas. It uses only graphics or pictures or both graphics and pictures to represent a large mass of data or to show their progression. It may be related to an individual or an institution, an object or incident, an idea or ideas which are represented for easy reference. For example, now-a-days, a large number of dowry deaths are published in the newspapers. One can compile and classify all information relating to dowry deaths over a period of a month or a year, datewise or monthwise and a particular variable, say time gaps after the marriages were held, is taken for a chart. Thereby it can show deaths taking place within a week, a month, a quarter, a half-year, a year or two, three, four, five, six, seven years. The chart can easily represent the progression of the incident.

Charts are useful at various stages of teaching and in different classes. Their importance lies in the very nature of representation and communication. The desired information, facts and numerical data relating to a particular subject or incident are visually represented in a beautiful and pictorial form. They prove more effective in the task of systematic presentation of facts, ideas and relationship than other graphics-pictures, graphs, diagrams and photographs. For instance, the inner structure of a coal mine, the functioning of various subsystems and their inter-relationships can be better represented in a chart than in a picture or a photograph. Similarly, a polling booth and its functioning can be better shown in a graph than in other traditional media or material.

Utility of Charts

The different uses of charts are given below :

- To present data and information in a summarised form.
- To show the relationships through comparison and classifications.
- To give the visual representation of the abstract ideas and facts.
- To enable learners to get clarification and meanings at a glance.
- To facilitate discussion and narration on a particular issue or problem.
- To create interest, draw pupils attention and provide motivation in a topic or issue.
- To generate awareness about the gravity and seriousness of the issue or problem.

Variety of Charts

There are, on the whole, six types of charts. These are development, pictorial, tabular, genealogical, flow and skills.The developmental or progress chart is very commonly used. The pictorial chart is used to present facts through interesting illustrations.The tabular chart is widely used to bring out a mass of related data in a compact form. The genealogical chart is extensively used in history and biographical books to show dynasties and generations. The flow chart is used to show a process or sequence in various subjects like political science, industry or government. It is also called organization chart for showing relationships and inter-relationships in an organisation.The skill or experience chart is an orderly presentation of skills and experience items prepared by teachers for showing language skills, planning skills etc., for evaluating pupils' activities.

In our situation we have the following six kinds of charts which are commonly used and are now discussed as follows:

i) *Tree chart :* The figures given in this chart look like a tree. Several roots of the tree show the sources or resources or reasons of an event or problem. Similarly the trunk and branches give an idea of the structure, dimensions, categories and classifications. The leaves and flowers of the tree may show the contributory factors and outcomes. All types of tree charts are utilised for showing growth,development and changes resulting from a series of factors combined, gradual development and final results.

ii) *Time Chart:* Time chart is used for showing the sequence of time of various events or for depicting chronologically all the happenings relevant to the development of a process, certain organisation or any problem.

iii) *Issues Chart:* This chart is used for highlighting the contrasting views of individuals and organisations on a burning issue or problem.

iv) *Flow Chart:* This chart is meant for representing an organisation or an industry or an hierarchy of structure administrative or supervisory. Various geometrical designs like triangles, quadrangles, circles and arrow marks are given to indicate the development of an organisation or a system.

v) *Table Chart:* This chart represents data in tabular form. The basic importance of this kind of chart is to indicate a mass of data precisely and represents time-relationship, contrasts as well as comparisons among various events and ideas.

vi) *Pictorial Chart:* This type of chart is very attractive with illustrations, diagrams, sketches etc., which represent various ideas and objects.

Preparation of Charts

Charts are comparatively cheaper and easier for construction than many audio-visual aids. Generally these are prepared by teachers and students. Now-a-days, commercial firms have come up for producing various types of charts on mass scale at cheaper rates. But specific purpose charts are produced more by teachers than these commercial firms. Involving students also in the process of constructing the charts provides effective learning experiences. In order to make charts efficient teaching aids and informative as well as interesting material, adequate planning and preparation are necessary. Inspite of variety in the nature of charts, there are common features viz., caption or title, the message or content. The message may be verbal, graphical or pictorial or a combination of both. Generally, the caption is mentioned in bold letters either at the top or bottom.

Charts are a very simple type of A.V. aids and their preparation is quite easy. Generally, charts are prepared on card paper or on mounting board. The following steps and aspects are followed in the preparation of charts:

i) *Verbal Message:* Suitable words should be selected. These words should be plain, precise and meaningful. Too many words in a chart make it clumsy and sometimes distracting. The size of the words should be quite visible and also readable by all students in a class. Important points need be highlighted in a chart. Sometimes different colours are used for differentiating one concept or idea from another. The difference in colouring also helps in catching attention and marking the differences.

ii) *Graphic Message:* Very often a verbal message is supplemented or reinforced by graphics such as graphs, diagrams, maps, pictures, figures, photographs and so on. The size of the graphics should be appropriate to that of the chart. Colours are used effectively in drawing graphics on charts or may be enlarged with the help of an epidiascope or overhead projector. Sometimes pictures, maps, graphs etc., from a newspaper or magazine or books can be pasted or superimposed on a chart. Necessary planning is made prior to preparing a chart.

Models

A model means an imitation, a replica or a copy of a thing, act or process. It is a three-dimensional aid with desired flexibility, size, complexity, safety and cost for effectively achieving instructional objectives. Models are the actual representation of the real objects. The original size or shape of the actual things is changed i.e., enlarge or reduced to suit the learning group. That is why, models are more advantageous and more convenient than actual objects or process. For example, a fly is so small in size in actual condition that it cannot be used as an aid in the classroom, but an enlarged model of a fly can easily show its structure and various organs very well. Similarly, a process or a phenomenon actually in operation cannot be explained to students, but models of the same can be effective aids in explaining the details of their functioning. Models are also most suitable from safety point of view. For instance, you cannot take your young students inside mines to show the actual functioning of the mining system. But it can be explained very well through models.

Utility of Models

To explain the details of actual objects in a clear and leisurely manner which is not possible in case of real objects:

- To show the minute parts of a system or a process through a model which cannot be done when it is actually in operation.
- To use models economically and effectively in the class-rooms.

- To use models more successfully than two dimensional aids like pictures and illustrations.
- To show the internal functioning of a system or objects which are not visible from outside with the help of cross-sectional or dissectable models.
- To use models with safety and convenience.
- To utilise models with adequate flexibility and freedom.

Various Kinds of Models

There are mainly three types of models:

i) Solid models, which are used generally for recognising external features viz relief maps (ii) Cross-section models which show internal structure like heart, brain etc. (iii) Working models which demonstrate functions or processes viz a machine, gear box etc. Each type of model has distinctive advantages and uses. Solid models are commonly used and easily prepared. Cross-section models are cutaway models that enable viewers to look into the inner design and structure of a system, say a gas engine or a coal mine. Working models are designed to show students how an organ or a process works. Sometimes, contrasting colours are used for showing different parts and how various parts are fitted to work or move together. These are very fascinating and provide exciting learning experiences to students. Engineering and medical students are familiar with such models.

Making of Models

Models can be prepared or procured from the market. Normally the solid models can be prepared by students and teachers. Previously, relief maps and models of various fruits etc., were prepared by them. But the other two kinds of models are difficult to be constructed. It is a valuable learning experience for pupis to participate in the preparation of models. Some teachers are very good in preparing models and are well-trained to do the job. They can take initiative and motivate students to collect the materials and participate in the construction of models.

Materials like cardboard, plaster of paris, wax, paper, thermocal etc., are used for preparing models. At the school stage, (in the past) students brought soft soil and teachers prepared models of various kinds, ofcourse, mainly of solid models. Even wooden models were prepared for showing the functioning of an object or system. Even in teaching Mathematics and Science, many things can be prepared to make abstract ideas concrete and real objects. In Engineering, Medicine and military training, a good number of models are prepared for making the concepts clear and meaningful.

Since models are three-dimensional, they are capable of representing the real objects in a better way than the two-dimensional graphic aids. It is also better to get them prepared in the schools, with active cooperation of students. A teacher, therefore, should acquaint himself with the steps and essentials of their preparation, which are discussed below:

i) At first the objectives and scope of preparing the models should be decided in relation to lesson.

ii) Decision about the materials to be used for preparing the model need to be taken carefully. The material may be clay, plaster, papermache, paper, card board.

iii) Real Object of the model to be prepared should ideally be kept in view or in its absence in mind. That is, at least a picture or photograph should be kept handy before preparation.

iv) A rough sketch or a rough model can be prepared at first before finally preparing the model.

Materials and Models

Since there are various types of materials ranging from cheap clay to costly plasters, we have to decide the material according to our financial provisions. Skills in preparing the model differ according to the quality of the material. These are briefly discussed as follows:

i. Clay Models

Clay available in the beds of lakes, ponds and rivers is found suitable for modelling. That clay should be without or little sand. No hard material like seeds, stones etc., should be there. At first dry clay is powdered and is added with water allowing three/four hours for softening, so that it can be squeezed in any manner we like. Then such soft clay can be immediately used for model making or be kept in fine-lined box or in an earthen pan, so that as and when we need it can be used for preparing a model.

Small models can be prepared with clay in the light of the object or graphic. In case of making big models, hay, wire, bamboo sticks or such other things can be used for giving strength to the model. Anyway, clay coating is to be given in the end and be dried or baked to add more stability. The baked clay models can be coloured according to our choice.

ii. Papermache Models

Papermache is made of any fibrous paper i.e., brown paper, news paper etc., by cutting into pieces and soaking them in water for some hours (can be heated also for getting quick results). Superflow water can be poured off and the soaked material be powdered for getting consistency and softness. A little glue and starch may be added to the pulp for making the mache more adhesive-like and unbreakable. And then models are prepared out of such mache by pressing it into a plaster of clay mould. Sometimes oil or any greasy substance is added to moulds for getting better results. Then models may be dried thoroughly and colour be applied according to our design. Occasionally, without moulds also models can be prepared out of mache making a structure with the help of bamboo sticks, wires etc., and then papermache coating is given to it.

iii. Plaster of Paris

Plaster of Paris can be used like clay and papermache for preparing models. Moulds can be used or prepared by hand with plaster of paris which is readymade for model-making with all softness and malleability. Wires and bamboo sticks were used for making structures or for freehand structuring or using moulds and plaster of paris is applied according to our requirements.

iv. Cardboard and Thick-paper Models

For preparing models, cardboard, thick paper, chart paper etc., are used with profit. Artists and artisans prepare designs of plants, animals, birds, human figures with necessary colours, costumes and other make ups. Bridges, tunnels, dams and other kinds of scientific and geographical designs can be prepared with these materials with required dexterity and skills. Various geometrical models can easily be prepared to explain the principles and formulae.

Slides

Slides are transparent pictures projected by shining light through them. The commonly used sizes of slides are 2" x 2" and 3-1/4 " x 4." Slides are used on a variety of materials-glass coated or etched or clear or sensitized. These are used as very effective teaching aids.

Advantages of Slides

Advantages in the projected pictures and photographs for effective teaching and learning are numerous. Slides-

- create interest and curiosity among students.

- explain the concepts very well.
- can be viewed by the entire class.
- can be shown in a semi-darkened room.
- can be used according to convenience.
- can be utilised according to the slow or quick learning needs.
- can be used according to our desired pace.

Two kinds of Slides

Slides are mainly of two kinds (i) handmade and (ii) photographic. Slides in series or linked together in a sequence make a film-strip or film slide or strip film. Film strip is a roll of 35 mm positive film which has sprocket holes in both sides and contains a sequence of pictures like slides.

Making of Slides

Slides are prepared easily and with inexpensive materials. That is why, in developed countries even the primary school students prepare slides not only as a learning aid, but also as a means of self-expression. Plain, coloured or etched glass, binding tape, cellophane, coloured pencils, and coloured inks are the materials needed for producing slides. With a little artistic skill, practice and ingenuity, slides can be prepared and mounted.

Photographic slides are printed on sensitized glass on a large scale by commercial firms. The teachers and students who have never developed or printed photographs/pictures, cannot prepare photographic slides so easily. These slides are made on glass plates coated with an emulsion similar to that used for making film negatives. The plates are developed, fixed, washed and dried as are other photographic plates. After the plates are fully dried, these should be projected in a lantern or small light for examination.

Then these should be mounted for making durable.

Slides can be printed from negatives by either contact, reduction or enlargement. Since contact printing is very easy, it can very well be printed by a camera. Any negative that makes a good print can make a good lantern slide. The photographic slide is merely a positive print from a negative. Thus a darkroom and ancilliary photographic facilities should be made available for developing, exposing and printing the slides.

Now-a-days, handmade slides are prepared by drawing/ writing on the transparent films. Then the film is cut into pieces and mounted on a cardboard or plastic mounts available in the market. Photographic slides can be prepared using positive films. Preplanning is necessary before preparation of slides. After selecting a topic for teaching through slides, we have to write a script. Then the filming is done to develop slides in a series of items/aspects of the topic.

The latest method of preparing slides is by using computer graphics on the colour screen and shooting the same directly from the screen. The computer provides a lot of flexibility in planning and preparing slides.

Transparencies

Overhead Projector (OHP) is an important electronic teaching aid. This machine projects an image from a transparency which is transparent. The graphic picture and message of transparencies are reflected on a screen. The teacher while teaching can use transparencies and show the graphics and message. Besides, readymade transparencies, very often the teacher can write certain important points and draw figures or pictures on glass or cellophane sheets with the help of a specific type of pen which can write various colours. The glass and cellophane can be wiped out and cleared with a cloth. Sometimes cellophane is available not in sheets, but in rolls.

Kinds of Transparencies

As discussed earlier, transparencies are readymade or are written or drawn on by the teacher in the classroom then and there in course of teaching. Commonly available cellophanes used for transparencies are in sheets. Cellophanes are also available in rolls.

Advantages of Transparencies

The advantages oftransparencies/OHP are as follows:

i. They serve as an attractive chalkboard/blackboard.

ii. While using transparencies, the teacher can face the class without any difficulty.

iii. The classroom need not be darkened for projecting transparencies.

iv. The teacher can write or draw extemporaneously on a 10" x 10" surface of transparencies.

v. Small objects can be shown on the machine simply by placing them on the projection stage.

vi. The graphics and writings on transparencies can be shown to students very clearly and colourfully.

Making of Transparencies

1. *Single transparency:* It can be prepared by writing on the

cellophane sheets with the help of an OHP pen. Even graphs, figures, and diagrams can be easily shown in different colours. Generally black, blue, red and green colours are used as they are more visible on projector screen. Coloured transparency can also be used in the classroom to give variety and attraction. Xeroxing from any printed material can be made on transparencies and magnified or reduced according to requirement. Tracing can be done on transparency from the original material.

2. *Roll Transparency:* Besides single transparency, we can use roll of transparency on which writings and pictures can be made in a sequence and can be projected on OHP in classroom while the teacher would be explaining/narrating/demonstrating. The role transferancy can be moved backward forward as required.

Whenever it is felt that something is to be added or shown alongwith the previous writing/graphics, we can make overlays by placing the addition on the OHP stage. Thus with ingenuity and dexterity, we can bring about effectiveness in the use of transparencies.

Cartoons

A cartoon is a novel way of using pictures or symbols or bold exaggerations for presenting a message or a point of view concering a personality, news, situations or events. At present, even in schools/ colleges cartoons are profitably used as a useful teaching aid for interpreting or highlighting some social, political, economic, literary and scientific data. Cartoon is more attention drawing and in a small space, gives a lot of imagination, particularly on the current happenings. Very often cartoon is blended with humour and satire.

Kinds of Cartoons

Cartoons are of different types and are prepared/used with imagination and creativity. These are used more and more in newspapers and magazines for foucssing attention of the public on certain social, political, economic and other problems and issues. Hence the types of cartoons can be innumerable.

Utility of Cartoons

Educational uses of cartoons are many due to their universal appeal irrespective of age, sex and cultural differences. The main advantages of cartoons are as follows :

i. These are very good attention-capturing devices and motivate the students.

ii. These can reveal the truth or reality about the people, events and incidents in an interesting way.

iii. These are useful in modifying behaviour and developing positive attitude, interests and character of learners.

iv. These are capable of creating humour and interest among the viewers and explaining various concepts.

v. These are helpful for providing opportunity for self-expression and creativity among children.

Making of Cartoons

Cartoons as useful teaching aids can provide information and knowledge about various subjects and current issues in an interesting way. Before preparing cartoons, it is essential to locate suitable topics and pictures from newspapers, magazines etc.. But the teacher himself should prepare cartoons according to the class room needs. Students need be involved in the process of preparation in order to maximise learning experiences.

The material for cartoons should be selected by the teacher who should keep the following points in view:

i. It should be suitable to the age, class and experience, level of students.

ii. The writing and graphics used in the cartoon should be meaningful and intelligible to them.

iii. Cartoons should be of adequate size, so that the details can be made visible to the entire class.

iv. The symbols used in the cartoon should be clear and understandable.

v. Cartoons need to be both ammusing and instructive.

vi. Students must be actively involved in the process of preparing cartoons.

vii. Cartoons should be prepared according to the educational objectives and background of students.

Teaching aids are now available in a wide variety and novelty ranging from traditional graphics to electronic materials and media. With a view to making the teaching-learning process more interesting and effective, it is necessary to select suitable teaching aids suitable to the instructional objectives and students' needs as well as their background. It is, however, desirable that besides commercially prepared readymade materials, students and teachers should join hands in preparing suitable aids according to their interests, expertise and resources available. Learner's participation and involvement enhance their knowledge, understanding and skills, and can make education more efficient and pleasurable.

Teaching Machines

Today Educational Technology is intended to make both learning and teaching processes effective as well as efficient. In view of the unprecedented explosion of knowledge in various disciplines and fields of education it is found necessary to make teaching as well as learning less time consuming and less laborious. It is also felt imperative on the part of educators to make the teaching-learning process motivating, interesting and exciting. Educational Technology does not mean only some machineries or equipment, but it consists of various means and methods as well. All the systematic approaches and techniques are put into educational practices as a part of educational technology in order to achieve instructional objectives with economy of time, money and efforts.

Teaching machines are usually hardware being used alongwith software like programmed materials. They are operated on certain fundamental psychological principles and are considered superior by many educationists on account of their better techniques and methods. The teaching machine is defined as a carefully prepared programme housed in some apparatus and presented to learners with indications whether and when their responses are right or wrong. Teaching machines are called feed-back devices as they supply knowledge of results when a student or a group of students are questioned on what they have learned.

Types and Functions

According to Norman Mackenzie, Michael Eraut and H.C. Jones (1970). "Teaching machines are normally divided into three categories: adjunctive, linear and branching. The adjunct machines developed by Pressey and his co-workers provide knowledge of results to students answering multiple choice test questions. Methods of giving feedback include lighting a bulb, allowing a punch in the corret answer space to penetrate more clearly and having chemically treated paper change colour. The term adjunctive is used because these machines are adjuncts to the main teaching-learning process. They only contain tests and they are used to test and revise material which the student has already encountered elsewhere. Linear and branching machines present original material as well as questions and answers and can, therefore, assume total responsibility for teaching a topic. The linear machines present questions step by step in a predetermined sequence, get the student to answer each question in turn and gives him immediate knowledge of results. The branching machine allows the student alternative routes through the material and uses his mistakes to determine his route, but it can only accept mutliple choice button pressing responses. None of these machines has so far been shown to have any learning advantages in higher education over programmed texts, and they impose considerable restrictions on the persons writing the materials." (pp. 50-51.)

Besides, many other resources like slide projectors and taperecorders may be used in teaching machines presenting material in media with considerable advantage. In many countries the computer is used as a teaching machine with all the flexibility which the traditional teaching machines lack. In discussing various types of teaching machines. Cream (1961, p.77) says, "There are constructed response machines in which the student writes his answer on a tape and compares it with the correct answer, which is exposed only when the students answer is covered with a plastic window (so he cannot change it after he sees the correct answer). A variation of this allows the student, after he has written his response, to uncover a clue (at the same time covering his response with a window). At this point he may write a second response if he wishes to amend the first one. The answer may then be unmasked at the same time covering the second response with the window) and both answers may then be compared with the correct answer."

There are constructed response machine in which the student does not write the response but rather constructs his answer mechanically by moving sliders.

There are multiple choice linear devices which require the student to push buttons, punch holes in paper with a stylus, pull tabs or type his answer on a keyboard all of which immediately provide some knowledge of results (i.e., right or wrong). There is a machine for branching programme which presents the programme on a microfilm viewer. The alternatives are selected by a choice of push buttons. Finally, there are computer-based systems which are still experimental but which have great promise of versatility for a variety of teaching objectives.

James W. Brown and others, (1964, p. 257) have given a comprehensive picture of different types of teaching machines.

1. This is a holder for linear constructed response (write-in) programme. It is perhaps the simplest teaching-machine configuration since its function is only to present frames one at a time and prevent cheating. It is most appropriate when writing an answer is the desired skill and where self-checking can be effectively done by the student. Research features appear in some models to provide an item analysis of student responses to guide the programme, write as he tests his programme.
2. This illustrates a typical linear multiple-choice device. It too displays frames one at a time and prevents cheating, but because the response is made mechanically, various kinds of "feedback" information can be given to the students. For example, lights or sounds may indicate correct or incorrect discriminations, correct responses may be counted automatically, so that the student may observe his record of progress. But most important, the student's knowledge of the results of his choice is instantaneous and the judgment of the correctness of an answer is made not by the student but by the machine according to the programme in it. This machine is used where recognition is more important than recall.
3. This drawing represents a device designed to present an adaptive programme. The programme which is presented to the student is modified on the basis of his responses. That is after a student responds to a frame stimulus the machine adapts to the student's background or progress or understanding as expressed through readiness. Such machines must necessarily be multiple choice devices because control of the student must be "inside" the machine. Thus far, the only way to achieve such control is through use of push-buttons to reveal the student's discriminations for the learning tasks involved.
4. This illustration suggests, the ultimate in adaptive programming devices leading towards truly automated instruction. A highly complex machine built around a computer with capacity for retaining and responding to vast amounts and infinite varieties of data. Such a device is conceived to be capable not only of accepting student responses in terms of multiple choice push-buttons, but also of accepting and responding appropriately to type written, handwritten and even spoken student responses and of adjusting its programme sequence accoidingly.

A set of criteria developed co-operatively by several nationi oorganisations of the USA stressed bases for appraising teaching machines. Since the teaching machine itself does not teach, but the programme in it does, the appraisal of any one machine must take into account the number and quality of programmes it can house and its mechanical efficiency. Teaching machines are looked upon as automatic tutors and auto-instructional devices motivating the student to play an active role in the learning process. That is why, they should be designed in such a way as to make the student an active participant in learning instead of a passive receipient.

Utility of Teaching Machines

1. In a teaching machine, feedback is immediate as a result of which the responses of the learner are reinforced without delay. This also helps in making learning more effective.
2. The subject-matter in a teaching machine is sequentially and systematically structured and presented in small steps called frames. The programmers make new material quite easy to understand as they organise the same on sound psychological principles of effective learning.
3. The use of teaching machine facilitates learning by motivating the student to work independently without the help of teachers. The continuous interaction between the learner and the programme in the teaching machine results in better learning.
4. The teaching machine is designed to be used as an auto-instructional medium making the learner an active participant in the learning process. Learning becomes effective when the learner takes an active part in the learning process. Hence the use of teaching machine promotes better learning.
5. The teaching machine maintains the accurate record of the responses of the learner on the answer tape locked inside. This objective recording helps in providing guidance to the learner and in the modification or revision of the programme for making it more effective from time to time.
6. The use of the teaching machine for rote learning and drilling is more successful as it helps in maintaining interest and motivation for a longer period. Particularly in learning certain intellectual abilities, linguistic and motor skills, teaching machine is extremely useful.
7. Teaching machine saves the teacher from a lot of drudgery resulting from drilling and routine teaching. This helps him to utilise his

energy and time so saved by the machine for better and more creative type of activities and teaching.

Limitations

Although teaching machines are getting popular with the teachers and educators and working as useful instructional aids in the advanced countries of the world, they have several limitations. Inspite of the fact that they are being introduced in the educational and training situations more and more and supplementing the teaching work in many respects, many fears and queries are raised at various quarters as to the use of this new instructional medium for better learning. The disadvantages in the use of teaching machine are as follows:

1. Teaching machines are expensive equipment and add maintenance costs on account of mechanical difficulties and disorders. Hence, the developing countries like India cannot afford to use teaching machines in their educational and training institutions at a reasonable scale.
2. Teaching machines have been developed on the principles ofoperant conditioning that mostly emerged from animal learning. Doubts are expressed as to how far these principles can be used for better and higher types of human learning. Even some recent experiments with the teaching machines in the field of human learning have revealed the lack of immediate reinforcement and feedback.
3. The assumption that instant feedback helps motivation in the learner is not accepted as a fact since the human beings, as the thinking animals, think over and over to find out his diffucluty in his performance.
4. The readymade structure of the programmes often fails to create curiosity and thinking ability of the learner. Even it becomes boring for the intelligent students who like to meet challenging tasks in learning.
5. There is loss of human touch and lively interaction in the learning process organised by means of teaching machine. This leads to lack of flexibility and interest in the system and fails to promote effective learning.

Teaching machines may be better, faster and more efficient than teachers, but they cannot replace them, not even the text-books and the other textual materials. They may help in solving the problems of quality and quantity that are so acute and massive at present. They may improve the classroom communication and the teaching-learning process. But they cannot be taken as perfect media or aids in education nor should be used for the types of learning for which they are best suited especially for rote memorisation and drilling in the language skills. The techniques and methods of reinforcement and feedback involved in the system may be introduced for effective learning. Attempts may also be made to minimize the disadvantages and remove the limitations in the teaching machines so that they can be effective self-instructional media and useful aids to teaching.

The development of teaching machines is mainly based on the psychological principles of Skinner, Thorndike, Pressey Crowder and others. The original teaching machine designed by Skinner employed simple mechanical devices to display programme frames and to reduce student responses. Pressey's early work also used a simple mechanical unit. BF Skinner at Harvard University emphasised stimulus response devices, whereas Pressy at Ohio State University laid stress on multiple-choice devices. Subsequently numerous theoretical and practical considerations entered into such dichotomy. But the common characteristics of teaching machines indicate that this device can tutor the students without assistance from a human instructor. Student's active participation is necessary and the device gives rewards to the student giving answers immediately. The learning theories and principles are also involved in the process. Pressey has devised his devices more as supplementary adjuncts to course materials and textbooks and Skinner's as replacement for texts and classroom instruction. Instead of all these developments neither Pressey nor Skinner would eliminate teachers both being interested in making more efficient use of the teacher's time in classroom.

The last development is not to use the machines at all but to use books and paper devices. Although lacking some of the control machines, there can be flexibility of rate, unit presentation and immediate knowledge of results. The student answers the question by referring to the appropriate page. The answer page tells where the choice is correct. If the answer is wrong, further instruction is given to be followed by a new question. If it is found correct, the next problem is presented.

References

1. *International Encyclopaedia of Education*, 1994, p.3886
2. *The Encyclopaedia Britannica*, 1964 p. 647
3. Reported in workshop on *Developing and Application of Learning Materials*, Tagaytej City, Philippines, 1976
4. NCERT: *Concept Access to Primacy Education Programme*, 1979

10

Computers and Software in Education

The Ministry of Education launched an important project of Computer Education in the country. It has been launched as a pilot project for introducing Computer Literacy and Studies in Schools (CLASS) in collaboration with the Department of Electronics. At the first instance, 250 schools all over the country were brought under the purview of this project and training courses were organised for teachers in the selected Resource Centres. Gradually all the schools would be covered in a phased manner. This has raised a wave of discussion in the country: Why computer in the field of education also? There has very often been hue and cry when computer has entered into the arena of industry, business, banking, examination and so on. It is usually complained that computer will replace the man and unemployment will be rampant as a result of this.

Applications of the Computer

Computers inspite of strong opposition are now extensively used in various fields of human activity. Application of the computer in industry and business is considerable. It is used in traffic control and in police investigation. But for its help, space journey would be impossible. It is utilised for student guidance as well as for marriage counselling. It assists the universities and Boards of Secondary Education in tabulating scores and grading students. Now it is also useful in sports and games at the national and international levels.

In data-processing, efficiency of the computer cannot be over-estimated. It can make very complicated calculations in a split second. It has proved its wonderful capabilities and is regarded as the most important invention after the birth of the printing process. It may be said that as the printing machine has enlarged the scope of communication, the computer has broadened the field of information and data processing. Its impact on food and material production, defence and remote sensing, scientific research and education is enormous in most of the advanced countries. The scientists and researchers having confidence in computers claim that no teacher ever born, no method ever adopted and no media ever utilised, can match the computer's efficiency.

In view of such increasing importance of the computer, students, the future citizens and employees in various walks of life, cannot afford to keep themselves aloof from this potential medium. Education even at the school stage has to provide for computer instruction. Profound technical knowledge and positive attitude as well as interest in the computer are essential pre-requisites for the successful citizens of the coming decades. Besides, some of the challenging job opportunities will be available to the young in near future.

What is a Computer?

The computer is an electronic machine working on the principles of prolonged learning that aim at individualised instruction to meet the special needs of individual learners. The computer is a flexible as well as powerful devise which can cater to these needs by storing, processing and retrieving information.

The computer is equipped with electronic circuits, keyboards recording and storage facilities. Although it is called "a dignified calculating machine", or a "glorified calculator", it has a unique capability of "memorising heaps of information and reproducing or retrieving" them whenever necessary. The procedures and languages used for recording and retrieving information are specific and peculiar. Hence, programming involves great knowledge and skills which call for training and experience for manipulation and translation of the information.

The computer usually has five important components: (i) input system, (ii) output system, (iii) a memory storage, (iv) processing equipment, and (v) a control system.

The input system converts our information into computer's language form and the output system retrieves the information into our language. The memory storage retains all the information that is fed into it through the input system. The processing system processes the data through manipulation and selects the information as required. All these functions are controlled and co-ordinated by the control system as per a particular programme.

Two kinds of information are normally fed into the computer and a programme consists of a set of instructions and an amount of information. Both sets of information are preserved in the memory storage.

Computer - A Teaching Machine

The computer is now regarded as a super teaching machine. Its use in education has been tried as an innovation and it has proved its teaching efficiency in many developed countries. The computer has been helping the teacher in the following areas: -

(i) Evaluation of students performance and classification of children according to abilities;

(ii) Preparation of timetable and schedules;

(iii) Allocation of learning materials according to individual needs and interests.

(iv) Maintenance of progress cards efficiently and confidentially.

(v) Providing information/data for guidance and reference.

(vi) Provision of direct interaction between pupils and subject-matter.

(vii) Engaging students in tutorial work;

(viii) Providing immediate feedback to students for better interaction and motivation.

Computer Assisted Instruction (CAI)

Computer Assisted Instruction, briefly known as CAI, is an interesting innovation in educational technology. Its marvels have been demonstrated and seem to revolutionise the whole spectrum of education. It has better flexibility and more versatility than any of the teaching machine. It can cater to the individual needs of many students at a time and record all the responses of all the pupils with reliability. The time taken by individual student in responding to a question and extent of correctness in the same are also recorded by the computer. All this helps the educator in planning instruction and providing relevant materials.

The CAI can deal the problem of quality in education more effectively and more flexible kind of branching is possible on the part of the computer according to the student's performance. A learner can make progress at one's pace, receive and choose the material, sequencing and level of instruction freely. Since each learner's performance is automatically recorded and can be fed back to the teacher, learner's performance can be evaluated and education be provided according to the strategy that is best suited to the individual. The teacher can be relieved from the daily routine and monotonous drilling activities. It has been experimentally proved that any lesson in any subject can be programmed for CAI if the objective is clearly defined and learning materials are represented in words, visuals and experiments.

The CAI installation usually consists of individual learning booths each with a console. Every student sits in front of the console with a television screen displaying information etc. A complete learning package suiting to his individual needs is presented, sequentially. This package may consist of video as well as audio tape-recordings, films, slides, film strips and so on. The student may make queries to the computer by means of a type-writer key-board and get answers in printed forms. The student may write the answers directly on the cathode ray tube display screen with a "light-pen" which can be evaluated by the computer. On completion of a programme, the computer records his progress and prints out a report for the teacher. Although CAI is developed on the principles of programmed learning, it also utilises the concepts of audio-visual education, communication theory, system analysis, data processing and learning theory. CAI produces learning experience effectively and efficiently. A good amount of information stored in the computer is made available to the learner more readily than by any other media. The interaction between the student and instructional programme is made more dynamic and more individualised in CAI than in any other system. But judicious pre-planning and careful programming are essential for this.

CAI is, however, extremely expensive. It is also mostly mechanical and deprived of human touch. Therefore, it is criticised on the ground that this innovation will dehumanise the educational system and the teaching-learning process will be lifeless and mechanised.

Educational technologists, therefore, suggest system approach representing an integrated, sequential and multimedia learning package. This systems approach should also consist of all relevant media, material and methods. It will not replace the teacher, but will relieve him of drudgery and dreariness. The Computer Assisted Instruction will rather bank upon the teacher heavily for constant analysis, curricular revision, better planning human guidance and counselling. A creative and committed teacher is more in demand than anything else when computer is available in education.

National Policy of Education, 1992

The provisions under the NPE, 1986 remained intact in the NPE, 1992 but more emphasis was given in the latter on Computer Education. In the beginning the coverage of schools under the CLASS Project was modest. But with a view to increase awareness of computer literacy among students, teachers and parents, more schools were taken up and more agencies were involved in the process. A notable initiative was triggered by the CLASS Project as private schools were allowed to charge fees for the said facility and professional agencies were contracted for providing the hardware and teaching inputs. The CBSE pioneered Computer Science Programme at higher secondary stage and some State Boards followed this lead. The UGC also started the Computer Education Programme by providing PCs, starting certificate, diploma and degree courses in universities and by giving computers for Central Institutions for research and higher studies. IITs and engineering colleges acquired computers and started computer science programmes in many institutions. The World Bank assisted the project for strengthening and modernising polytechnics and giving other facilities.

The CLASS Project expanded and covered many thousands of senior secondary schools and many advanced schools which implemented the CLASS Project effectively. Computer education with adequate facilities was encouraged in secondary and higher secondary schools. Access of students to computer facilities in universities, colleges and technical institutions was encouraged and computer facility was made available to students and researchers round the clock. With the resources available, computer platforms for MCA students and researchers were upgraded. The polytechnics and professional bodies were accredited by the Departments of Electronics. UGC formulated a concrete programme for motivating and encouraging teachers of Computer Science to commercially link up with the professional agencies for mutual benefit. The UGC set up effective training arrangements for college teachers and initiated the programme for starting a support paper at Master's level.

The MHRD worked with the Ministry of Information and Broadcasting, Department of Space, Department of Electronics, and Finance Ministry for augmentation of transmission facilities for educational programmes and opened a new educational channel. The CIET and UGC continued a co-ordinating role and assisted the State agencies more meaningfully both financially and academically.

Problems and Prospects

As reported earlier, computer education has assumed immense significance in the education system of the country. But it is found that people are more interested in acquiring hardware, particularly computer sets and not in developing and utilizing software suitable for the various groups of clientele. The MHRD, UGC and even the foreign agencies have come forward to finance the projects relating to computer education. But necessary steps need to be taken for giving training and providing necessary facilities for developing and using software in the teaching-learning process. Many educational institutions at school and higher education stages are now equipped with computers. Prof. S.K.Khanna, Vice-Chairman UGC rightly pointed out that there is need to look at computer education in its totality starting from school education to higher education keeping pace with changing technology. He stressed that for imparting proper training, the educational institutions must posses necessary hardware and software. In the CLASS Project computers were provided with a few CAI software, while colleges were provided with computers without any software. The CAI software is almost absent, and lack of provision of suitable software has led to gross under-utilisation or no utilisation of computers.

The manpower requirement in computer education is wide ranging i.e. from data entry operator and technician to designer and engineer of computer configuration and programmes. It goes without saying that computers can be used effectively for providing good quality education and for removing disparities between slow and bright learners as far as possible. Besides teaching various subjects, there can be versatile use of computers in research experiments and innovations for enriching curricula and improving the standard of education. Unfortunately there is lack of imagination and co-ordination in the planning, management and utilisation of computer education and unless this is removed there would be huge wastage of resources both material and human and instead of computers becoming functional and useful would be ornamental and great wastage. Therefore, adequate steps need to be taken in utilising this potential and expensive equipment for improving our education system as early as possible.

Software in Audio Production

Production is an important stage in the process of audio development. Planning production, distribution, utilisation and evaluation are five significant steps of educational broadcasting on play-back of cassettes/ tapes. These steps are inter-related, and efficiency in all these stages results in good and suitable educational radio/audio programmes. Deficiency at any one or two stages spoils the entire radio/audio programmes. Although no stage is less important, production is found to be very significant and its success largely determines the effectiveness of these programmes.

In this unit we intend to discuss the software development's various features of production, importance of audience profile, scriptwriting, tryout of the script as well as the radio/audio programmes in order to make these material effective and interesting.

After going through this part, you will be able to

- know the need and importance of software for radio/audio
- realise the importance of production of these programmes
- acquaint yourself with various features of production
- identify the need of audience profile for good production
- feel the significance of scriptwriting
- know the need for editing the radio/audio programmes

Audio Production

Among the stages of planning, production, distribution, utilisation and evaluation, production is most important step of audio/radio broadcasting. The curricular needs and objectives should be identified and planning has to be made for production of suitable audio/video programmes. Audience profile is found useful at this stage to know the needs and interests of the clientele group. After planning, suitable script is prepared by subject experts on a particular topic and then production takes place either in the studio or outside. Various steps are taken by the producer to see that the programme is recorded properly. Sound being the main strength of the radio/audio programme, the "clarity and the quality of what is heard is fundamental to the understanding of the listener" (John C.H. Ball 1974).[1]

Software Development

Hardware and software are like two wings of audio-production. All kinds of machines and equipment are essential, but the material therein on the academic input of the programme is called software. Both of them should go hand in hand to make the programme meaningful and effective. Hardware has its origin in physical and engineering sciences and software owes its origin to the social and behavoural sciences. Software is developed according to the principles of these science and is used for modification of behaviour known as learning.

Software development is closely related to psychology and pedagogy. It is very much associated with the principles of programme learning and is characteristed by task analysis, identifying objectives, selecting suitable strategies, reinforcement etc. The software approach is often referred to behaviour technology aiming at modification of behaviour or enriching learning experiences. Achievement of educational objectives is possible only through adequate use of software inputs and organisations. Procurement of hardware is one-short activity but software production is a time taking process which has to be continuous and academic by nature. Software had to be need-based, need-specific and relevant. Teachers and students can easily produce software and also programmes according to the curricular needs and provisions. "One of the major lessons of SITE is that the planning for software rather hardware requires more time. Hence the planning for software aspects must start many years prior to the planning of hardware aspects." Therefore, preplanning should be made for software development much before hardware planning and production. A systems approach to software planning and production is desirable and the entire teaching learning process should be viewed holistically with reference to the curricular needs and interests as well as abilities of the clientele group. Optimum achievement of the instructional objectives has to be emphasized for software development.

Software production for audio programmes requires a combination of content knowledge, production teachniques and communication strategy to reach the target audience. It is rightly said that as merely copying a picture from a book into a large sheet of paper does not make a good illustration, similarly just recording a chapter or story of a book does not give an audio programme. Some basic questions should be answered for understand ing the production needs. Some of these questions are-

i. Software for whom?

ii. With what needs?

iii. With what objectives?

iv. With what background experience and knowledge?

v. With what means and medium?

vi. By which agencies?

vii. With what infrastructure?

viii. With what advance preparation?

ix. What targets are set in terms of time and money?

Answers to these questions are very relevant for properly planning and producing the audio programmes. Sometimes while answering these questions we see that change in one does not suit the needs of audio production. .The stereotyped ways or outdated rules and regulation do not promote creativity and productivity. The objectives of software production may be one or more of the following.

i. To inform

ii. To entertain

iii. To impart skills

iv. To instruct

v. To solve problems

vi. To generate thinking and curiosity vii. To stimulate imagination and creativity viii. To change aptitude and interests

vii. To modify behaviour

Some of these objectives can be easily realised, but some are not so easy to be achieved. Some objectives are quite challenging and some are very stimulating. The production process is long drawn-out and adequate insight into the process is developed for ensuring effectiveness of the audio programme.

Features of Production

Before producing any programme, its medium of production, its nature, its strength and weaknesses have to be properly understood by the personnel concerned including scriptwriter and producer. Otherwise due justice cannot be done to its potentialities, nor its deficiencies can be made up and limitations can be overcome, so that programmes can be meaningful and interesting. The strengths and weaknesses of radio and audio programmes have been discussed before. Inspire of its potentialities, it suffers from a few limitations and steps are taken for effective audio production. The following points need be taken into account for production of suitable audio programmes. These are (i) Instructional Objectives, (ii) Audience Profile, (iii) Content, (iv) Format, (v) Sound/ Music Effects.

Instructional Objectives

In the curriculum, there are various provisions which are dealt with in the textbooks presented in radio and television or audio/video programmes. Some topics are identified for radio programmes in view of their presentation facilities in the same medium. There are some specific objectives and teaching points which are dealt within the audio programme and attempts are made to realise those objectives. To the extent these objectives are realised, the programme is proved to be a success proportionately.

Audience Profile

Before production of an audio programme it is essential that the producer and scriptwriter should have a clear concept about the background knowledge, experience, attitude, interests etc. "Know your audience" is the basic motto of the electronic media production. Radio/

audio programme can be planned and developed successfully with adequate knowledge about the audience. Broadcasting on audio programming without this prerequisite is a dull diction or a dry exercise. The psycho-socioeconomic and political background of audience for whom the audio programmes are mainly meant, should be given prior attention, so that the programmes can be produced effectively.

Content

As mentioned above, curricular content/provision should constitute the backbone of the programme. The audio programme should be based on the subject matter or main highlights. It may be merely a syllabus-based or an enrichment programme.

Format

The styles of presentation called format of the audio programmes should be varied. Some of these are stories, talks, discussion, interviews, demonstrations, dramatization and so on. Some topics are very good for dramatization, but not for discussion or demonstration. Some are quite effective in interviews, but not suitable for other styles. The scriptwriter should have the necessary skills and competence in developing such formats. Any interesting audio programme should be produced in a suitable format.

Sound/Music Effects

Since sound is the most important strength of the audio programmes, it is essential to make use of various sound effects and musical effects at appropriate places.

Importance and Implications of Scriptwriting

Script is the backbone of the audio programme and the basic material for the audio programme. It is not the final product, but the basis for the audio programme. It is aptly said that if you have a good script, half of the battle is won in making a good audio/ radio programme. A script is prepared to communicate a theme or an idea to listeners through radio or audio programme. The link between the scriptwriter and listeners is established through the producer who translates the script into sound. Necessary instructions should be given by the scriptwriter to use relevant and meaningful sound effects and musical sounds at appropriate places. For example, if the scriptwriter wants a boy to participate in a dialogue for a specific reason, this should be indicated in the script. If the scene on the deck of a ship is given in the script, sound of sea waves, singing of sea-gulls etc., should be suggested.

Every radio programme is introduced by a compere or an announcer. If the scriptwriter is to tell specifically to the listeners, it can be mentioned by him in the beginning very clearly. It should be indicated in the script, whether it should form a part of the script or just an announcement. But such an introduction should be brief and catchy. After making an interesting beginning, occasional attention-catchers must be used for making the programme interesting.

Similarly, the end of the script should be natural and not abrupt. But climax should not be the end. Care should be taken for a smooth, but heart touching end. In the educational audio programmes, it is desirable to make some repetitions for reinforcement and recapitulation. Such repetition should not be made haphazardly, but in a planned manner repeating only the important highlights.

Some activities can be suggested for the listeners who should not be just passive participants. Appropriate support materials may also be suggested by the scriptwriter for ensuring efficiency.

It is not desirable to show off the knowledge or use any technical jargons and very bombastic words. Simple language and style are to be preferred. No moralisation or sermonising is to be encouraged.

Too many teaching points should not be in a script and too many facts and figures are to be discouraged.

Audio Scriptwriting

Script being the basic framework of educational audio programme, utmost care should be taken to make it suitable for reflecting the above concepts and principles. In this context, the guidelines developed by the British Council Media Departments, London are found to be quite relevant as well as comprehensive. These are given below:

1. The script is the most important of an audio programme. Unless it is excellent, every other aspect of production is useless.
2. To be successful it must be written in the right language for the listener.
3. The right language is the language the listener can understand. So it must take into account the listener's background, education and interest. The writer must therefore think carefully about the structure he is going to use and the vocabulary.
4. The words the scriptwriter uses are not read by the listener-they are listened to. So the words must appeal to the EAR, not to the EYE.
5. Writing for the EYE relies on the conventions of writing-punctuation-paragraphs-type sizes-columns-headlines. The reader can go at his

own speed. He can go back to check any point of difficulty. He can stop reading, put the writing aside and return to it later.

6. Writing for the EAR is quite different. The listener can not be given too many facts. He cannot be given too many figures. It is essential to sustain his interest - therefore the script must be presented in an interesting way. It must develop logically. The radio writer may have to repeat, expand and reinforce. He must use the form of language which is simple and informal. It is SPOKEN LANGUAGE. The listener must be held - otherwise he switches off mentally.

7. How is the listener held? The radio writer must think of the listener as his personal friend....

He must talk with the listener, not at him.

He must hear in his mind all the tones of voice that will communicate the script.

He must visualise the listener.

He must read the script aloud to himself and ask -

"What do I sound like?"

"What do I mean?"

Current Status of Audio Production

As discussed earlier, the script is the basis of all work in educational media including radio or audio cassettes. It contains ideas and content to be presented in an interesting way on a particular medium - here, radio/audio. The script for radio/audio programme would be different from one for television. Scriptwriting for any medium requires an understanding of the potentials and limitations of the medium, production and distribution processes. In India, workshops are organised for developing scripts of various kinds with or without any knowledge of the medium, production and distribution technicalities. Even though they might not have heard good examples of audio programmes or audio materials like audio tapes/cassettes, the writers would be exposed to some good programmes/materials and production machines and processes. They, under the guidance of experts develop scripts of their own. They should ask and answer all the questions before they start writing scripts.

It is natural that a few drafts would not be upto the standard, because the quality of an educational audio script is not judged merely by the correctness of its information/content. That is essential but more than that the format, use of sound/music effects, ect., are also of great importance. A good script might have undergone three or four revisions and modification before it emerge as the final script.

Audio programme is dependent on an aural medium quality of what is heard and clarity of recording is of paramount importance. Reception on short waves due to variable conditions in the ianosphere, can adversely affect speech clarity. R.L. Hilliard writing about school broadcasting observed, "The conscientious radio broadcaster aims to transmit sound in such a way that the listening public will be able to understand speech clearly and enjoy the reproduction of music- After leaving the transmitter, sound is subject to all sorts of losses and quality degradations before it reaches the listeners' ears. Therefore, it is necessary to keep the technical quality of the sound as high as possible at all times while it is under the control of the station."

John C.H Ball in this context said, "By quality here we mean quality directly in relation to audibility. It is of first importance than the producer of programmes is aware of the reception conditions in the area to which he is broadcasting and that he takes them into account."[2] It is therefore, necessary that proper recording of the audio programmes and their broadcasting or play-back should be-made under favourable and congenial conditions. Hence besides production quality, listening conditions need to be suitable.

Audio programmes should be interesting any way. Otherwise these cannot be heard at all or heard, not received adequately. Ball has aptly said therefore, "The class teacher may consider the programme useful and so switch on the radio, but unless it is also 'interesting' the children will switch off their ears." Besides, content and format of the programmes, the quality in production, broadcasting and playback has to be ensured for increasing effectiveness in the educational institutions and distance education system. In the AIR we have a quite well-developed infrastructure for production of audio cassettes/tapes.

Although *Akashavani* is responsible for production of educational radio programmes, it depends on the outside resource persons for preparing scripts. However necessary editing of the script is made by the producer. A case-study of school broadcasts at Delhi revealed that "It is mostly of the nature of substituting some difficult words with simpler ones, and/or curtailing/adding the spoken matter. The accuracy of facts presented in the material is generally accepted, as no other subject matter specialist is consulted in the matter. This practice allows a material passed off for broadcast without providing a safeguard for checking its accuracy at the editing stage" This practice at New Delhi holds good for all the Akashavani Stations and the instances of errors in educational programmes are also not rare.

Hence writing of scripts free from all errors thematic as well as linguistic is very important for success of the educational broadcasting. It may be regarded as a specialised job. The script-writers are usually appointed from among subject experts which does not always happen well. Therefore care should be taken for preparing fool-proof scripts for the purpose. It is better to get them approved by subject experts and then use for production of programmes in presentable form by the producer who is a media man.

It was thought desirable as well as more practicable to train the specialist to write scripts for educational radio. In order to write suitable scripts, besides content knowledge the writer should have knowledge about various formats, audience profile, different techniques for attracting attention and sustaining interests, ability in creative expression, proficiency in language and presentation styles and techniques. During a training course or workshop, the prospective scriptwriters should be exposed to these theoretical as well as practical aspects of the programme. It should be realised that good scriptwriters are not born, but made through sincere efforts, long practice, keen interest and love for the job.

At present a good number of institutions like IGNOU and UGC through their production centres are producing many kinds of educational audio cassettes/tapes. These are being produced by groups of subject experts, and media experts and the audio materials are sold at no profit no loss basis. Besides, some private firms are also engaged in producing audio tapes for various educational courses/classes. They produce these audio tapes on commercial basis and the quality of their production is not always satisfactory.

As discussed earlier, audio tape/cassettes and radio are aural media and these programmes have their own limitations. Some people have aversion to listening only. They dislike to hear only words, words and words. Again what is heard is fleeting and changing from moment to moment. That is why, radio/audio programme is called evanscent and taxing to its audience. In view of these handicaps, attempts are being made to provide support to the spoken words. Illustrations are used to explain, to create interest, to motivate and to help concentration.That is, vision is supplemented with audio or radio. This is done in many ways - viz., by showing pictures or flash cards or by projecting slides or film-strips even by organising activities. France Berrington and Anne Gibson (1978) have rightly observed in their paper "Radio and Audio - Vision in the British Open University: Towards Individualization", "At the simplest level, having a visual support does seem to help concentration. It is easy enough for the mind to wander during a twenty minute radio talk or discussion. To support what is said by an illustration or an activity helps to concretise the subject matter."[3]

Research conducted by Gallagher (1977) has revealed that students prefer radio-vision to radio alone and this justifies more of it in the advanced countries of the world. Radio-vision has become more popular day by day and the latest trend is towards more audio-vision in the field of educational broadcasting.[4]

Experiences in Radio/Audio Vision

The British Open University is a remarkable achievement in educational technology and has been using various kinds of media for providing its students with rich learning experiences. It has developed multi-media packages for various units in all subjects-arts, sciences, technologies and humanities. Particularly, its attempts to support radio-programmes with print materials, posters, coloured post cards, slides, film strips and realia are quite laudable and enlightning.

Since 1964 the BBC have started with radio-vision programmes systematically. In Sweden, Norway and Denmark, radio vision series are specifically brodcast along with educational radio programmes in general. Even in Kenya, its Ministry of Education used to broadcast radiovision science programmes in conjunction with the Centre for Educational Development Overseas (CEDO), London. In 1976 the Audio-visual Media Research Group was asked to evaluate several programmes with special emphasis on a radio-vision programme. But it was found that there was a wide range of materials being used for radio-vision programming. At that time there was no record of the number of courses or programmes using radio-vision and no way of measuring the cost of this medium to the OU. It was therefore decided to carry out a study to discover the range, extent and cost of radio-vision in the university. According to the study undertaken by Berrington and others (1987) radio-vision described the simultaneous use of radio and vision which promotes better utilisation.

The extent of radio-vision showed that Mathematics made most use of the medium. The second most extensive use is in Science. The range of materials used for radio-vision includes diagrams or tables in broadcast notes, charts, maps, samples or specimens, film strips and transparencies. Radio-vision materials in the Arts Faculty consist of coloured or black and white photographs, colour postcards, drawings and plans etc. It is interesting to know that 62% of all Open University courses in 1977 were making use of radiovision. But 23.33% i.e., a quarter of all radio programmes made use of the technique in some way or other. Thus the innovation has made a headway in the visual area and has shown a significant development in the educational broadcast.

The experience in use of radio-vision of OU shows that much more effort has been devoted to the provision of eloborate visual support material for radio-vision than to the design of the sound component. Berrington and others have in their study rightly pointed out "Many radio-vision programmes overload students, requiring sustained concentrating as well as expecting a great deal of pre-broadcast preparation to assemble materials. Often programmes seemed to race through the material, allowing in sufficient time for the detail to be located, or observed" (1977).[5]

Besides, many radio-vision programmes are designed with a predetermined work pace, when broadcast makes no allowance for individual learning styles and varying speeds of comprehension. This is, of course, due to the very inherent limitation of the sound broadcasting. Once the listener fails to locate a reference, he is likely to lose concentration and miss valuable information.

Indian Experience

During the Satellite Instructional TV Experiment (SITE) period (1974-75) an in-service training course in Science was organised by the Centre for Educational Technology, NCERT in collaboration with the Educational Technology Cells ofAndhra Pradesh, Bihar, Karnataka, Madhya Pradesh, Orissa and Rajasthan for the teachers of the elementary schools. A Multi-Media Package was developed by the CET for this course which included radio-vision programme in its sound broadcast component.

Explaining these radio-vision programmes to the teacher monitors who were to conduct the course it was mentioned by the CET (1975), "Radio-Vision means a radio-programme accompanied by visuals which may be on flash cards as in this case (shadows)/or as posters as in the case of next programme "Vikas aur Vigyan" or on slides/film strips. A topic like "shadows" needs visuals. In the materials sent to you, have included "Sketches/ diagrams as eleven cards numbered serially. You should display these cards one by one, the programme will cue you for such display by announcing look at card no. so and so? Please ensure that the participants are made to sit in such a manner, at such a distance that where these sketches, they could easily see them while listening to the radio-feature. The teacher monitor here has to be alert to change the sketch when next sketch is referred to."[6]

It was found that with the help of these suitable graphics accompanied by commentaries from radio, the principles of shadow in various situations were well-explained to the trainees. Similarly, few posters used in the other radio programme "Development and Science in Villages" helped to clarify certain difficult concepts and made the radio teaching interesting and meaningful.

The question "In the age of TV, has pedagogical Radio a future?" stimulated the Department of Education, South Gujarat University, Surat to take up a research project "Radio-Vision as a Partial Substitute to Educational TV." The experience of SITE programme provided further impretus for the venture. Although TV is considered to be a better medium of communication for the rural masses, the question arises, "Are we in a position to provide TV to all the inhabitations of our country?" Secondly, "Have we been able to exploit fully the potential of Radio as an educational medium? "Loud thinking over these questions further stimulated to examine the "effectiveness of Radio-Vision as a medium of instruction." As reported in the Newsletter of the Indian Association of Programmed Learning (1978), the major aim of the project was to study the efficacy of radio-vision as a medium of instruction in formal and non formal education situations (1978). The findings of this study were quite encouraging.

Production of audio/radio programmes is a significant process. It assumes special significance when such programmes are educational. Although hardware and software are two wings of audio production, software is more important, because we can procure the machineries and equipment from the market if funds are available. But software materials need to be developed with the help of persons having adequate knowledge in psychology, pedagogy and content areas. Software is to be need-based and need-specific relating to a particular group of clintele.

Important features of audio production are instructional objectives, audience profile, content, format, sound and music effects. Importance of scriptwriting cannot be overemphasized. A few basic guidelines should be followed in developing suitable scripts for radio/audio programmes.

In the AIR there is quite a well-developed infrastructure for production of audio programmes. Besides scriptwriting which is quite significent a number of precautions need to be taken for sound recording, editing, broadcasting etc., to ensure better quality and higher reception.

Some innvoative measure have been taken for overcoming the deficiencies and limitations of audio programmes. Radio/Audio-Vision is one of such innovation for providing visual support to aural presentation through the use of slides, illustrations, maps, charts etc. The BBC and other agencies abroad and in India NCERT and South Gujarat University have made some notable experiments in radio/audio-vision.

Software in Video Production

Like any other media, video production requires both hardware and software and these two components call for more or less amount of time and money according to the nature and quantity of these requisites. But software is given more importance than hardware due to the fact that the former is developed by the experts with adequate knowledge in pedagogy, psychology and content subject. Knowledge in learning strategies, reinforcement techniques, reading readiness, attention and interests and content is felt essential for developing suitable video programmes for the clientele groups. The software approach is often referred to behaviour technology aiming at modification of behaviour and enriching learning achievement. Maximization of learning experiences can be possible through the adequate use of software inputs in man-machine systems.

Procurement of hardware, even production and transmission services are more or less one-shot activities, but software development is a continuous process and purely academic in nature. Software must be relevant to the curricular needs specific to the courses/clientele. Teachers and students can interact and develop the material according to their capabilities and requirements. The entire process must be taken as integrated and inter-related. The objectives should be precisely identified and software has to be developed by educationists and academics. These useful material can be utilised in video production.

Software Development

Software production for educational TV or video cassettes requires a combination of knowledge of subject matter, media production techniques and communication strategy to reach the target audience. Just recording a chapter of the book cannot make a good video tape. The video/TV productions are only tools for communication and some basic questions need answering and understanding before production. Some of these questions are :

(i) Who is the target group?

(ii) What is their socio-cultural background?

(iii) What are their needs?

(vi) What are their experiences?

(v) Material to be produced by what means/medium?

(vi) By which agencies/personnel?

(vii) What advance preparation is needed?

(viii) With what infrastructure?

The production personnel, especially the scriptwriter should answer these and other allied questions and understand the production techniques before developing the software for the video programmes. The infrastructure for administration and production should be quite adequate and oriented to produce good quality video programmes without much hindrances and handicaps.

Software Objectives

The objectives of such communication may be one or more of the following:

(i) To impart relevant knowledge

(ii) To inform

(iii) To entertain

(iv) To teach skills

(v) To present concepts

(vi) To generate curiosity and interest

(vii) To stimulate creative and imaginative ideas

(viii) To develop problem-solving ability

(ix) To bring about change

These objectives are to be realised through the scripts. Some objectives are very easy for realisation. These objectives are also not hierarchical. Media communication to be effective needs insight and understanding of the target auidence and their needs according to which scripts and materials for video programmes are developed for realising the specific objectives.

Process for Software to Video Programme

Scripts are tne basis of all production activities. These software materials need to be translated into action i.e. video programmes. Sometime scripts for educational video programmes are developed through workshops where writers of various abilities, experience and insight, discuss the programme briefs, objectives, audience profile and prepare drafts in a rough proforma. These drafts prepared under the guidance of experts are presented and discussed in the workshops. Again the scripts are revised, redrafted and utilised for video programmes. These scripts undergo several revisions before good quality materials are ready for video production.

Scriptwriting

The process of writing a script for ETV and video programmes is essentially the same as desiging any learning activity. But writing video scripts means using your "ideas and imagination in a different way." i.e., giving visual treatment to your ideas. The first thing, therefore, to understand and learn about video Scriptwriting is that it is not a process of writing words or sentences and thinking of pictures to accompany them. On the other hand, it is an imaginative and creative process and is essentially and basically an art of imaginative programme creation, using the available resources. It is because of this reason that it is said that television programmes are evolved from the combined or pooled talents of the producer, the scriptwriter and occassionally others directly involved, such as desginer, graphic artists etc. Satisfying success can be achieved in this exercises more conveniently and confidently, if we look upon the process of evolving an ETV video script as a cyclic process.

Scriptwriting for ETV Programme

Before going into the details of each of the steps involved in the process of evolving an ETV script, it is, however, essential to point out the two important facts that all scriptwriters must always keep in mind.

1. Television is a one-way medium
2. Television is a mass-medium

Both these factors exert considerable limitations on the designing of ETV programmes. One has to bear in mind that there should be no gap in the content and the script should, as far as possible, be self-sufficient in communicating the desired messages. This limitation makes scriptwriting a difficult job which demands special care and attention, better imagination and visualisation, mastery of the subject and mature experience in identifying the requirement of the viewers. So the script should evolve step by step and different steps be presented vividly and linked so smoothly and naturally, one after the other, that the average viewer undrstands and follows the total content without any difficulty.

Secondly, because television is a mass medium, an ETV programme will be viewed by a large number of students, including the talented, the average and the below average. It may be very difficult to cater to the needs of all the three categories simultaneously throughout a programme. Therefore, the programme has to be planned and prepared in such a way that all the three categories benefit to the optimal extent, providing involvement and satisfaction to each one of them. This can be achieved by devoting the major part of the programme to the average students and also offering some satisfying material for the talented as well as the below average ones, so that the interest of all the three categories is sustained and the programme attracts and serves viewers from all sections of audience.

Introducing the entertainment element in a television programme is useful, but a balance is to be maintained by the scriptwriter between entertainment and education. In case of younger age group audience, entertainment programmes are desirable but this element must be exploited cautiously and carefully so that children are not carried away by the entertainment part so much that the actual message is not at all received by them. Thus, a successful scriptwriter always keeps in mind the psychology, interests and needs of his target audience. He has also to remember that visuals are the main carriers of the message and sound effects and words have a role to play but only in support of visuals, Television scriptwriting is thus the other name of thinking in terms of visuals to convey the intended message, combined, of course, with sound effects, music and words to make it a continuous programme in order to achieve the desired objectives.

Different writers follow different methods and techniques for writing scripts and it varies from writer to writer. However, for purposes of explanation and convenience of beginners, the process of scriptwriting may be described under the following main steps:

Stages in Video Production

Defining Objectives and Selecting Content Outlines

Once the topic for writing a script has been assigned, the scriptwriter should be informed about the target audience, their age-level and specific objectives and the programme.

This is to be followed by deciding the content to be presented in order to achieve the established objectives. Specifying objectives and visualising content in detail is an essential discipline in the production process. At this stage, the detailed visual ideas on which the programme will be based are evolved. "How can we convey that concept visually?" "How can we grasp the attention of the viewers?" This stage demands creativity and imagination. The success of the programme will heavily depend on the care taken at this stage.

Research and Selection of Materials

Research is important to all programmes. Finding information from books, periodicals, reports, atlases, encyclopedias, dictionaries and from experts in the field, checking details, locating pictures, selecting film locations, etc., are the part of research. Once the materials have been collected after research, the relevant materials which match the content and lead to the achievement of the desired objectives, can be finally selected for making the programme.

Selection of Resources to Present the Content

The scriptwriter has to be very imaginative in his selection of resources to match the content and the objectives. It is the most important step in the porcess. Success of the programme depends on the imaginative use of visual resources, keeping in mind the time and money available for the programme. This process of selecting resources implies the conversion of the programme content into suitable and appropriate visual terms, i.e. how the content tan be presented visually. It needs imagination, research and experience to accomplish this job successfully and to achieve the desired quality of the programme.

Organisation of Resources into a Programme Structure

This is the process of giving the programme a shapc and a form-visual treatment. It includes deciding how the programme will vary according to the needs, interest and how the parts of the programme will be linked together and knit into a natural sequence, so that the programme may have varying interest level and appear to be evolving from one sequence to another. In this process, each sequence would have to be linked with the previous one in respect of content, visuals, sound effects and other demonstration materials. But at the same time, care may be taken to see that there is a good coherance in the whole programme, something to bind everything into one natural and effective unit. At this stage, it is helpful to draw a time-line of the programme, showing how much time is to be spent on each element of the programme keeping in view the way the selected resources are to be used.

Developing a Story-Board/Draft Script and the Final Script

All the visual themes alongwith necessary links thought out and planned by the scriptwriter need to be communicated to the producers for understanding the shots and logical sequencing of the programme. This could easily be communicated if the scriptwriter presents his ideas in the form of a story-board. For developing the story-board, the scriptwriter may divide the white sheet of paper into two vertical columns. Pictures in sequence may be described within different rectangless (ratio 3:4) drawn on the left hand side of the paper. The supporting words,sound effects and music may be indicated in the right half of the paper.

From the story-board and final script, the producer writes the camera script which contains the technical information necessary for the production of the programmes.

To sum up, the following guidelines should be borne in mind by the scriptwriter while writing a script for an ETV programme.

i) First of all, the scriptwriter must realise and accept the factual position that scripts are not writtern but they are evolved.

ii) He should always keep in mind the target audience and their needs.

ii) The script must be simple, direct and personal.

iv) It must be written with full knowledge of and involvement of programme visuals.

v) It should constantly pick up, stress and reinforce its educational points using different resources.

vi) It should involve the audience , as far as possible, actively.

vii) The commentary should be informal and not book type.

viii) It should not attempt to say too much in limited time and space.

ix) It should end with a simple summary of the main programme points, with a different visual presentation.

x) It should have a variety of pace and rythm and must give breathing space ocassionally.

xi) Above all, it should attempt to take its viewers/audience on a journey of discovery and not merely give information.

Resources for Video Production

Television or video is primarily a visual medium. Naturally, therefore, the quality of any video programme will be determined by the quality and variety of visual and other resources that have gone into its making. A scriptwriter must, therefore, have a thorough knowledge of different visual and other resources of television which may be available to him to evolve a programme.

For puposes of convenience, the resources for video production can be classified into the following major categories:-

i) *Picutres:* By pictures, here, we mean any kind of visuals that can be put in front of a video camera. These may include still photographs, slides, filmstrips, overhead transparencies, especially prepared graphics such as charts, diagrams, maps, outlines, summaries, pictures from books, cartoons, captions' with letterings on them. We call all such pictures or photographs as captions or photo-captions. Sometimes, we can prepare special captions in which things and words can be made to move, appear and disappear. These are known as animated captions. All drawn pictures and photo-captions are usually made in a standard size of 12" x9", unless the camera is required to move about for showing different parts of the picture.

ii) *People:* Most television is about people, people telling us things, people being interviewed, people acting, people laughting, people weeping, people playing instruments and dancing, people singing, people playing games, people doing all kinds of things from mending bicycles to telling jokes, and people trying to persuade us to take to their point of view. They also include presenters, demonstrators, guests, teachers and class children.

iii) *Things:* The range of things shown on television is infinite, elephants, puppets, models, machines of all kinds toys, furniture, bridges, buildings, aeroplanes, the sun, the moon and so on. Television provides a unique opportunity to bring together a huge variety of things, new and old, mundane and unusual.

iv) *Drama:* Drama is also classified by many as one of the important resources for television. It may be very simple with no studio set or very complex ones using several settings. Drama does have elements of people, things and sound included in it, yet it may be classified as a separate resource.

v) *Film:* Films constitute a very important resource for television. The film can be put on a projector and beamed straight at a television camera. Things that are - impossible or impracticable to shoot on television - such as under-water photography and complicated cartoon work which we call Film Animation - can be shot on film. Films can also be used to slow down or speed up actions, as you might have seen in programmes shown on games, sports and races. All such specially prepared films can be fed into'a TV programme. (The technique of making films and television programmes are in themselves very different, of course).

vi) *Set and Lighting:* It is also an important resource of TV which gives it reality.

vii) *Sound:* Sound is an important resource for television though it is often under-utilised. Imaginative use of music and appropriate sound effects can certainly go a long way in making a good TV programme.

This classification of resources into PICTURES, PEOPLE, THINGS, DRAMA, FILM, SET, LIGHTING and SOUND, is particularly useful and convenient for beginners who, while trying to evolve ideas for video programmes, can refer to this broad classification.

Technical Terms in Video Production

Pictures are of paramount importance in video programmes. The Central Institute of Educational Technology, NCERT has identified the following, mostly related to pictures.

A video programme consists of a series of pictures, i.e., the pictures keep changing in quick succession. This change is not just for variety, but each picture has its own message. All the pictures must synchronize with sound.

Picture Types

Types of pictures (shots) depend on the focal length of the lens and the distance between the camera and the subject. Following types of shots are used commonly:

i. Single Shot - a shot including one person
ii. Two Shot - a shot including two persons
iii. Three Shot - a shot including three persons
iv. Crowd Shot - a shot including a number of people
v. Wide Shot or Very Long Shot (VLS) - a shot which includes along with the principal subject a large amount of the background in the picture.
vi. Full Length Shot or Long Shot (LS) - a shot in which the subject occupies about 3/4 of the vertical height of the picture frame.
vii. Medium Long Shot (MLS) or Knee Shot - a shot in which the subject is seen from the knee upwards.
viii. Medium Shot or Mid Shot - a shot in which the subject is seen from the waist upwards.
ix. Medium Close Shot (MCS) or Medium Close Up (MCU) - a shot which includes the subject's head and shoulders. It is also called the chest or Bust Shot.
x. Close Shot (CS) or Close Up(CU) - a shot which includes the subject's head and neck only
xi. Big Close Shot (BCS) or Big Close Up(BCU) - a shot which includes only a section of the subject's head from chin to forehead.
xii. Over-Shoulder Shot (OSS) - a shot of a subject or subject taken over the shoulder of person in the foreground.

Changing of Pictures

For maximum effects, the change of pictures must be brought about in the right manner. The following are certain conventional methods of changing the shots.

The Cut - This is an instant change form one picture to another. It is used when the action is continuous in time. A cut should be motivated by an action, by the dialogue or both.

The Dissolve or Mix - This is a gradual change from one picture to another. While the first picture is vanishing slowly, the second one is gradually appearing on the screen. At a point both pictures are visible on the screen simultaneously. It is used when a lapse of time is to be indicated, when there is a change of screen, and in getting to and from captions or telecine.

The Superimposition: This is the imposition of one picture over another one which is already on the screen. It is used for showing written captions over persons or objects in order to identify them, in teaching to reinforce the visual with the verbal, and for special effects, e.g., to show a person dreaming or thinking.

The Fade In and Out - These are the gradual apperarance of a picture on a blank screen and the gradual disappearance of a picture from the screen. These are used at the beginning and the end of a programme and instead of a mix when there is longer lapse of time to be indicated.

The Pan - Here the change of picture is brought about by panning i.e., moving the camera head left or right in the horizontal plane while the base of the camera remains static. It is used when following a moving person or thing and for moving from object to object in order to build up a particular effect or to provide background for a series of captions.

The Tilt - Here the change of picture is brought about by swinging the camera head up or down in the vertical plane without moving the base of the camera.

The Crab - Crabing is like panning except that here the whole camera is moved left or right from the base.

The Zoom In - Using a zoom lens, a wide shot of an object or person is changed to a closer shot. This is used for focussing attention on a particular part of the whole picture and for special effects (horror, surprise, excitement, etc).

The Zoom Out - Using a zoom lens, a close shot of a person or object is changed to a wider shot. It is used for establishing the relationship between the object or person with the surroundings, when a person in close-up moves or is joined by someone else or is going to talk about something next to him but not visible at the moment.

The Track In-Out - This has the same effect as the zoom in and out except that here in the absence of a zoom lens the whole camera is moved forward or backward from the base. This not only requires great skill on the part of the cameraman but a very smooth studio floor. It cannot be used for a quick change of shot and the range between the two shots would be limited.

Video Scriptwriting

1. Use active voice as far as possible.
2. Use specific words and examples, wherever possible, to establish specific relationships.
3. Try not to start with a negative sentence.
4. Sometimes, we may write just one sentence as commentary and then change three/four similar slides/ shots in succession.
5. There is no need to describe pictures which must speak for themselves.
6. Words should coincide with pictures where they make sense.
7. If you have a marvellous speaker in your programme, let him do the job. It will give your programme some "credibility." So, let it come from horse's mouth.
8. Make your audience see the 'pictures' you want them to see in a long shot.
9. Use just one line of commentary and let the noises take over. Avoid too much use of words. Try to forget your bombastic vocabulary and get rid of words only.
10. In general, the less you write, the better it is. So, learn to get rid of your vocabulary and use simple words only.
11. Never cover all the really dull stuff like facts, figures etc., in commentary. These can be really handled much more amusingly when they are presented graphically.

So we learn

Software is more important than hardware and is very local specific, objective based and academic in nature. It must be relevant to the curricular needs and is developed with the knowledge and skills based on pedagogy, psychology and content subject. The objectives of software are to impart knowledge, inform, entertain and so on and learners' experience and interest are taken into account for suitable software development. Scriptwriting for video production is of paramount importance and is evolved through the efforts of the writer, producer and other associated personnel. In view of the limitations of the video programme, better visualisation and imagination, careful selection of content, appropriate format and language, etc., are used for scriptwriting. A well integrated and inter-dependent process is adopted for developing suitable script and video production. Various resources like pictures, content about people, things, drama, film, set, lighting, sound etc., are utilised for video production. Since visuals are of crucial importance, great caution is taken for selecting spots and taking shots relevant to the content. Besides, producers and scriptwriters need to be acquainted with various technicalities including production strategies, terms and techniques used in video production. A number of guidelines are followed for writing suitable scripts.

References

1. Ball, J.C.H., 'School Radio: The Future' *Educational Broadcasting International*, London, June, 1974.
2. *Ibid.*
3. Berrington. F. and Gibson, A "Radio and Audio Vision in the British Open University: Towards Individualisation", In their research group paper no. 85, 1978.
4. Gallagher M. "Broadcasting and the Open University Students' IET Paper No. 44.
5. Berrignton F. and Gibson, A. 'Radio/Audio vision in Open University' 1977.
6. NCERT, Centre for Education Technology, *Teacher Monitors Handbook Pt. II* for 12-Day inservice Teacher Training Course. New Delhi, 1975.

11

Mass Media and Other Relevant Aspects of Education

A man as a social being cannot help but communicate with others. He communicates to express his feelings, needs, ideas and opinions about himself, environment and other people around him. He communicates, because he feels and he feels not only for himself but also for his fellow-beings. When such communication is meant for the mass, the media used for the purpose is called mass communication media or mass media in brief. The history of man and the history of communication seem to be synonymous. One cannot be separated from the other. The differrent types of inventions and discoveries that man has so far made are all to enhance his ability to communicate and to make his work better and easier. Emerson in his famous essay "Works and Days" has aptly said,"All the tools and engines on earth are only extension of its (mankind's) limbs and senses." Samuel Butler in his "Erewhor"(1872) develops the same idea "that machines were to be regarded as a part of man's own physical nature, being really nothing, but extra-corporeal limbs, every past invention being an addition to the resources of the human body." In The Study of Invention" (1928) HendrikVan loon has illustrated the tools as the extensions of man - his hand, foot, mouth, skin, eyes and ears(Dale, 1969, p.612)[1]

Thus, history of humanity is an account of the extension of man's powers. Particularly, the invention of alphabets, printing from movable types, invention of radio and television are landmarks not only in the history of mankind, but also in the development of mass communication media. It has therefore been observed that "In this age of science and technology, importance of mass media cannot be over-estimated. It is felt difficult to spend a single day without the use of mass media. Different aspects of our life-social, political, economic and personal, are being influenced by mass media."

Like Industrial Revolution many people call the present day changes "Communication Revolution" James Kinder (1959 p.2) had pointed out, "Today the mass media of communication reach millions of people scattered over the face of the earth. Through the mass media, every working hour of everyday, modern man is entertained, is informed, is urged to act this way or that way, and to spend money on an infinite variety of goods and services."[2]

Mass media of communication are the results of the modern age of science and technology. Previously, there were traditional modes of communication like meetings, conferences, fairs, yatras, beating the drums, blowing the trumpets and so on. Then the manuscripts with many limitations acted as a medium of communication. But printing of the book with movable types brought about a significant change in the communication system. Lately, electricity and electronics started a revolution in the communications. Radio, television, films and newspapers acted as the effective mass media of communication. Mass media are many and to describe their development here is far more difficult. However, attempts will be made to discuss briefly the development of some important mass media like folk art and music, printed materials, including newspapers, radio political and economic life of her people.

Traditional Arts and Music

Traditional arts and music dominated the scene of mass communication in India. They were, of course, associated with the cultural festivals and religious rituals. Folk songs, folk dance, folk drama, puppet shows, kirtans, palas, daskathias, yatras etc. were used both as the media of information as well as entertainment. These were of universal appeal, crossing the barriers of religious and economic backgrounds. These folk arts and music were quite indigenous and appealing to all sections of the society.

During the freedom struggle also these art forms were utilised for creating patriotism and nationalism among the people. The poets, dramatists and writers also contributed their mite to this noble cause through their creative activities. Folk musical forms were found effective for fostering heroic spirit and scacrifice in the hearts of the people. These were oral and aural mass media of communication. Although entertainment is emphasized, education is also promoted by the use of folk art and music.

Newspapers and Journals

Books, journals and newspapers constitute the whole gamut of printing materials. These are comparatively less expensive and more popular. Prior to this, there were manuscripts namely "Pothis" in palm-leaves or Bhurja leaves which were very limited in number as well as in use. At first the European Missionaries brought printing technology to India, two centuries ago. The first newspaper was published in Calcutta in 1780. Indian newspapers with Indian editorship and proprietorship started during the period of renaissance under the inspiration of Raja Ram Mohan Roy. The first Indian newspaper in English was the Bengal Gazette (weekly) published in 1816. Although it died after a year, the era of Indian journalism was opened and by 1823 the country had atleast three newspapers published in Bengali, three in Persian and one in Gujarati.

During the struggle for freedom the press restrictions were harsher and the Anglo-Indian press defended the government by belittling the people's fight and aspiration for freedom. On the other hand the Indian leaders like Aurobindo, Annie Besant, Lajpat Rai, Bipin Behari Pal, Surendranath Benerjee, Tilak, Gandhi and Gopabandhu were the shining luminaries not only in politics but also in journalism. Mahatma Gandhi launched his Non-cooperation Movement soon after the First World War and demanded fearless criticism from the press. This led to the enactment of the Press (Emergency Powers) Act of 1931 for dealing with the terrorist activities and crushing the Civil Disobedience Movement.

After Independence the "freedom of speech and expression" was recognised as a fundamental right under Article 19(1 a) of the Constitution. Although there is no special provision on the freedom of press as such, it is covered under this fundamental right.

The Registrar of Newspapers was appointed 1956 for regulation and collection of authentic statistics regarding all aspects of the press. Some other Acts and amendments were also passed for control ling the press and during the Emergency of 1975. Severe restrictions were imposed for curbing freedom of the press. Most of these restrictions have been removed by the amendments to the constitution.

Printed materials made education available to a vast population. In place of "class education" it became - "mass education." Printed materials in fact became the most popular means of education. Textbooks, handbooks, guidebooks and journals are used as very useful teaching-learning materials. Inspite of electronic advancements, printed materials are felt indispensable.

Radio, Television and Films

Radio - Since 1924, the era of radio broadcasting began in our country as a Radio Club at Madras which started a broadcasting service. In 1926

Government granted a license to the Indian Broadcasting Company to establish broadcasting stations in the country. The company got the monopoly of broadcasting earning revenues through licences. The first station was set up at Bombay on July 23,1927 and the second one at Calcutta on August 26,1927. The Broadcasting Company was, however, liquidated in 1930 and the Government of India took over the broadcasting service. Originally, it was called the Indian States Broadcasting Service and in 1936 it was redesignated as the All India Radio.

Lienel Fielden took over the office of the Controller of Broadcasting from the beginning and Government of India provided a sum of Rs.40 lakhs for development of the service initially. With an impetus from the World War, broadcasting developed considerably. The AIR, however, had to face a lot of administrative problems on account of foreign rule, multiplicity of languages and economic backwardness. Menon(1976) has rightly pointed out, "It was only after Independence that broadcasting was organised as a national service. In the last twenty years the growth has been both in quantity and quality, steady, if not spectacular. The orientation in outlook, the shift in emphasis of values, the transformation of an existing set-up into a national service, these take time. And the wheels of Government grind slowly."

With a view to formulating programme policies, advisory committees were attached to the radio stations from the very beginning of the service and such committees are still continuing with every station. The AIR always functions under a code of conduct. News involving sex, crime, religious fanaticism, communalism, personal attacks, threats to public place are generally avoided.

Television - Television service was inaugurated in Delhi on September 15,1959 and was operated from a small improvised studio. It was telecasting programmes twice a week for a duration of one hour each. Only 21 TV sets were installed for community viewing and a UNESCO assisted project was implemented to assess the effectiveness of social education programmes. Since the report was quite encouraging the Government of India started telecasting educational programmes since 1964 with the Ford Foundation assistance.

An innovative project in television was the SITE (Satellite Instructional Television Project Experiment) during the year 1975-76. The international communication experts like Wilbur Schramm pleaded for mass medium like satellite for India and the Indian scientists with vision and zeal like Vikram Sarabhai made the project of satellite communication a success. The SITE was inaugurated on Aug. 1,1975 and TV progrmmes produced by the

Doordarshan and ISRO (Indian Space Research Organisation) were telecast to 2400 selected villages of 6 states - Andhra Pradesh, Bihar, Karnataka, Madhya Pradesh, Orissa and Rajasthan. The satellite which was loaned by NASA of USA to India for a year was called ATS-6 (Applications Technology Satellite-6).

After the SITE, the Government of India decided to provide TV viewing facility in 40 per cent of the SITE served villages by setting up terrestrial transmitters in the six SITE States. The project called Community Viewing Scheme was implemented in these States at different times during the years 1977-80. Then detailed planning was made for another ambitious project named INSAT (Indian National Satellite) which is an experiment of great national importance in the field of multipurpose communication system. The INSAT-IA was launched on April 10,1982 in order to provide TV service in the states of Andhra Pradesh, Orissa, Bihar, Maharashtra, Gujarat and Uttar Pradesh.

After its mechanical failure in September '82, INSAT-IB was launched in August 30,1983 and was made operative from October 15,1983. It is successfully providing facilities of nationwide coverage by direct telecast to low-cost community receivers, television and radio programme distribution, disaster warning, and relay of meteorological data. About 4000 community viewing TV sets have been installed in these States and television programmes were being broadcast daily for two hours and forty-five minutes in the morning for Primary schools and two hours in the evening for adults.

TV is now the magic carpet being used as a means of exploring the mysteries of the universe and a magic box for providing education and entertainment simultaneously. It is now a window to the world and a very potential and pragmatic medium of education catching the attention of all- high and low, rural and urban, students and teachers.

Films - Films are a very effective mass media of communication and provide education as well as entertainment. India entered into the era of film production in 1912 with "Pundalik" a silent film produced by R.G.Torney. The age of silent films came to an end in 1931 when the talkies began to be produced. Over these years thousands of films have been produced and the majority of them in a few important centres of film production like Bombay, Madras and Calcutta.

Documentary films are useful for mass communication and most of these films are produced by the Film Division of the Government of India. Its headquarters is at Bombay and branch offices in different States for distribution of such films. Films are produced almost on all subjects of national interest and include documentaries, cartoons and TV films in almost all important languages of the country.

Educational films are a very interesting medium of education. On a wide canvas we can see the real world or imaginary world with keen interest and rapt attention. Educational films produced with specific academic theme and suitable methods as well as techniques, are helpful in imparting instruction and happiness. They provide reality and imagination, variety and novelty, motion and animation by making instruction interesting. Students learn from educational films without tears, without boredom and without any strain. They enjoy and get themselves enlightened. Children are quite sensitive and creative. They are to be "warmed up" or motivated to get information, develop positive interests and attitudes so that their education becomes effective.

Impact of Mass Media

Impact of mass media is felt on every aspect of the modern life-social, economic, political and so on. A man in the society is a man in communication with others - his kith and kin, his friends and fellows. He is always exposed to the lifestyle of others, ideas and opinions of others, news and views conveyed through all kinds of media-newspapers, radio, television, films etc. He is influenced by them and cannot keep himself aloof from the effects of mass media. The entire people, may the whole mankind is shaped according to the mass media that are available at the time. R.K.Chatterjee(1979) has rightly remarked, "The activities of the mass media follow closely the development in various fields, informing people, reacting to policies and creating the social climate in which development and nation-building programmes can take place. They cannot operate in a social and political vacuum, nor do they deal with obstruse philosophies. Mass media are every day dealing with problems that affect the destiny of the nation and in the wider context, of humanity as a whole. Mass media not only inform, but also entertain. They promote cognitive as well as affective development of students. They transmit knowledge and understanding very economically and interestingly. That is why, they are very cost-effective and impact-effective. They are forceful media, influencing education of all groups of clientele-children, youth, adults, teachers, farmers, students of both formal and non-formal systems.

System's Approach

After independence, it has always been demanded that educational system has to be revamped and geared to the emerging needs of the nation. The Constitutional Directive to secure universalisation of elementary education is yet to be implemented fully; democratization of education is yet to be realized; equality of educational opportunities is yet to achieved and eradication of illiteracy is still an unfinished task. Although various endeavours have been made both at the national and state levels to realize those objectives and spectactular progress has been made during the last three and half decades, the country has still to go a long way in reaching the target.

With a veiw to reorienting and reforming the educational system, a large number of suggestions have been made by different committees and commissions and the Government of India as well as the State governments have been trying to implement these recommendations. But these steps have been more sporadic and less systematic in the shape of patch-works only. Instead of overhauling the entire system, we are merely tinkering with the casual changes here and there according to expediency and exigency. This has resulted in unsatisfactory progress and impermanent solution.

Therefore, as suggested in the Report of the International Commission on the Development of Education, "Learning To Be", new educational strategies must proceed from an overall vision of educational system and must conceive of education as an enterprise transcending the framework of school and universities overflowing its constituent institutions. Flexible, integrated and systems approach has to be adopted for bringing about desirable changes in education.

Understanding Systems Approach

Educational system may be compared with an organism or a machine in which all the parts or components are interdependent and their interaction is dynamic. In an organism there are living cells which are acting in different directions individually and contributing towards common goal at the same time. In a machine, there are various parts like engine, wheels, steering, chassis and so on which have their individual functions and at the same time helping the machine to do its job. Both the organism and machine have a particular purpose or goal to realize and all their parts are tuned or oriented or geared to achieve this goal. Thus, inspite of individual entities and functioning a common goal is aimed at co-ordination, co-operation and integration.

UNESCO has also given the example of human body in explaining a system. Besides a large number of living cells, different sub-systems and units like circulating system, nervous system, digestive system, seeing and hearing system function within the large system of the human body independently and jointly for existence of the body itself.

The system is thus "a complex", a set of "connected things" or "organised body of materials or things." !t is an assemblage of objects or units with regular interactions and inter-dependence collectively contributing towards an overall complex function.

Systems approach or systems analysis is a systematic way of identifying goals of any system and scientifically working out different steps to move towards these goals. It has been aptly mentioned in the "Learning To Be" that "It is precisely a characteristic of systems analysis to integrate uncertainty into daily action. Be this as it may, to the extent that it enables us to orchestrate many agents into a unified process leading to the greatest possible efficiency, systems analysis would appear to be an intellectual instrument which may be applied to an overall critical study of existing educational systems and is likely to suggest new scientifically calculated pedagogic patterns."

The systems approach generally consists of the following steps:

(i) an analysis of the existing situation;

(ii) setting up goals for the desired situation;

(iii) defining machanisms to evaluate the achievements of goals;

(iv) generating alternative solutions;

(v) choosing the best possible soltuion through cost-benetit analysis;

(vi) detailing out the design of the system;

(vii) outlining the monitoring mechanisms for the system;

(viii) working out for introducing the solution.

Systems Approach as applied to Education

Systems Approach is an innovatie and rational problem-solving method of analysing the educational system and making it more effective. It views the educational process as a whole with all its dimensions and components like pupils, teachers, curriculum, teaching media and materials, instructional strategies, physical environment and evaluation of instructional objectives.

According to the systems approach in education, the entire teaching-learning process is taken as cybernatic or organic which is self-generating as well as self-controlling. As the general health of an individual depends upon working conditions of different sub-systems like respiratory, digestive circulatory, etc., so also the educational achievement and progress at a particular stage is proportional to the functional efficiency of various sub-systems like teacher, supervisor, administrator, librarian, evaluator and so on. Integration and interaction among all these agencies are to be promoted for overall efficiency.

The following steps are adopted in the systems approach to education:

(i) Definition of instructional goals, behavioural objectives and stating them in operational terms;

(ii) Determination of functions for achieving these objectives through the use of various media and materials;

(iii) Identification of learners needs and characteristics;

(iv) Selection of suitable methods for effective learning of the topic;

(v) Selection of appropriate learning experiences;

(vi) Choice of relevant materials, media and resources for such experiences;

(vii) Assignment of appropriate personal roles as teachers, students AV, personnel, librarian etc.;

(viii) Implementaton of the programme starting with a try-out under typical conditions;

(ix) Evaluation of the learning outcomes in the light of instrument/ instructional and behavioural objectives; and

(x) Redefinition and revision of the goals, objectives, content methods, strategies, etc., for improving learning experiences.

With a view to improving the teaching-learning (input-output) process at the outset the instructional objectives should be formulated and the operational behavioural objectives must decided in the light of instructional objectives. Adequate linkages should be established between the inputs and outputs and a feedback system be developed. This process is not merely conginitive. It operates in a social, emotional and affective environment. According to Panda, motivational and affective considerations have occupied a signficiant place in the learning process and outcomes.

Implementation

The systems approach should be introduced as an integral part of the whole educational environment and accepted by all concerned with the environment. Otherwise, it will not be effective and its implementation cannot bring about improvement. Formative evaluation and benchmark survey may be necessary for formulating objectives, subject-matter and strategies, training and orentation of teachers and generating adequate awareness and imparting necessary knowledge as well as skills. The teacher has to plan for utilization of resources, organisations of activities, use of media, etc. He should have a good knowledge of the subject limitations of the environment, individual differences of children and suitable methods as well as materials so that he can plan the system accordingly. The systems approach involves continuous evaluation, the results of which contribute to the revision of the plan wherever necessary.

Advantages

Sampath and others have enumerated the following merits in the systems approach:

1. It provides a conceptual framework on which to build plans for implementing change for education.
2. It helps to identify the suitability or otherwise of the resources to achieve the specific goal.
3. It helps to assess the resources, needs, their sources and facilities in relation to quantities, time and other factors.
4. Technological advance could be used to provide integration.
5. It permits an orderly introduction of components demonstrated to be required for system's success in terms of students.
6. Rigidity in plan of action is avoided as continuous evaluation affords desired beneficial changes to be made.

Role of Teachers

The teacher has to play a pivotal role in effectively adopting the systems approach not only in his teaching process, but also in organising various projects, both curricular and co-curricular in the school situation. But there is ample truth in the old saying that it is difficult to teach the "old ones new tricks." It is also equally easy for the new teachers to forget the "tricks of the trade" learnt during the pre-service training period. Therefore, systems approach should be first in the educational planning and administration itself, so that no constraints and adverse situations are faced by the teachers. The teacher should act as a "friend, philosopher and guide" of students and implement all projects according to the principles of systems approach both in theory and practice.

Flanders' Interaction Analysis

The distinguished historian - philosopher Henry Adams once said that "the teacher effects eternity, he can never tell where his influence stops." His personality, his teaching and his conduct in the calssroom and outside influence his students and through them others innumerable in this world in so many ways. The very purpose of teaching to bring about changes in the students behaviour is served to a great extent through his activities in the calssroom. That is why the Kothari Commission (1964-66) have aptly said in the opening sentence, "The destiny of India is being shaped in her classrooms."

A number of researches conducted in the field of teaching effectiveness have revealed that the teachers classroom behaviour generally decides what is called the "classroom climate" concomitant of his interaction with the students. The classroom climate is the true measure of his success or failure in teaching and is also the result of his personality and conduct.

An Observation Technique

Interaction analysis is an observation technique or a specialised research procedure which provides information about a few aspects of teaching. It helps capture the quantitative and qualitative dimensions of teacher behaviour in the classroom. It measures the classroom events systematically and objectively. It is designed to record the behaviour of a teacher which is not only complex, but also variable, in an accurate manner as far as possible. As the observer's perceptions may be subjective due to a number of psychological factors, Flanders has developed an Interaction Analysis Category System (FIACS) for objectively assessing the teacher's verbal behaviour. According to him, "Interaction analysis is an observation procedure designed to minimize these difficulties, permit a systematic record of spontaneous acts, and scrutinize the process of instruction by taking into account each small bit of interaction."

Teachers' behaviour, particularly his verbal expressions/acts in terms of predetermined concepts are recorded by means of Flanders Interaction Analysis with a view to analyse his influence pattern in the classroom situations. They refer to the control of students' freedom of action. With the help of 10 categories, those acts which require more creative and voluntary participation are discriminated from others that result in compliance. Since the observation categories are based on some sound psychological principles, interaction analysis is used as a process of abstracting the intent of an act from the act itself. It is mostly concerned with the verbal behaviour which is assumed to be total behaviour and the impact of verbal behaviour is taken approximately as the impact of the total behaviour.

Category System

Flanders has developed 10 categories for describing the communication pattern in the classroom. Out of these categories, 7 are related to teachers' talk, 2 to students' talk and one to pause, confusion or noise. The categories pertaining to teachers' talk are classified into direct and indirect influences. Categories from one to four are meant for indirect influence and from five to seven are intended for direct influence. Flanders has believed that indirect influence encourages students' participation and thereby increases their freedom of action. This also changes the communication pattern which must be different from that of the situation where students listen passively.

Flanders' category one represents the ability to use the feeling tone of students, category two stands for praising or encouraging greater students' participation: category three means to say how the teacher accepts, clarifies, or uses the ideas of students constructively. These acts, according to Flanders, "tend to increase student participation and to give students the opportunity to become more influential." Consequently, greater freedom of action is promoted for the students.

Flanders perceives direct influence to increase the control of the teacher and stimulate conformity and compliance. Category five represents lecture through which students have to listen to the teachers' ideas. Category six stands for giving directions or commands intended to direct activities of the class for obtaining compliance. Category seven explains when the teacher tries to justify his authority or criticizes students' behaviour. The net effect of direct influence is the reduced freedom of action of the students.

The categories eight and nine stand for students' talk. These two categories pertain to students talk in the sense that there is greater students' talk if the teacher does not impose many restrictions on them. Category eight is directly related to students' talk in response to the teachers and category nine has been assigned to students' talk which is self-initiated and also inspired. The category ten stands for pause, silence or confusion in the class. It is, however, not used to record longer periods of silence or confusion. The continuous use of this category for periods longer than 2 minutes does not serve any purpose desired under this concept. This interactive process is found to be most suitable, when students and the teacher are actively engaged in discussions concerning school work. When verbal communication is not continuous or separated by long periods of silence or dominated by lectures or characterised by confusion of observation, it should cease by noting down the time and reasons for distrubance.

A summary of Flander's Interaction Analysis Categories (FIAC) is given below. It is to be noted that each category is classificatory and does not fall on a scale.

Teacher Talk and Pupil Talk

1. *Accepts Feelings:* Accepts and clarifies the feeling tone of the studens

in a non-threatening manner. Feelings may be postive or negative. Predicting or recalling feeling is included.

2. *Praises and Encourages:* Praises and encourages student saction or behviour jokes that release tension but not at the expense of another individual nodding head or saying "un hm' or 'go on' are intended.
3. *Accepts or Uses Ideas of Students:* Clarifying, building or developing ideas suggested by a student, as a teacher brings more of his own ideas into play, shift to category.
4. *Asks Questions:* Asking a question about content or procedure with the intent that a student answers.
5. *Lecturing:* Giving facts or opinions about content or procedures expressing his own ideas, asking thetorical questions.
6. *Giving Directions:* Directs, commands or orders with which a student is expected to comply.
7. *Criticizing or Justifying Authority:* Statements intended to change student behaviour from non-acceptable to acceptable pattern; stating why the teacher is doing what he is doing; extreme self-reference.
8. *Students Talk Response:* Talk by students in response to teacher. Teacher initiates the contact or solicits student statement.
9. *Students Talk Initiation:* Talk by students which they initiate. 'Calling on' student is only to indicate who may talk next. Observer must decide whether the student wanted to talk. If he did, use this category.
10. *Silence or Confusion:* Pauses, short periods or silence and periods of confusion in which communication cannot be understood by the observer.

There is no scale implied by these numbers. Each number is classificatory; it designates a particular kind of communication event. To write these numbers down during observation is to enumerate, not to judge a position on a scale.

Observation Procedures

It is essential that the observer should understand as well as remember the categories well. In the classroom he must take a position which is the most convenient to observe and listen to the participants. He has to decide about the category at the end of each three seconds and record them on the sheet intended for the purpose. Thus, the whole communication system should be recorded at the rate of 20 to 25 observations per minute. The original sequence of events is to be recorded by the members representing different categories from top to bottom on a sheet with marginal notes to explain unusual circumstances. A double line is drawn and the time is indicated in case of a major change in the communication pattern or the subject under discussion. On completion of the observation the observer gives a general description on each separate activity period demacrated by the double lines.

Teachers can know the effectiveness of their behaviour or teaching in the classroom with the help of interaction analysis. Pupil teachers can study their own teaching and get an insight into their own classroom performance. They will be able to analyse and evaluate their work and practise the individual teaching skills, getting feedback from their peers and supervisiors through interpretation of recordings by means of interaction analysis techniques. The research studies have shown that there is significant gain in the classroom behaviour of pupil-teachers through training in interaction analysis. The impact of teachers' behaviour on students' attitudes can be ascertained by this method. A scale can be developed to measure the personality, traits of dependence and other proneness of students on the findings of the Interaction Analysis System. The technique can help teachers in grouping of students and improving their patterns of influence through interaction.

Simulated Social Skill Training, Role-Play and Training Group

To improve the quality and efficiency of teaching is an important objective of teacher education. This objective is not properly realized in our country due to so many factors. Absence of adequate feedback devices in our teacher education system is felt to be the greatest shortcoming in the way of modifying as well as improving teacher behaviour. A number of techniques have been developed and introduced during the last decade for providing feedback and modification of teacher behaviour. Simulated Social Skill Training (SSST) is one of these techniques and like a few others it has been tried out as an innovation in teacher education for providing suitable feedback and modifying teaching skills.

SSST Techniques

The pioneering effort in the development of this technique is attributed to the State University Research Foundations, Columbia, USA where originally a taxonomy of teacher behaviour was developed. The SSST techniques include four dimensions-sources, direction, function and sign. In fact, this technique is utilised for training in role-perception and role-playing.

The fundamental assumption underlying this technique is that there are certain patterns of teaching behaviour which are essential for effective teaching. It is also assumed that these patterns can be identified and described in certain behavioural outcomes. Like any other skill they can be practised, and used in teaching appropriately and effectively. A particular pattern of teacher behaviour can be called a social skill for the training purpose and can be identified and practised intensively for its acquisition. This will facilitate modification of behaviour for professional growth.

Simulated Social Skill Training has been the basis of role-playing, socio-drama and psycho-drama. The general objective is to place a person in a situation which provides spontaneous interaction to enable him to practise a certain pattern of behaviour. The person who gets the training is called the actor, the individuals providing the spontaneous environment are called foils and one or two supervisors recording behaviour for professional or maintaining notes for later evaluation are known as supervisors.

The objectives of simulation exercise are as follows:

i) Modifying student behaviour,

ii) Motivating learners,

iii) Bringing about changes in attitudes,

iv) Understanding one's role properly,

v) Realising other's role and responsibilities,

vi) Helping students to assume emerging roles,

vii) Discussing crucial social problems and generating awareness.

Simulation exercises promote free expressions and participation in situations that are very close to reality without involving them in the actual circumstances. The participants are encouraged to understand real problems and freely think and decide themselves for improving their conditions-social, psychological, educational and so on.

Steps in SSST

The following procedure is usually followed for SSST exercise:

1. Each trainee in the group may be designated as a lecturer and all have to be prepared for changing their roles. That is, everybody must have a chance to play the role of an actor, a foil and an observer.
2. Each skill may be discussed and practical topics be suggested for suiting the skills. One topic may be selected for the first exercise and additional topics for other exercises. Each trainee should select a topic convenient to him for playing the role of an actor.
3. A schedule may be drawn up as to who will start teaching, who will introduce the actor and who will stop the interaction and when they should be stopped.

4. Prior decision may be taken on the procedure of evaluation, on the kind of data for recording and how best the data and views can be presented to actor.
5. The first practice session may be conducted and the actor be provided with feedback on his performance. If necessary, the procedure may be changed for the second session for improving the training procedure.
6. The procedure may be modified and topic be changed so that each actor takes it as a challenge and interest is sustained. Thus, the task should neither be too easy nor too difficult.

SSST exercise, in order to be successful, requires the following abilities of the trainees:

1. The ability to ask open or closed questions and to know when each is appropriate in classroom teaching.
2. The ability to ask a question which lifts the current level of abstraction or a question which lowers it and the ability to ask a series of questions which gradually lifts or lowers the level of abstractions.
3. The ability to ask questions in which the concept and logical connectives have previously been expressed by pupils.
4. The ability to summarise what pupils have said and then end by asking a question which moves the discussion into the next step in logical sequence of problem-solving.
5. The ability, both to demonstrate and to explain the rates of logic in classroom discourse, including helping to maintain consistency in the meaning of words, and helping to distinguish matters of fact, opinion and value.

Role-Play

Role-playing refers to special kinds of memorised, often imprompt, dramatization put on by a group of students. This may be planned and practised or may be spontaneous outgrowth of the study of some important problem in class. Socio-drama and psycho-drama are also taken as role-playing. They are used to probe into deeply rooted prejudices and behaviour patterns which are difficult to change. Socio-drama relates to social problems whereas psycho-drama is used as a device to provide scope for change of behaviour and reception of suggestions for doing better.

In short role-playing aims at the following:

a) Illustrating interpersonal problems;
b) Adopting simulation techniques to solve problems;

c) Developing insight into personal attitudes, values and behaviours;

d) Understanding adequate awareness about social and psychological issues;

e) Understanding feelings and opinions of others;

f) Developing interpersonal communication skills; and

g) Enabling even the shy and introverts to express their views.

Role-playing comes naturally to children. Without rehearsals or coaching they assume various roles through which they project themselves into adult experiences. It is an excellent medium for conveying new information or practising a skill. It can integrate with other learning techniques and materials.

On the whole, the important steps in organising the role-playing as follows:

1. Identifying a suitable problem situation;
2. Selecting the pupils for playing the roles;
3. Assigning roles to the students;
4. Orienting the students to the techniques-identifying with characters, understanding the issues, playing the characters etc;
5. Allowing time for preparation;
6. Playing the roles as actual characters;
7. Encouraging peers to express their views on the role-playing;
8. Giving remarks and summing up by the teacher.

The most effective role-playing situations are those which grow out of problems concerned with people, their actions and their beliefs. Role-playing skills and the disposition of students/ trainees to participate in such an activity are improved by good playing and organisation. The role-playing techniques prove successful with older children and adults as well as with young children. Through these they get rid of shyness and develop social poise, ease and smartness. In order to bring about adequate solutions to social problems and psychological problems sociologists and psychologists respectively adopt role-playing techniques like socio-drama and psycho-drama. Teachers also find them as effective devices for teaching attitudes and interests to children most naturally and interestingly.

The advantages of role-playing may be summed up as follows:

i) Generating awareness and sensitising the students to learning problems;

ii) Minimizing shyness and inhibitions through role-playing;

iii) Gaining insight into behaviour patterns;

iv) Helping students in adjustments;

v) Giving scope for free expression of feelings.

Role-playing does not prove successful on account of the following:

a) Shy and introvert students do not play the roles properly and spontaneously;

b) They cannot articulate well and give bent to their feelings and views;

c) The technique is found to be time-consuming and wasteful exercise if roles are not played realistically.

Teachers can cleverly find out solutions to current problems and gain insight into the real feelings and opinions of the students who are likely to play thier future roles in the present simulated situations.

Training Group

The Training Group is briefly called T Group and is used as an exercise in human/social relations. Participants in this Training Group get the opportunity not only to share their perceptions of each others behaviour, but also to get an insight into their own behaviour. This helps in bringing about an awareness which provides suitable feedback for modification of behaviour.

Procedure

Training Group consists of eight to twelve trainees and one or two experienced trainers. No agenda is fixed nor any leader is appointed for conducting a meeting/discussion which is extended over 2 or 3 hours. This may be held once or twice a week.

Discussion will be initiated on a topic by a trainer. Some trainees may express dissatisfaction with the set up and some may find fault with the tariner. Thus in the initial meetings conflict and frustration increase to a great extent.

The trainees are however, encouraged to give bent to their feelings. In subsequent meetings they become sobre, honest, frank and introspective.The trainer will give necessary guidance through suggestions and clarifications. He will help the group to come to effective interaction.

The Training Group Technique enables the experienced teacher to improve his behaviour and the pupil teacher to improve his skills and abilities as a good teacher. The training group gives opportunities to live through enquiry in order to improve one's own behaviour and to get perception of the group behaviour. This technique has the justification for creating efficient means of continued self-assessment and adequate readiness in teacher education. It provides a context of a human relations programme to make the teacher more receptive and more sensitive to the problem of social interaction. With proper feedback devices developed through this training, the teacher will not only improve his behaviour, but also increase the effectiveness of his teaching programmes.

Evaluation and Research

Educational Technology is the application of scientific knowledge and skills about learning to improve the effectiveness and efficiency of the teaching-learning process. It is a systems approach aimed at optimization of learning. It implies a behavioural science approach to teaching and learning and making use of relevant scientific and technological methods and principles developed in psychology, sociology, communications, economics, linguistics and other related fields. It includes the development, application and evaluation of systems, techniques and aids in the field of learning. In short, educational technology consisting of all modern methods, media and materials is used for effective as well as efficient learning.

According to Eric Ashby[3] mankind has already passed three revolutions in education and now it is in the midst of the fourth revolution. The first revolution took place when the task of educating the child was shifted from parents to teachers and from homes to schools. The second revolution occurred when the written word was adopted as a tool of education. The third revolution came with the invention of printing and use of books in education. The fourth revolution was initiated with the development in electronics particularly invention and use of radio, television, tape recorder, computer and other communication media in education.

This fourth revolution implies in the words of Eric Ashby-"Any technology which increases the rate of learning, would enable the teacher to teach less and the learner to learn more."[4] In this new context, learning is more emphasised in place of teaching and learner is given importance more than the teacher. Consequently, mathetics, the science of behaviour of the pupil undergoing the process of learning gets priority over pedagogy, the science of behaviour of the teacher while instructing pupils. The mathetic principles are now used to plan methods, media and materials for optimization of learning taking the nature and needs of the learner into consideration. Thus the shift in emphasis from the teacher to the pupil as the central figure in the process of education has resulted in evaluation and assessment of instructional media and materials with the realization of specific learning outcomes.

Evaluation in Media

Previously, evaluation was defined and interpreted in very narrow terms - a kind of assessment of examination of achievement or effects or programmes. A sort of adhoc reporting was done by the concerned officers and inspecting officers on the utilization and problems of media and materials. This concept was, however, broadened to include more scientific reporting procedures based on sampling techniques, questionnaire forms and statistical interpretations. Evaluation should be considered as a form of continuous monitoring, the findings of which are taken as feedback for modifying and improving the media system.

It is not possible on the part of producers and managers of educational media to have direct knowledge of how their programmes are actually used in the school or home. It is very important to know not only the extent of media utilisation and their contribution to realizing learning objectives, but also the necessary conditions for effective and efficient media system. Since the fields of knowledge in particular and the conditions of society in general are dynamic, the educational media system must be flexible enough to meet the demands of such changes. Therefore, continuous review of media design, their utilisation and effectiveness is felt imperative as well as essential.

Objectives

According to Alan Hancock[5] media evaluation must consequently -

i) Ensure that there is as much knowledge as possible of what is happening,

ii) Suggest possible changes that are likely to lead to improvements in the system,

iii) Provide adequate information to assist and make possible rational policy making.

Hancock has then spelled out the objectives for an evaluation system as follows[6]:

a) Providing information to assist these election of appropriate policies for an educational media system,

b) Providing information on the success or failure of educational media in meeting their educational objectives,

c) Providing information on the effectiveness of the various production and management elements involved,

d) Increasing knowledge of how to integrate media most effectively into an overall teaching context, in terms of both course design and production formats,

e) Increasing and spreading knowledge of the most appropriate production tecniques in various educational context,

f) Increasing and spreading knowledge of how to use media to their best advantage in actual teaching situations.

Out of these there are some short-term and some long-term objectives and attempts need to be made to realize these objectives according to needs and conditions of the evaluation system. Important short-term objectives are adjustment of programme-content, adjustment of production techniques, provision of teachers notes and monitoring programmes. Some of the long-term objectives are programme planning to integrate with curriculum changes, allocation of priorities for planning programmes to meet the specific needs and planning for expansion of transmission facilities, planning for effective pre-service and in-service programmes of teacher education.

Types of Evaluation

Evaluation of media is still in its infancy. It is a complex subject calling for specialist discipline and complicated technicalities. It involves some sensitive areas of operation and touches various points of media planning, production and utilisation. Different agencies should be associated as well as involved in the process of evaluation. John Mayo, Robert Harnik and Emil Me Anany from Stanford have outlined mainly three kinds of evaluation: (i) Planning, (ii) Formative and (iii) Summative.

(i) Planning Evaluation: This entails the collection of essential data on the media system before it is implemented and often before a decision is made to undertake it. Among the most common methods of data collection are feasibility studies which survey the key aspects of an educational environment specifying the technical requirements for the media transmission of radio or television broadcasts and estimating how much effort will be required to develop content outlines, prepare learning materials and train personnel. Planners of media collect the relevant information regarding age and achievement levels of students and what Ueachers as well as pupils expect of media. Teacher attitudes towards media must be understood and training opportunities be designed to equip teachers adequately for utilising the media.

(ii) Formative Evaluation: This is a process of data collection during the development and production of media so that modification can be effected in order to improve functioning. Such evaluation touches decisions at every level for example, whether to spend more on printed materials or classroom activities; whether to produce a series of radio or television programmes for a given course and whether a feature or dramatization

format will be suitable. Formative evaluation is used to collect background information about the target audience, their profile of needs and condition and to diagnose the problems for taking corrective steps.

(iii) Summative Evaluation: This is a process of data collection designed to provide planners and policy makers with a more comprehensive understanding of how a medium succeeds or fails in reaching its goals. The findings of this kind of evaluation assists the decision-makers to take long-term decisions and formulate plans for production of media over a long time and with specific objectives. This evaluation is required to assess how far the medium in question is effective in the teaching-learning situation. It is also conducted during or at the end of a course implementation for certification or validation.

The summative evaluation differs from the formative one in time perspective and is usually aimed at those decision-makers who control funds to continue or discontinue the medium. The need for immediate information to guide short-range decisions justifies formative evaluation whereas the need for long range decision and policy making require summative evaluation. Due to its long range effects and importance, data in the case of summative evaluation are gathered in more scientific and systematic manner. When a programme or project on media is of repetitive value and formative evaluation has not been possible at the initial stage, summative evaluation is more justified to be conducted for bringing about desired revision in the project. It is, however, wise to conduct formative evaluation in time and improve upon or modify the media programme in the process of production on the basis of its findings.

The two approaches, nevertheless, overlap in many ways. The variables, and effects studies in both the evaluation methods may be quite similar. Formative evaluation of learning and attitudes often do contribute to summative evaluation of the same phenomena.Therefore, when gathered in a systematic way, the data from formative evaluation also provide the basis for the long-range analysis and conclusions characteristic of summative evaluation.

Tools and Techniques

Each of these evaluation types utilises various tools and techniques for collection of data. Some of them are objective and statistically based, and some are subjective and qualitative in nature. Even some techniques are in the process of development or an intermigling or mixture of the two. The important elements of these techniques are given below:

Data Collection: A good amount of information is required for evaluation to work effectively on media as well as on educational situations.

Some agencies make routine statistical collection of the educational data. But there are gaps in data on media. One of the means of making economic use of the data is to put them in a central data bank and use the methods of coding and retrieval in common with similar agencies and it may not be available from any other source. This will include statistics relating to number of programmes, support materials, report figures, delivery, maintenance, repair, budgetary analysis and so on.

Survey and Questionnaires: Prior to the inception of a media service, a general survey of viewing and listening habits should be carried out. A base-line data survey is required to be undertaken for gathering statistics regarding number of schools, classes, students, school-timing, holidays etc.

Special surveys are also carried out when there are proposals to serve a new audience or to introduce a new series. Regular daily or weekly questionnaire surveys need to be undertaken to provide an ongoing picture of media use. The audience can directly be approached either in person or through a form of questionnaire. Of course, this is more successful in case of the limited audience than a larger one.

In a large area, however, a sample is taken which should be statistically based. The sample can also rotate in order to involve each school only a few times each year. For this, random sampling is adopted and say, for a total universe of 200 schools (The total number of viewing schools) 50 schools may constitute the sample as per one-in-four principle, which is sufficient to ensure valid results. Adequate precautions need be taken for developing the questionnaire properly for getting responses unambiguously and for assessing statistically. Scaled responses are therefore preferable to enumerate a whole range of possible responses for various shades of opinion.

Performance Testing: Performance and ability tests usually constitute a part of the evaluation studies undertaken in connection with the media. The main advantages of such tests is that teachers and pupils are likely to take the broadcasts more seriously. These tests enable the teacher to identify the major learning points easily and to plan the follow up activities accordingly. When the pupils responses are sent to the programme designers and producers, these data can help them in bringing about improvement in the media. In view of the extra labour and cost involved, it is recommended, that a regular system of performance testing is first piloted on one or two programme series to see if it can be extended to the rest of the system conveniently.

Observation and Interviews: The statistical approach has its own limitations. It can enlist reactions, but cannot interpret them qualitatively.

With a view to getting over this difficulty, individual or group discussion, direct observation, personal interviews are conducted with teachers, pupils, supervisors and management. Predesigned information sheets and interview schedules should be used for the purpose. The points dealt therein will be as regards theme and quality of programmes, reception, teachers preparation, pupils participation and reaction, difficulties faced, attitude and suggestions of the teacher and pupils follow-up activities.

Content Analysis: Surverys and Statistics cannot measure the range of programme formats and the teaching style used in the programme materials. Therefore, specific content analysis techniques have to be used for these puposes. An examination of the relationship between programme format and level of interest and learning is felt necessary. It is generally assumed that a variety of formats within a series of programmes will lead to increased interest and learning. Further, it is assumed that certain formats are more suitable for some subject areas than for others. This kind of evaluation is useful for introducing new methods of teaching and innovative approaches. In order to use media as a support to curriculum development and renewal, new teaching styles need to be utilised in the programme for promoting individualised learning, teacher-pupil and pupil-pupil inter-action in the classroom, for both these forms of evaluation. Scripts of all these programmes preferably tapes of these programme should be made available.

Media and Operations Research

Measures of media effectiveness are positively related with student and teacher acceptance, cost factors and other sociological and psychological variables. Therefore, operations research studies are undertaken in order to evaluate the factors of effectiveness, acceptance, costs and equipment variables. These studies involve different disciplines of education, psychology, mass communication, engineering, economics and sociology. As the Encyclopedia of Educational Research has pointed out, "such operations research studies consider all factors involved in the introduction and operation of media in an instructional situation. They are also concerned with the size of the change required to affect significantly the total operation and the administrative changes required to carry out the new operation."[7]

Educational planners who want to employ media and materials on a large scale feel an obligation to conduct research study to demonstrate that the quality of instruction is better than or superior to that which prevailed before the introduction of such media. The need accounts for a large number of research studies in which instruction involving media is compared with instruction conducted in the conventional manner. Media effectiveness is ensured after the target audience is exposed to the programme. This can be done under "case study" experimental design, which appear to be the weakest of evaluative research designs. It is, however, commonly used by evaluators to establish the fact that every programme has a positive impact. The greatest limitation of this design is the absence of baseline data for comparison with post-programme measure.

A comparatively better research method is "a Single Group Pretest-Post-test Design" which refers to baseline data of the target group before the programme takes place and then post-programme assessment data. The differences between pre-programme and post-programme assessment is taken as the index of impact or the amount of effectiveness. The limitation of this evaluation design is that there is no scope to trace extraneous factors of events which might have their impact on the group simultaneously.

Another evaluative research design is known as "Static Group Comparison." According to this, performance of two separate groups of subjects are compared-one having been exposed and the other not exposed to the programme. When the exposed group shows higher evidences of the desired behaviours, it is generally attributed to the effect of the programme. The limitation of this design is that it is not possible to know whether the two groups were equivalent or not before the programme.

The "Pre-test Post-test Central Group" is regarded as the best experimental design. In the beginning of evaluation, two equivalent groups are identified through random sampling. Then a pretest is administered on both the groups to get the baseline data before the programme. This also ensures a check on equivalence of the two groups. One of these two groups exposed to the programme is called experimental group and the other not exposed to the programme is called as the control group. Mutual contact and inter-action of these two groups are avoided as far as possible. After the programme is completed, post-tests, are administered on both the groups and the results of the pre and post-tests are compared. The difference of the pretest and post-test result is the index of the programme effectiveness.

Some evaluators are interested to compare the effectiveness of a medium programme over a long period. This evaluation process is called "Longitudinal Study" design which is an important model of continuous evaluation. Since evaluation is made at different points of the media process, check on progress of the media towards desired objectives is ensured and the results of evaluation are used as feedback into the programme.

Cost-Effectiveness

Media may be effective and acceptable to teachers as well as students.

But the educational planners and administrators may find the cost too high and do not want to continue the system. Economics of media is of great importance to them and cost effectiveness is the deciding factor in installing and utilizing the media. A large number of variables enter into media costing: salary and price changes are so rapid, so many hidden costs are to be taken into account and so many differences stem from local conditions, labour, markets, taxes and on on.

In this context, therefore, any standard media costing is not possible, but clear understanding of these concepts like capital or development costs, recurrent costs, cost breakdowns into the production, transmission and distribution, unit costs and cost benefits, is extremely essential. For example, educational planners and administrators are to be convinced of cost efficiency through the concept of the unit cost. For than, the total costs of the media system are calculated and divided by the number of students exposed. This can be related to a unit of time (per annum or per hour) to a programme unit or to a total project. The advantage of this approach is that equivalent unit cost can be claculated for alternative channel (open education system with traditional formal education) and a basis for comparison found. The disadvantage here is that the calculations of many items are likely to be omitted or given undue weightage.

Although measures of cost-effectiveness or cost benefits are often reguired to show economy of media, it is very difficult to calculate particularly when media are used as a qualitative supplement. But when media are asked to provide alternative solution to the educational problems such as are envisaged in open or distance learning system, a valid basis of comparison is found since we are faced with true options, not.hypothetical cost comparisons. In Mexico, for example, the unit cost per annum of the teleschool project was calculated at 151 dollars compared with an estimated 200 dollars for regular schools. Similarly, in the Open University unit cost per annum is 1,174 dollars compared with 1,666 for regular university courses in campuses without a high postgraduate enrolment and 1,999 for campuses with professional courses. It is to be noted that with higher enrolment and scattered rural population, unit cost for utilisation of media like radio and TV (particularly when satellite is used) comes down and cost benefit increases as compared with traditional or formal system of education.

Research and Evaluation

Evaluation should be considered as a process. All the tools and techniques, methods, and approaches of evaluation are all parts of a whole process which is again a part of the overall media system. Evaluation is called upon to provide answers to certain questions, fundamental or operational, economic or psychological, pedagogical or mathetic, educational or sociological. There are learning objectives which are to be realized through media and various tools are used to evaluate the extent of their realisation or effectiveness. Further, if such effectiveness is to be considered from the economic point of view, calculation of cost effectiveness or cost benefits is felt imperative. Users of media, their needs and conditions are the focal point and evaluation process aims at reaching the same most efficiently.

Distinction between research and evaluation is a matter of convenience. There are no water-tight compartments between them. The puposes of both are overlapping or identical. The same methods and techniques are adopted by both. But their overall perspectives and objective are different. Hancock has aptly observed, "Evaluation seeks a continuous monitoring of the media system, research tries to answer specific queries, or concentrate upon a social subject problem or audience. Research is, in this case, particularly, concerned with new development, with areas of experimentation of fields where insufficient is known upon which to base planning strategies."[8] Studies of innovative approaches to media integration programme formats and techniques, socio-cultural effects and attitudes are a few examples of research.

Limitations of Media Evaluation

Media evaluation has its own limitations. The tools and techniques of traditional evaluative research are found inadequate. Methodology adopted for media evaluation is not sensitive to study the children reactions and feelings. According to Schramm (1973) there are over 500 experimental studies of instructional media in the research literature. The greatest number of studies deal with instructional television, the next largest number with film, a considerable number with programme instruction and computer-assisted instruction, relatively a few with radio, very few with the simplest media such as film strips or audio tapes and almost none with textbooks. Most typically these studies compare learning from media with learning from conventional teaching without media. Only small proporation compare one medium with another. And unfortunately, a high proportion of all the studies are not entirely satisfactory in terms of scientific design.

Most of the students of media are "judgemental and subjective." The findings and suggestions of the evaluator "rarely helps a project director to improve his system." The results of some studies on effects and teacher attitudes about media "are of little use in suggsting pragmatic changes and may irritate rather than guide producers." The objectives and strategies of evaluation are often determined by the evaluators and not by decision-makers, "Evaluations are often exercises planned by an academic with little empathy for the needs of the manager."[9] All evaluations are taken as threatening to the working of the producer who is always under heavy pressure of schedule. Hence, any findings or recommendations of the evaluator do not find favour from him. Political and non-academic considerations intrude into media planning and utilization in a very big way. The media with which evaluation is concerned are proposed, installed, funded and implemented through political decisions.

References

1. Dale, Edgare. *Audio Visual Methods in Teaching,* The Dryden - Rinehart and Winston Inc. New York, 1969, p. 612.
2. Kinder, J.S. *Audio-Visual Materials and Techniques,* American Book Co., New York, 1959, p.2
3. Ashby, Eric. Quoted in *The Fourth Revolution, Instructional Technology in Higher Education* - A Report of Carnegie Commission on Higher Education, McGraw Hill Book Company, New York, 1972.
4. *Ibid.*
5. Hancock, A. *Planning for Educational Mass Media,* Longmans, London, 1977.
6. *Ibid,* pp. 322-24.
7. Ebel, R.L. *Encyclopaedia of Educational Research:* 'Educational Communications Media' The MacMillan Co., London, 1969.
8. *Ibid,* p. 334.
9. Shramm, W. *Big Media - Little Media,* AID Studies in Educational Technology, Stanford University, p. 41.

12

Managing Educational Technology

Herein an attempt has been made to properly plan, procure and utilise the various components of Educational Technology (ET) including modern media, materials and methods in the educational process. Selection, procurement, preparation, planning and utilisation of all the wide-ranging media make the process very much complicated, and the procedures call for extreme care and caution, skills and strategies for maximizing learning experiences. All this implies not only effective management but also proper management of ET. Hence, the discussion has been made on the planning, organization, co-ordination, monitoring and application of ET by developing suitable infrastructure for acquisition, maintenance, utilisation, networking and support system for ensuring effectiveness and efficiency. After going through this chapter, you will be able to-

- know various aspects and implications of management
- plan and execute the E.T. application in various formats, types and methods.
- organise E.T. in different types of schools.
- coordinate various aspects of E.T.
- develop infrastructure for procuring media and manpower recruitment and posting.
- maintain media of different types properly.
- provide networking and support system for effective utilisation of E.T.

Management of Educational Technology

Management of E.T. involves different activities and processes aiming

at effective and efficient functioning and application of various media. The E.T. application and operations seek to achieve higher levels of satisfaction and quality in education. Efficiency of E.T. requires a high degree of perspective planning and execution of technology, improvement of teaching-learning skills and greater motivation of the learners. Modern management is goal-oriented and result-based. It envisages a constant and continuous process of change to generate new ideas, insights, methods and techniques to cater to the needs of different clientele groups. The educational manager can prove effective if he knows the fundamentals of educational management and technology and takes decisions appropriately in time to meet the goals.

Management is controlled by certain general principles like planning, organising, coordinating, monitoring and evaluation. It deals with multifareous resources, human, physical, ideational or academic which have to be handled properly to realise the instructional objectives. It is a systems approach in which all elements are interlinked and interdependent. If one link is weakened or broken, the entire, process can be damaged or adversely'affected. It is, therefore, desirable that there should be harmonious coordination and efficient organisation. Since E.T. includes a wide range of media and materials, its managment requires a series of activities relating to planning, organisation, coordination, monitoring and evaluation for maximising the learning experiences. These are as follows:

Planning of Educational Technology in Schools

Planning is the pre-requisite exercise for any effective activity. It implies a basic function 'do how' I that is how the aims and objectives need be realised. Before launching upon a particular job or enterprise or implementing any project, the manager is required to take decisions about the methods and strategies for effectively and efficiently achieving the objectives. This implies that for ET planning the school management has to have the basic data, facts and figures, background information and audience as well as the school profile at hand and take decisions on the basis of such fundamentals.

Modern planning needs to be democratic, scientific and decentralised. There must be adequate participation of all concerned-teachers, students, media experts and E.T. specialists or E.T. trained personnel, in the planning process. The persons not only at the helm of affairs, but also at the grassroots level must be consulted for planning effectively. In view of the objectives, expenses involved and size of the E.T. project, the plans/ projects may be long-term or short term or medium-term. This kind of democratic planning becomes more productive and creative, promoting high morale, motivation and commitment of teachers as well as students.

Educational Technology in Vertical and Horizontal Schools

E.T. has to be provided to all types of schools, rural, urban, tribal, non-tribal, primary, high or higher secondary schools. The resources available in these institutions vary in range, quantity and quality. The roll strengths of students and teachers also range very widely. Similarly, E.T. also comprises all kinds of media and materials, ranging in vast complexity and control, expenses and distribution. Hence, after planning, the next important phase of organisation of execution comes into play. Both human and material resources are to be well organised for achieving the instructional objectives set for various media and materials.

Effective organisation ensures maximum utilisation of resources. Otherwise, there would be wastage of resources and duplication of work. Interpersonal relations need to be improved for making an organisation efficient to apply ET according to needs, abilities and interests of students. Therefore, one E.T. application must be strengthened and supported with other kind of media and materials. Formal and informal contacts and linkages must be established for mutual cooperation.

There must be decentralissation and delegation of powers and greater autonomy can ensure better functioning. Vertical structure of relations must be flattened and horizontal linkages and relation should be expanded. Adequate consultancy and advisory services should be provided for improving the tone and morale of personnel and efficiency of the systems.

Staffing: Recruitment and Training

For organising ET effectively, it is essential that suitable human resources are deployed in time and adequately. The personnel should be recruited in time and they must be equipped with required knowledge and skills. There should not be any mismatch of persons with the specific skills required of them. The right man should be posted at the right place. He should know how to operate the media or utilise the materials. Now-a-days the work is becoming more complex, more skill-based and more knowledge/expertise-based. Management should, therefore, be quite active and responsive to matching human resources with particular/specific job and work place.

The first step in matching jobs and individuals is to make job specifications or descriptions available to the management. A job description sets for the objectives, duties, relationships and results expected of a person on the job. An operator of the projector, overhead or film, for example, should have adequate training and experience in handling the machines effectively. In order to match job and individuals, job descriptions or job-chart should be more explicit and specific. That is, for example, in case of a projector operator, it may be specifically mentioned that he can be able to do minor repair in case the machine goes out of order. The second step in matching jobs and individuals is translating the duties or spelling out 'individual specifications'. In considering an individual for a particular job, his qualification, past experience, accomplishments and conduct in the past or in earlier positions must be taken into consideration. In case of a fresher, his behaviour and conduct in the viva voce or practical test have to be appraised with more care and objectivity.

After a person is recruited and posted, it is felt necessary to guide and supervise his/her peroformance and ascertain his/her strengths and weaknesses. It is to be assessed whether in order to make him/her more capable, any specific on the job or in-service training is essential or desirable. He/she has to keep his/her knowledge, skills etc., abreast with the latest trends and innovations. Therefore, very often in-service education/training is to be provided continuously and systematically. Introduction of new machines or media makes it imperative on the part of the manager to provide suitable training to the incumbent. The in service education/training may be of various types as follows:

a) Refresher training courses for giving advanced knowledge and skills.

b) Orientation on training for wider exposition and better acquaintance with latest developments.

c) Staff discussions/faculty meetings.

d) Participating in professional meetings, conferences, seminars, workshops etc.

e) Making various distance education courses and career development programmes available.

f) Encouraging staff members to take up researches, experiments, extension work and publication activities.

Coordination, Monitoring and Evaluation

Since machines/media as well as materials of multifareous nature and types are to be utilised, adequate coordination is necessary to avoid wastage and duplication of work. In any kind of organisation, inspite of all resources available, without proper coordination, the entire process gets plugged because of a little negligence or through-oversight. All facilities and services should be properly unified and harmonised for promoting effectiveness in operation or execution. The plans and programmes should be made operative only through proper coordination of various resources, both human and physical. To ensure adequate coordination, communication has to be vertical as well as horizontal and any gaps or lapses in this communication process can spell disaster or wastage of resources. The responsibilities assigned to different individuals are to be coordinated through written or verbal communications without hindrances and bottlenecks. Inter-human relations should be properly maintained and monitored, so that their activities and assignments can be properly streamlined, coordinated and accomplished. Proper understanding and cooperation should be ensured and sharing of information, joint discussion, staff participation and rapport should be promoted among different functionaries and personnel for effective functioning and implementation of E.T. programmes.

Last, but not the least is the importance of monitoring and evaluation which are essential for effectiveness of management. Since there are various agencies and sectors involved in the process, it is imperative that timely and proper monitoring are really necessary. There are mainly two kinds of evaluation from time perspective. One is short-term and another is long-term. But evaluation should be continuous. It may also be formal or non-formal. It may also be formative or summative or both; evaluation can be done internally and externally. In order to bring about improvement in the system, it is necessary to study the strengths and weaknesses, deficiencies and difficulties in the implementation so that suitable steps can be taken to high light the strengths and success, take remedial measures for avoiding weaknesses and deficiencies encountered and experienced in different factors and segments of management. Short-term evaluation is necessary for periodic check-up and getting feedback on the progress made. If the project is a major one implemented over a long time and involves a good number of persons and agencies, it is felt desirable to undertake long-term evaluation.

Formative and summative evaluation is conducted for ascertaining the needs and for assessing the effectiveness of the programmes. For example, before producing ETV programmes, the needs and conditions, background experience and knowledge are to ascertained. It may be in the form of audience profile or survey. This is called formative evaluation which is required for planning. On the other hand, after producing and telecasting the programme, summative evaluation is taken up for measuring the effectiveness or success of the programme or a series of programmes. On the basis of the evaluation results, planning can be made either to continue the programme if found suitable or discontinue the same, if it is found a failure. But the findings must be useful for bringing about improvement or desirable changes in the process for ensuring more effectiveness. Similarly, in order to ensure impartiality and objectivity, evaluation should be done by an external agency. But in order to check up any lacunae or progress in organising a programme, it is desirable to conduct evaluation internally. The persons working in the same organisation can evaluate the programmes being implemented or were implemented.

Management

In the management of E.T. a number of problems are experienced at various levels and in different sectors. These problems may be related to infrastructure i.e., facilities, human resources, procurement of media, financing and maintenance of media, networking and support services. These are discussed below:

Infrastructure

Infrastructure is the pliysical and human resources which are basic requisites for managing a particular institution or a project. For smooth functioning of an organisation both human and material resources are necessary. But in this context, we are going to discuss infrastructure as regards material or physical resources which are required for transaction of curricular and cocurricular activities from planning to evaluation. Hence, the infrastructure includes buildings, equipment, media, furniture, laboratory, library, studio, auditorium and so on. For planning and developing the necessary infrastructure, the following factors are taken into consideration.

(i) Determination of material resources.

(ii) Specifications of the facilities according to requirements.

(iii) Quality determination.

(iv) Quantification of facilities.

(v) Development of indicators for per capita requirement.

Determination of Material Resources

Many kinds of physical facilities are required for organising the programmes in an educational institution. Besides buildings, other resources like media, equipment, studio, auditorium etc., are to be provided for various activities. With a view to making the teaching-learning process effective, all these material facilities are to be determined appropriately and in time, so that the programmes will not be affected adversely.

Specification of the Facilities

The material facilities should be determined as per prescribed standards and specifications. The specification of facilities implies the description of materilas in the context of their quality, utility and standards. Unless specifications of these facilities are made clear and specific, there is a possibility of wastage and underutilisation. Hence exact specifications can ensure proper utilisation or resources.

Quality Determination

Now-a-days materials and media are available in a wide variety of makes and brands. Some of them are of high quality whereas others are of poor standard. It is, therefore, felt desirable to determine the nature of the materials in order to optimise their use. Unless the quality of the products or materials is specified and standardised, there will be difficulties not only in procurement but also in using and maintaining the same. Poor quality materials, for example, leads to poor functioning and maintenance, which again calls for frequent replacement affecting the output very badly.

Quantification of Facilities

Management of material resources includes the quantification of facilities on the basis of per capita requirements. The quantum of materials of different types has to be assessed and full deployment and utilisation of resources are to be made at the right time. Time and space management in terms per capita and per hour need to be calculated for quantifying the facility requirement.

Development of Indicators for Per capita Requirement

With a view to ensuring efficient management of material resources alongwith quantification of per capita need, it is necessary to develop material requirement indicatiors. This should be done as the amount of material facility is required to produce a given amount of output. It can be possible if combinations of material facilities are shown in an input matrix and various combinations are found out to see whether they have influenced the outcomes.

Procurement of Media

After the basic infrastructure is developed, specifications are determined and requirement of various types of media and materials are estimated. Steps need be taken for procurement of media which are of multifareous grades and quality, uses and expenses. In every organisation there are fixed and formal procedures and principles for procurement of media and materials. These are to be followed scrupulously as far as possible and procurement should be made in time in adequate amount and quality.

Now it is essential to see that these media and materials are properly used in implementing different programmes. In this context, the following two considerations need be made for ensuring adequate utilisation of the facilities.

i) Planning the Utilisation

ii) Optimum Utilisation of Material Resources

Planning and Utilisation

For streamlining the procurement and utilisation of material resources, it is felt essential to know what type of material facilities are available and how they are being utilised in the teaching-learning pocess and various co-curricular activities. Sometimes we procure materials that are not used adequately and on the other hand, we cannot procure the materials which are sufficiently required. Thus, on the one hand there is inadequacy and on the other hand, there is wastage of resources. Hence a checklist can be prepared to show the time of their procurement and use, by whom used and on what occasions. This will help not only in knowing the extent of utilisation of various materials, but also for providing these facilities adequately.

Optimum Utilisation of Material resources

It is the duty of the management to see that material resources are used to the maximum. We find that in most of the educational institutions, media and materials are not adequately used. It has to be ascertained which media and materials are over-utilised, under-utilised or properly utilised. Planning has to be made for optimum utilisation of physical resources.

Maintenance of Media and Material

Since media and materials are expensive and useful, we cannot afford to neglect their proper upkeep and maintenance. Unless they are kept in right condition, in right places and in right amount, difficulties are experienced in production and utilisation of curricular programmes. Suitable steps need be taken for saving them from wastage and under-utilisation.

Saving physical facilities from wastage is an important aspect of infrastructural management. It has two aspects (i) the media and materials need be protected from damages like wrong uses, wrong storage etc. (ii) they should be saved for future repeated uses. Students coming in batches or one generation after another must be given adequate facilities for their learning and skill development. Particularly valuable machineries and media need be used and preserved carefully.

Again there are two dimensions of proper maintenance (i) it lengthens the life of the media and materials and (ii) it keeps them in readiness or in good condition for repeated uses. As the prices are increasing by leaps and bounds, maintenance has assumed a greater significance. But it poses a serious challenge to both personnel working in an organisation and the clientele for whom media are to be used.

The personnel in charge of the material resources are actually the custodians who should be knowledgeable and vigilant. The media can have better longevity through proper maintenance and meticulous attention. Different caring and curing mechanisms like lubrication, watering, warming, cooling, repairing and renewing from time to time are to be adopted scrupulously.

The first step towards better maintenance is to train the persons concerned. Due to explosion of knowledge and technology many media are getting obsolete and complicated, unless the persons who are custodians of media and materials are trained and oriented properly in time. They must have-

i) a thorough knowledge about various media and materials for cleaning and caring them.

ii) an adequate skill in using various tools and materials, and

iii) a positive and scientific attitude towards the study of various custodian services at different phases.

In order to effect efficiency and economy of time and energy, it is essential that the custodians should have adequate knowledge, skills and attitude. The media and materials are sometimes unused, under-used or over-used and at times misused also. All this cuts down their longevity. All the media and materials procured must be mentioned in stock register or in the directory with specification, gradation and utilisation possibilities. The media should be used with proper recording about the date, time and purpose. Maintenance and storage procedures should be mentioned in a register.

It is also felt necessary to maintain a condition profile of each item of media/materials which can give a status account of all important ones in terms of quantity as well as quality. On the basis of the data given here, decisions will be taken for repair, replacement, maintenance or even write-off of the unusable and damaged media. Besides, a detailed checklist of various items of facilities can be maintained for the purpose.

Manpower

Man behind the machine is more important than anything else in the management. Persons need to be deployed for managing, operating and maintaining all relevant activites. Persons with requisite qualification and experience have to be recruited according to the job requirements. Today work is becoming more knowledge and skill-based and the management has to be active and responsive to emerging needs of media and matching human resources with various work places and jobs. Manpower planning and management has therefore assumed a great significance now-a-days.

The first step in this direction is to make job specifications and descriptions available which mention the objectives, duties, relationships and results expected of a person on the job. Job description should be more explicit and concrete in terms of work and outcomes. It should also spell out, for instance, how decent relationshiphis intended, what innovative and renovative measures are to be taken or what management technique need be followed for getting better results.

Another major step in manpower planning is to translate the alloted duties into activities. Individual specifications are to be chalked out and a job chart should be given to every incumbent about the work expected to be done by him to achieve specific objectives or reach targets. An 'individual specifications chart' may tell about the training and education, past experience and achievement, personality traits and characteristics which are important points for considering his work and performance.

Manpower management should take into account the following:

i) The knowledge, understanding, values, attitudes and skills required for proper performance.

ii) Manpower requirements should be estimated well ahead of recruitment.

iii) Development needs should be assessed periodically and steps for appointment of additional hands should be taken accordingly.

iv) Persons on jobs need to be motivated to maintain adequate levels of performance. v) Appropriate rewards and incentives should be provided through career advancement programmes and promotion.

Further, the following steps need to be taken for developing manpower.

i) Refresher courses giving advanced knowledge and skills should be organised from time to time.

ii) Orientation courses should be wider organised for better and further exposition to wider facilities.

iii) Staff/faculty discussions and deliberation should be organised regularly. iv) Persons have to be deputed to professional meetings, seminars, workshops and conferences.

v) Various distance education courses can be availed of, for career development.

vi) Staff members can be encouraged to conduct research studies, extension and publications.

vii) Personnel may be given certain amount of freedom and flexibility for taking initiative.

viii) Periodic review may be made for ascertaining the rate of progress and problems, if any.

ix) Continuous interaction, feedback and monitoring are essential for better performance.

x) Strengths of the employees can be capitalised whereas weaknesses can be considered for sorting out the problems or overcoming the hurdle.

xi) An objective system of awards and punishments should be developed in manpower management.

Networking

With a view to promote effectiveness in our educational system, it is desirable that proper networking of agencies and facilities should be developed. Now-a-days a large unmber of agencies and organisations have been set up to perform the same kind of jobs at different levels. Unless suitable steps are taken for establishing linkages for coordination, cooperation and collaboration, there will be duplication of work, wastage of resources and loss of time and energy. Inspite of all our developments, we are still facing constraints and crunches at the financial level, particularly for academic and educational programmes. Therefore, it is imperative that adequate networking of institutions and services should be developed at different stages for ensuring economy and efficiency.

Support System

Media and materials are gradually multiplied and getting sophisticated. Every new brand and generations are bringing with them new changes and improvements. Unless a proper support service system is developed it will be difficult to maintain the media of all types. Wear and tear of the machines is a must due to their uses and utilisation. Sometimes expensive media are damaged due to mishandling and wrong storage practices. They have to be repaired or cured and cared for their smooth functioning. Otherwise the programmes depending on the same media will be seriously affected or cannot be implemented properly. Hence suitable men and machineries for operation, repair, care and curing of the media must be deployed in time and adequately.

To conclude the above discussion, it may be mentioned that this unit has focussed on the need and importance of management, its types and implications for bringing about efficiency and effectiveness in the E.T. system. We have tried to discuss the planning and organisation of E.T., recruitment and training of personnel coordination, monitoring and evaluation which are essential parts of management.

Bibliography

Alien, W.H., "Media Stimulus and Types of Learning" Audio-Visual Instruction.

Apter, Michel J., *The New Technology of Education*, Macmillan, London, 1968.

Balcomb, John., "Communication for Development: From Propaganda to Dialogue and Entertainment" in the UNICEF News 84/ 1975/2.

Bloom, B.S. et al., *Taxonomy of Educational Objectives: The Classification of Educational Goals*. Handbook 1-Cognitive Domain and 2-Affective Domain, New York Mackey, 1965.

Bloom, B.S., *Human Characteristics and School Learning*, Harper, New York, 1976.

Beiggs L.S. et al. *Instruction Media*, Fittsburgh American Institute for Research, 1966.

Brown, J.W. Lewis, R.B. & Hercleread, *A.V. Instruction Materials and Methods*, McGraw Hill Book Co., New York, 1964.

British Council, *Radio Writing*, Media Department, London,1972.

Cream, David, *Explaining Teaching Machines and Programmes*, Featon, San Fracisco, 1961.

Chatterjee, R.K., *Mass Communication*, National Book Trust, India

Dale, Edgare, *Audio Visual Method in Teaching*, Dryden Rinehart and Winston, New York. 1969

Faure Edgar et al, *Learning To Be*, UNESCO, Paris, 1972.

Frankling, D, *Television in our Schools*, Bulletin No. 12, 1972.

Gagne, R.M., *The Conditions of Learning*, New York, Holt Binsort and Winston, 1965.

Goodman, Loster, *Educational Radio*, CET, NCERT, 1977.

Govt. of India, *National Policy on Education*, 1986/92, MHRD (Education), New Delhi, 1986/92.

Govt. of India, *Programme of Action*, 1986/92, MHRD (Education) New Delhi

Govt. of India, *Annual Report*, 1999-2000, MHRD (Educatrion) New Delhi.

Government of India, Report of the Working Group on Autonomy for Akshvani, Doordarshan, New Delhi, 1978.

Government of India, Report of the Study group on IN SAT, Television Utilisation for Education & Development, Ministry of Education & Culture, New Delhi, 1981.

Government of India, *The Constitution of India*, Manager of Publications, New Delhi.

Government of India, Report of the Secondary Education Commission, 1952.

Government of India, Report of the Education Commission on Education 1964-66, Ministry of Education, 1966.

Haban, Charles, F. (Jr), *Movies that Teach*, New York, The Dryden Press, 1945.

Hancock, Alan, *Planning for Educational Mass-Media*, Longmans London, 1977.

Kinder, James. S, Audio-Visual Materials and Techniques, American Book Company, New York, 1959.

Kothari, O.S. et al, Report of the Indian Education Commission, 1964-66, New Delhi, 1966.

Kulkarni, S.S., *Teaching Learning Process: A Systems Analysis*, UNESCO Regional Office for Education in Asia, Bangkok, 1975.

Kulkami, S.S., *Introduction to Educational Technology*, Oxford Publishing Company, New Delhi.

Kaul, B.N. & Others, *Studies in Distance Education*, Association of Indian Universities, IGNOU, New Delhi, 1988.

Lowman, J., *Mastering Techniques of Teaching, Parentice Hall India*, New Delhi, 1987.

MacJver, R.M. & Page, C.M., *Society*, Macmillan, London, 1950.

Mackanzie, N. Eraunt, M and Janas, HC. *New Resources for Learning*. In Prospects in Education. Vol-I No. 3, UNESCO., Paris, 1978.

Mathesan, Alastair, *The Communication Materials and Methods*. McGraw Hill Book Company, New Delhi, 1964.

Menon, Narayan, *The Communication Revolution*, National Book Trust, India, New Delhi, 1976.

McWhinnie Donald, *The Art of Radio*, Faber & Faber, London, 1961.

Mukhopadhyay, M., *Educational Technology*, Year Book, 1988, AIAET, New Delhi, 1989.

Munn, Norman L., *The Fundamentals of Human Adjustment*, Houghter Miffm Co., Boston, 1965.

NCTE, *Self Instruction Modules for Teacher Education through Distance Mode*, New Delhi, 1997

NCERT, A Case Study of School Broadcasts in Delhi, Centre for Educational Technology, New Delhi, 1980.

NCERT, Teacher Monitors Hand-Book Part-11 for 12-1 Inservice Teacher Training Course, Centre for Educational Technology, New Delhi, 1975.

Ottaway A.K.C., Education and Society, Routldge and Kegan Paul, London, 1962.

Panda, K.C., Role of Motivation in School Learning, Current Issues in Euducation, Vo. 2, RCE, Bhubaneswar, 1978.

Perlberg, Arye, "Micro-Teaching : An Innovation Laboratory Procedure." *Prospects in Education,* Vol-I, No. 3, 1970.

Rahman, S, *A Study in Educational Television*, Orissa, 1972.

Rewntreu Desk, *Educational Technology in Curriculum Development*, Harper and Row Publishers, London.

Schramm, Wilbur, *The Process and Effects of Mass Communication*, University of Illinois, Urbane.

Schramm W., *Big Media, Littel Media*, Agency for International Development, 1974.

Schramm, Wilbur, Programmes Instruction : Today and Tomorrow, *The Friends of Advancement of Education*, New York, 1962.

Schramm, Wilbur, New Media: Memo to Educational Planners UNESCO, 1967.

UNESCO, APEID, Report of the National Workshop on Educational Broadcasting, Ministry of Education & Culture, New Delhi, 1980.

UNSECO, *Learning To Be*, International Commission on Development of Education, Paris, 1972.

Warwick, D., *Modular Curricula: International Encyclopedia*, Pergamon Publications, Exter, UK, 1994.

Index